C000111996

SPIES
OF THE
DEEP

SPIES
OF THE
DEEP

The Untold Truth
About the Most Terrifying Incident
in Submarine Naval History
and How Putin Used the Tragedy
to Ignite a New Cold War

W. CRAIG REED

PERMUTED
PRESS

A PERMUTED PRESS BOOK

Spies of the Deep:
The Untold Truth About the Most Terrifying Incident in Submarine Naval History
and How Putin Used The Tragedy To Ignite a New Cold War
© 2020 by W. Craig Reed
All Rights Reserved

ISBN: 978-1-68261-801-1
ISBN (eBook): 978-1-68261-802-8

Cover art by Cody Corcoran
Putin cover photo credited to Kremlin.ru
Interior design and composition, Greg Johnson, Textbook Perfect

PERMUTED
PRESS

Permuted Press, LLC
New York • Nashville
permutedpress.com

Published in the United States of America

This book is dedicated to the 118 Russian submariners
who were aboard the *Kursk* in August 2000
and are now on eternal patrol,
and to their families and loved ones.
Also, to all those who have served under the sea
as submariners.

CONTENTS

CHAPTER 1

THE TRAGEDY

*"There are three kinds of people: Those who are alive,
those who are dead, and those who are at sea."*

—ARISTOTLE

On the evening of August 10, 2000, a fierce Arctic wind whipped across a barren fjord near Murmansk, Russia. Scattered beads of rain dotted the back of an oddly shaped beast as sailors scurried about the deck, clearing lines, stowing gear, and securing hatches. Tugboats pulled alongside and guided the vessel into the channel.

From high up in the sail of the *Oscar II*–class submarine, forty-five-year-old Captain First Rank Gennady Lyachin released the tugs and scanned the fjord. Navigation lights winked through the damp fog surrounding the Russian naval base. The pungent scent of diesel fuel filled the night air. Lyachin ordered turns for six knots. Steam from the sub's twin reactors turned two massive propellers, which struggled to overcome inertia. The sub lurched forward, and a dark blue wake formed across its bow. The topside crew bid farewell to the tugs and scurried below. Inside the channel, Lyachin requested course 020, toward the Barents Sea, and a speed increase to "all-ahead standard."

Smooth and quiet, the submarine *Kursk* sped through the channel and passed by the mouth of the bay. Dry tundra lined both sides of the kilometer-wide inlet. Outside the passage, gliding through the deeper Motovsky Gulf, the boat rolled to and fro atop the restless waves.

Lyachin scanned the horizon, ordered the deck crew below, and shimmied down the bridge ladder. A starshina "petty officer" slammed the hatch shut and slid to the deck. Beads of water dripped from his cap. In the rigged-for-red central main command post (GKP), bent over the navigation table, Senior Lieutenant Sergei Tylik confirmed there was enough ocean beneath the keel and Lyachin gave the order to dive.

Main ballast tank vents popped open. Cold seawater displaced high-pressure air and allowed the *Kursk* to submerge. Hydraulics hissed as the sub's diving planes, mounted on either side of the bow, swung outward. In the control room, a starshina pushed a half-oval steering wheel forward, which tilted the planes downward and allowed the *Kursk* to descend into the darkness. Once below the surface, Lyachin ordered turns for twenty-eight knots, unaware that the command had brought his crew one step closer to death.

On Friday morning, August 11, Lyachin barked an order to bring the *Kursk* to periscope depth. The sub crept toward the naval exercise firing zone, more than fifty kilometers from port, and lined up for a missile shot. The meaty smell of freshly baked piroshki drifted from the compartment-four galley and filtered into the GKP. Stomachs growled. Lyachin turned toward twenty-two-year-old Senior Lieutenant Alexei Ivanov-Pavlov and told him to prepare for battle readiness two. The new head of torpedo control repeated the command and hurried to ready a P-700 Granit missile. Designed in the 1970s and appropriately called Shipwreck by NATO, the thirty-three-foot-long missile stood at attention in a side-mounted tube. The projectile typically carried 1,700 pounds of high explosive, but the unarmed practice version had an empty warhead.

Ivanov-Pavlov completed preparations to fire the Granit and then stepped through the GKP hatch into the compartment-one torpedo room. There, he inspected a "Fat Girl" torpedo in a rack on the port side of the boat. The weapon's nickname had been inspired by its odd, bulging shape. Designated as a Type 65–76, the thirty-six-foot-long cylinder was heavy and difficult to handle. In a weight class equivalent to an eighteen-wheeled truck, Fat Girls were the largest torpedoes ever built.

Russian submariners knew this formidable weapon was feared by NATO, and for good reason. Each torpedo came loaded with enough TNT to split a warship in half. If enemies shivered at the sight of a Fat Girl, they were not alone. Russian torpedomen also felt threatened by the unstable weapon. The Russians had opted to use a volatile hydrogen peroxide (HTP) fuel instead of the safer combination of liquid fuel and compressed-air oxidization. Designers touted faster speed and a lack of rubles as the main reasons for selecting HTP as the propellant. American experts refused to consider the less expensive fuel as an option, stating that "you get what you pay for."

The 85 percent hydrogen peroxide solution in Fat Girls had a bad reputation of eating through rubber gaskets and valves and working its way into the torpedo's sealed casing. HTP was also chain reactive and easily agitated by almost anything found in a torpedo room, up to and including the metal sides of a torpedo tube. Fat Girls needed frequent ventilation and inspection to ensure they didn't "go Chernobyl." Glass tubes positioned near the weapons kept a constant vigil and triggered alarms in the event of a threshold breach. Should that occur, ocean water sprayed down on the casing to cool off the weapon. If all else failed, torpedomen were trained to eject the torpedo within six hours or risk being ripped apart by an explosion.

Lyachin aimed his bow toward the target and positioned his vessel to fire a Granit. For the experienced captain, this war game was old hat. He'd graduated from the Higher Naval School of Submarine Navigation in Leningrad (now Saint Petersburg) in 1977 and served as the weapons officer on the *Juliett*-class diesel submarine K-58. His competence led to a stint as the captain third rank, an executive officer, on the K-77, also a *Juliett*. He received his first command in 1988 on another *Juliett*, the K-304, and remained onboard until after the fall of the Soviet Union in 1991. The Russian Navy promoted Lyachin to captain first rank in 1996 and gave him the keys to the K-141, a Project 949A *Oscar II* named after the Russian city of Kursk. Now, four years later, he and his crew of 117 operated at the peak of efficiency as best allowed by budget cuts and personnel turnover.

Lyachin continued his approach toward the missile launch zone. First Submarine Flotilla Commander Vice Admiral Oleg Burtsev, now aboard the *Pyotr Veliky* (*Peter the Great*) *Kirov*-class battle cruiser, validated the *Kursk*'s exercise parameters. Lyachin keyed the radio mic to communicate with Burtsev and verify the exercise code of "*vintik*," which translates into English as "little screw." Vice Admiral Burtsev confirmed a "T-time" of noon to launch the first practice missile. He also reminded Lyachin to follow the command table and rendezvous with the control ship, maintain communications, and use the proper exercise signals.

Lyachin ordered the watch officer to submerge the *Kursk* to a depth of fifty-five meters. He then asked the "Acoustic Cutting" sonar team for an update on the target's bearing and speed. Using this information, he made a quick calculation and maneuvered his craft into firing position. Now ready to fire, he ordered Acoustic to "prepare the first measurement."

An Acoustic Cutting operator replied with a bearing update.

Lyachin responded with "Acoustic...zero. Measurement mode...one minute."

Following procedures, having heard their captain start the ball rolling with the word "zero," Acoustic started feeding bearings every minute to the weapons attack crew, which included the navigator, electronics officer, and fire control team. Michmen (warrant officers) assigned to the team entered the range data into the digital weapons systems using measurements called *cabeltovs*. Ten *cabeltovs* equals one nautical mile of distance to the target.

Ivanov-Pavlov verified the readiness of the Granit cruise missile and Acoustic reported that the target, a dilapidated craft from the Cold War, was now two thousand *cabeltovs* away. Lyachin raised his right arm. In one quick move, he lowered his arm and said, "Fire!"

The *Kursk* shuddered as the Granit screamed from its tube. The missile flew upward, broached the surface, lit off its rocket engine, and sped away. Traveling at more than two times the speed of sound, the seven-ton projectile streaked across a blue sky. A yellow-orange trail marked the path of the assassin, now en route to a kill.

Within minutes, radio bursts from the *Peter the Great* announced a direct hit. Cheers erupted in the *Kursk*'s GKP. Lyachin held his smile. They had one more missile to fire. Executing the same moves as before, he lined up for shot number two. He brought his arm down again, only this time, nothing happened. The fire control team reported a problem with the second Granit. Lyachin informed his superiors of the failure using the sub's underwater hydrophone system.

At 1400, the *Kursk* returned to periscope depth and contacted the flagship on the radio. Vice Admiral Burtsev dismissed the second shot failure and congratulated Lyachin and his crew for a successful first launch. Despite his boss's elation, Lyachin understood that failure of any kind, regardless of the cause, reflected badly on a Russian captain. He'd been forced to borrow personnel from another *Oscar II* submarine to complete his crew complement, and the coordination effort had been a struggle. Lyachin also knew that several Russian "brass" officers would be watching the next exercise, scheduled for the following morning, and it was imperative to ensure his crew was ready.

He keyed the shipwide comm and said, "Attention, crew, this is the commander. There have been many personnel failures while readying the submarine for sea, specifically in the material readiness of the boat. Two warning bells have already gone off. Therefore, all personnel are to remain at their posts and carefully inspect their spaces. Report the slightest sign of leaks to Control. Report any signs of smoke immediately. All emergency measures should be set to 'ready.'"

The following morning, on Saturday, August 12, while gliding through Arctic waters in the Barents Sea, the *Kursk*'s crew completed preparations for another battle. The three other submarines participating in the naval exercise were scheduled to fire their slew of practice torpedoes toward the *Peter the Great* flagship, followed by the *Kursk*. Unarmed volleys from the subs were programmed to pass underneath the keel of the Russian battle cruiser and then float to the surface for eventual retrieval.

At 0608, Lyachin radioed Vice Admiral Yuriy Boyarkin and said the *Kursk* had arrived on schedule and was preparing for the next phase of the exercise. Boyarkin radioed back, "The ships are opening up, and we will give you an opportunity to change the plan. You should descend immediately and head to the waiting area. How copy? Over."

Lyachin confirmed the new course and replied, "I am proceeding according to the mission. Over."

"You understood me," Boyarkin responded. "Report when you have completed the exercise."

Five hours remained before Lyachin's attack sub was scheduled to fire its salvo at the flagship, consisting of one Fat Girl followed by a USET-80 heavyweight torpedo. Captain Lyachin no doubt wanted the Fat Girl off his sub as quickly as possible. Torpedo Chief Murat Baigarin had expressed concerns earlier that the weapon's oxidizer tank was starting to "sweat." The HTP bubble-sensor monitor had twitched, causing Baigarin to do likewise.

Baigarin entrusted the job of making the Fat Girl go away to Michman Abdulkadir Ildarov. Experienced, easygoing, and over four decades old, Ildarov had shoved more than a few Fat Girls into the water. Operating slowly, so as not to anger the "bitch in heat," Ildarov and his team of torpedomen took almost twice the normal time to load the torpedo into one of the 650-millimeter tubes. They were aided by two civilian engineers from the Dagdizel military plant who had come aboard to ensure a successful test-firing.

At 1005, after completing a simulated practice attack, Acoustic reported bearings to four contacts. Lyachin acknowledged and slowed the *Kursk* to six knots. Acoustic confirmed the turns on one contact and classified the vessel as a fishing trawler. Another was a battle cruiser. The two additional contacts were classified as escort warships. Lyachin knew the battle cruiser was the *Peter the Great*, but in keeping with the rules of the war game, he treated this contact like a hostile American warship.

Lyachin called down to the torpedo room and received assurances that the Fat Girl's fever was under control. However, if the temperature were to increase, Baigarin and Ildarov would immediately jettison the weapon. Thirty minutes later, Lyachin turned the *Kursk* northwest onto course 320 to line up on the target. In less than one hour, he'd give the command to fire.

Several shore-based staff officers stepped through the aft hatch and wedged their way into the crowded GKP. Lyachin knew they'd report every misstep in the torpedo exercise, no matter how trivial. He trusted his seasoned crew, but given the questionable condition of the Russian Navy, he knew well the dangers involved in a torpedo exercise. Success relied on too many unknown variables. Had the fleet reused the test torpedoes one too many times? Had they followed proper procedures when storing and loading the weapons? Had the cheap high-test peroxide fuel in the Fat Girl turned it into a long stick of dynamite?

A half-dozen sailors sat on benches with their backs straight and their eyes glued to digital readouts. A helmsman and planesman gripped plate-sized wheels near the front of the compartment. They gently operated the rudder and diving planes to steer the massive submarine and maintain depth control. A current of excitement and fear surged through the veins of everyone in the GKP. Successful firings usually brought accolades and rewards. Failures brought severe punishment...or worse.

Lyachin issued an order. "Acoustic...prepare the first measurement."

Using the bearing and speed information reported by the Acoustic Cutting sonar team, Lyachin directed the *Kursk* to line up on its prey. He then planted his right eye against the rubber socket on the attack periscope and moved the aluminum cylinder back and forth. Without removing his eye, he initiated the firing sequence. Michmen updated the range to the *Peter the Great* in the digital weapons systems to three hundred *cabeltovs*, the equivalent of thirty nautical miles. At its top speed of fifty knots, the Fat Girl would close the distance to the target in about thirty-five minutes, giving the *Kursk* plenty of time to disappear into the deep and evade detection.

In the torpedo room, Baigarin heard a strange hiss. He turned toward the torpedo tube housing the Fat Girl. The low hiss ramped into a loud whine. He looked at the watertight door leading into compartment two, open to alleviate the pressure buildup that accompanied a torpedo firing. With the Fat Girl screaming in his ear, he knew he should shut the hatch.

He also knew he was about to die.

The torpedo tube housing the Fat Girl erupted with the roar of a cannon. The eight-hundred-pound breech door blew off its hinges, flew into the air, and whisked a seaman off the deck. The door slammed against the aft bulkhead. Blood oozed from around the edges. Shattered pieces of the Fat Girl ricocheted about the compartment like shrapnel from a grenade, slicing through flesh and bone. Intense heat from the HTP fire enveloped Baigarin and his shipmates in a fiery hell. As the flames sucked the air from his lungs, perhaps Baigarin's last thoughts were of his home, his family, and the life he would never see again.

In the GKP, Lyachin felt the shockwave before his ears registered the boom. A gush of hot air and flames rushed through the open hatch with the fury of a tornado, engulfing anyone in the forward part of the compartment. The thunderous shockwave threw Lyachin and his crew against nearby piping and systems and rendered them unconscious or dead.

A wall of water from the frigid Barents Sea rushed through the gaping hole in the bow and pulled the *Kursk* toward the ocean floor. Two minutes later, the wounded giant slammed into the sand and silt and slid along the bottom.

A secondary explosion, twenty times stronger than the first, shredded the hardened steel around the bow of the submarine like an explosive bullet ripping apart a beer can.

Several thousand yards away, aboard the USS *Toledo* attack submarine, a sonarman's eyes flew open and a quartermaster watched his coffee cup crash to the deck.

THIS IS THE TRAGIC STORY OF THE DEMISE of the *Kursk* as proffered by Russian and NATO government officials and reported around the world by the mainstream media in August 2000. A decade after the Cold War had ended, they claimed an explosion caused by an unstable and outdated torpedo aboard the Russian *Oscar II*–class submarine had sent her to the bottom of the Barents Sea.

In the chapters to follow, this manufactured lie and many others told by Russian and U.S. naval and government officials will be shattered. For the first time in print, the shocking truth about what really happened will be exposed. Never-before-told firsthand accounts from submariners who were aboard U.S. nuclear submarines involved in the incident will be revealed, as well as candid interviews with military and government officials, former Russian naval officers, and many other witnesses and experts.

Also brought to light will be indications of a secret deal later struck between President Vladimir Putin and U.S. President Bill Clinton to avert a serious conflict. When overwhelming evidence of a collision was uncovered after the incident, Putin's military staff demanded retaliation—up to and including a nuclear war. What settlement did Putin negotiate with Clinton, and how did this unprecedented agreement spur a new and even more dangerous Cold War? How did this incident incite Putin to fire or demote many of his senior advisors and military staff, wrest control of large energy firms from oligarchs, rebuild Russia's navy, and dominate Arctic resources and sea routes? How did Halliburton, while its former CEO was running for vice president of the United States, win the bid to train and equip the Russians so they could recover bodies from the *Kursk*? How did Russia use this training and equipment to build massive underwater oil- and gas-drilling platforms to bolster its wealth? How is Russia using it today to threaten underwater communication lines and potentially cripple the U.S. economy?

How did the *Kursk* incident create a domino effect that propelled the world's superpowers into another cold war, sparked conflicts in the Arctic, and fueled a resource war that could create an economic nightmare not seen since the Great Depression?

Looming on the horizon are potential naval conflicts with China as its leaders build "sand islands" in the South China Sea and reverse-engineer the top-secret weapon that sank the *Kursk*. Using this technology, they have developed supercavitation submarines that can go from Shanghai to San Francisco in less than a hundred minutes. What other secret weapons are the Chinese building? What is the Assassin's Mace, and how can it destroy an entire aircraft carrier flotilla within minutes?

Also using supercavitation, what "doomsday" weapons and platforms have the Russians built? How can the new Status-6 torpedo, which carries a one-hundred-megaton nuclear warhead, cause worldwide economic upheaval? How can such a large weapon silently travel over 6,200 miles without refueling?

While the media have focused on North Korea's aggressive rhetoric and land-based missile launches, what is rarely discussed is Kim Jong Un's real threat, which comes not from the Korean peninsula but from underwater. How is it possible that North Korea has amassed a force of seventy submarines, six of which carry nuclear-capable ballistic missiles? How did U.S. and South Korean forces lose track of several of these subs for almost a week in 2013?

All these questions and more will be answered in the following chapters. But first, to understand what really happened to the *Kursk*...and how this impacts our world today...we need to take an excursion into the past. We need to ride alongside U.S. and Soviet submariners and government operatives who played dangerous games of cat and mouse during the Cold

War. We need to step inside submarine-mounted compression chambers and watch saturation divers, trained to breathe helium, prepare to wiretap communications cables a thousand feet deep off the coast of Russia. We must also learn why submarines operating in the Arctic face greater challenges and dangers than in other world oceans. Due to unpredictable and harsh conditions in this icy domain, accidents and collisions are far more likely...and far more dangerous.

CHAPTER 2

THE COLDEST WAR

*"That was the longest minute of my life.
I really thought it was my last."*

—HARRY HALL, Petty Officer
USS *Queenfish*

For submarines, the Arctic Circle is the most dangerous region on the planet. While battling Germany, U.S. submariners noticed that Arctic conditions prevented their sonar, navigation, weapons fire control, and other systems from working normally in this region. This made it nearly impossible to detect or battle German U-boats operating in the Gulf of Saint Lawrence.

To solve this problem, the U.S. Navy enlisted Dr. Waldo K. Lyon to lend his expertise in underwater and Arctic sciences to the Navy Radio and Sound Laboratory in 1941. Lyon and his team dove into the task and designed new sonar systems for Arctic operations. They eventually tested the equipment aboard the USS *Boarfish* (SS-327) while coordinating the boat's under-ice dives. Excellent initial results led to an initiative destined to impact the Navy's ability to dominate underwater polar warfare.

After World War II, Lyon's work led to the creation of the Arctic Submarine Lab (ASL), which was first housed in a converted World War II mortar emplacement at Battery Whistler in San Diego, California. Lyon became head of the Submarine Studies Branch in 1947 and designed a special pool at Battery Whistler to test equipment for deep-submergence vehicles, such as the bathyscaphe *Trieste*. Lyon's team equipped the pool to grow its own sea ice so they could study the physical properties of a frigid environment, but they soon reached a knowledge barrier, overcome only by sending men into harm's way.

Freezing to Death

In the fall of 1947, nineteen-year-old Harry Hall knew something wasn't quite right aboard the diesel submarine USS *Queenfish* (SS-393). With an overhaul in Pearl Harbor, Hawaii, just completed, rumors started spreading. Petty Officer Hall's buddy, engineman Joe Prince, whispered that he'd seen the sub's commanding officer (CO), Commander Ralph Lockwood, stride across the brow after returning from a briefing with the mucky-mucks at Command Submarine Force U.S. Pacific Fleet (COMSUBPAC). Prince said the CO had a worried look on his face. Hours later, Hall and Prince were heaving lines onto the pier. The *Queenfish* rounded Oahu, turned north, and cranked the diesels up to flank speed.

The sub went deep and slowed to one-third speed. Hall sauntered into the control room (Conn) and stole a glance at the navigation table. His eyes lit up when he saw the plot line running past Little Diomede. Once known as Krusenstern Island, this speck of land housed around one hundred people and sat smack in the middle of the Bering Strait between Alaska and Siberia. Big Diomede lay a few miles to the west, and although the population was larger, they were all Russian. The nav line ended several miles west of the island, well inside Soviet territorial waters.

Hall shivered, and not just from the cold. They had left Hawaii sans any warm clothing. No foul-weather jackets, gloves, wool undies, or thick socks. Hall and his mates had taken to layering on khakis to keep from freezing in the Arctic waters. "Blue nose" *Balao*-class diesel boats were notorious for having less-than-desirable heating systems.

A day later, Hall finally found out why the *Queenfish* had been cordially compelled to wander into "Ivan's" backyard. Apparently, COMSUBPAC had been asked by some guy named Waldo Lyon at the Arctic Submarine Lab to take temperature and density readings at various depths in the Bering Strait. Explanations as to why they needed these readings were not offered. Then again, they never were, at least not to the common crew.

"Somebody smarter than me decided they wanted to take all these ocean readings in the Arctic," Hall says. "But somebody dumber than me forgot to consider how we'd accomplish that."

The *Queenfish* had left port in such haste that no one had thought to bring aboard instruments suitable for taking the readings. As the sub's auxiliary electrician, Hall pondered the dilemma for several hours before coming up with a plan.

"I jury-rigged a hydrometer," Hall says. "Diesel boats run on batteries, and part of my job was to maintain the 'cans' [batteries] so they didn't die, explode, or kill us with poison gas."

Doing so required instruments and diligence. Batteries were filled with triple-distilled water, and inspections were made frequently to check for hydrogen buildup—which could cause an explosion—or salt, which could create deadly chlorine gas. Hall "borrowed" a battery-checking hydrometer, ripped it apart, and removed the lead shot so the instrument could be used with saltwater. Resembling a turkey baster, the meter consisted of a glass tube bottomed by a red rubber bulb.

"It worked just fine," Hall says. "We were able to take readings at different depths and strata variations to see how the Arctic might affect sonar beams."

Hall later learned that Lyon and company needed the information to help save lives. Submarine skippers are trained to hide under thermal layers, which can reflect enemy active sonar pings. ASL staff needed to know how Arctic waters might affect various strata so they could recommend different tactics in relation to passive and active sonar. Gathering the data took Hall and the *Queenfish* crew two days. While they were down, the sub started rolling from side to side. The officer of the deck (OOD), Lieutenant A. E. May, ordered the diving officer to descend to two hundred feet. The rolling didn't stop. May called Commander Lockwood to the control room.

"Lieutenant May was worried," Hall recalls. "He said there must be a huge storm above us 'cause we were getting batted about at two hundred feet down. We were starting to run out of air and some of us were getting dizzy from the CO2 buildup. We also needed to fill the cans."

Even with the boat's cans near depletion and the air almost unbreathable, Lockwood chose to stay down another day and go slowly to conserve the batteries. He didn't want to risk trying to surface in a bad storm.

"If you come up in the middle of a huge wave," Hall says, "you might capsize the sub. With our heavy ballast on top versus underneath, the weight could send us to the bottom. The captain was also worried about surfacing underneath a Soviet ship. In a bad storm, our sonar jockeys might not hear them until it was too late."

After three days down, Lockwood had no choice. Sub commanders are chosen for their ability to make life-or-death decisions. When faced with disaster to the right or left, they must have the guts and intelligence required to select the lesser of two "deads." Lockwood decided to surface.

"1 was in the control room when it happened," Hall says. "The diving officer gave the order to surface and we angled up at the bow."

Freezing and wheezing, dizzy and scared, Hall stood near the gyro compass in the Conn. His eyes shifted downward, and he noticed that the glass cover on the compass housing had been removed for repairs. Knowing that the gyro contained mercury and concerned that a jolt might spill the metallic liquid onto to the deck, Hall craned his neck to see where the cover had gone. He spotted the metal plate on the port side.

The diving officer yelled a report: "One hundred feet, ten degree up bubble."

Standing near the number one periscope, Lockwood acknowledged the update. The boat shuddered and rolled while the helmsmen struggled to maintain control. Grabbing onto the overhead piping, Hall tried to pull himself toward the compass cover. He didn't make it far.

"Sixty feet, ten degree up bubble."

The sub lurched as the bow sliced toward the surface. Hall's stomach fluttered. His feet and legs shot upward. Centrifugal force flung him toward the starboard side of the boat. Someone screamed. An officer slammed against a three-thousand-pound air line with a dull thud. Hall whacked his head on a two-hundred-pound air manifold. The sub rolled farther to starboard. Hall bit his lip. His temples throbbed. He saw a half-dozen sailors and officers pinned against the starboard bulkhead. The diving officer, chief of the watch, and helmsman remained strapped in their seats but were powerless against the wrath of Mother Nature.

Panic welled up in Hall's throat. He knew the sub was close to a thirty-degree angle. If they rolled much farther to starboard, they'd capsize. If that happened, they'd all drown near the Siberian border.

The sub continued to roll. At about forty degrees over, mercury flew out of the open gyro compass and splattered about the control room. A large glob smacked Hall on the cheek and shoved its way into his nose. The smell reminded him of a morgue. Men nearby swatted at the silver orbs that rolled across their faces and uniforms.

The boat rolled even more. Hall figured they were close to forty-five degrees. Through clenched teeth, Lockwood barked out an order. The diving officer forced a strained reply. The boat whined and groaned. Hall muttered a silent prayer. He wanted to live to see twenty.

Thirty seconds passed, then another thirty.

"That was the longest minute of my life," Hall says. "I really thought it was my last."

Mother Nature and God ruled otherwise. The USS *Queenfish* finally pulled out of its death spiral and crashed into the trough of a massive wave.

"We were out of the fire," Hall says, "but back into the frying pan."

Tossed about in a bad storm, absent a working compass, unable to dive again due to low batteries, the *Queenfish* flailed about for two days on the surface. Lost and alone, still in Soviet waters, the crew were far from safe.

"We wanted to get spotted," Hall says, "but not by the enemy."

Praying for a miracle, Hall worked with the crew to gather up the spilled mercury. "We used every silver coin and object we could find to pick up the globs. We looked like a bunch of kids in science class."

Several anxiety-filled days later, a U.S. plane homed in on the *Queenfish*'s radio signal and helped the crew find their way back to Alaskan waters. The navigator managed to use star fixes to get them home to Hawaii.

"That was my first time in the Arctic," Hall says. "And I'm glad it was also my last."

Hall ended his enlistment shortly after that mission. His buddy, Joe Prince, tried to talk him into going into the reserves, but Hall had experienced enough excitement to last him a lifetime.

"I decided on a career as far away from the Arctic Ocean as possible," Hall says.

Despite the near catastrophe suffered by the *Queenfish*, Waldo Lyon and his team at ASL were ecstatic. The readings brought back by Hall and crew proved invaluable in understanding more about Arctic conditions. Hungry for more data, Lyon established a field station at Cape Prince of Wales, Alaska, in 1951.

OVER THE NEXT FEW YEARS, researchers at ASL measured brine content and ice elasticity to provide submarine designers with data to create boats that could surface through thick ice cover. Cold rooms and calibration facilities were used to study ways to eliminate icing on snorkel head valves—a problem that could prevent diesel submarines from sucking in enough air to run their engines and charge batteries. All this research led to the first submerged transpolar voyage by the nuclear submarine USS *Nautilus* (SSN-571), followed by dozens of additional under-ice scientific excursions to further Arctic operations.

When the Soviets launched the *Sputnik* spacecraft in October 1957, President Dwight D. Eisenhower was humiliated. Other free countries started questioning their alliances with the U.S., and the military wondered if they now faced a technologically superior enemy. To address these concerns, Captain William Anderson and the crew of the *Nautilus* were ordered to complete a dangerous voyage to the North Pole, traversing under the polar ice cap for the first time in history.

The public heard about some of this but never knew what really happened under the ice in 1958. After the release of heretofore classified information and logs, and after retired submariners divulged their stories, we now know the *Nautilus* conducted two top-secret missions in the Arctic known as Operation Sunshine I and Operation Sunshine II.

The *Nautilus* made the first trek to the geographic North Pole by crossing underneath the ice in August 1958. Navigating accurately beneath a sheer wall of frost was no easy task. The boat's gyrocompass didn't function well above eighty-five degrees north longitude, and Anderson's crew referred to the risky excursion as "longitude roulette." In fact, Anderson almost blew a hole in the ice with a torpedo to allow the boat to surface so he could gain an accurate bearing.

The *Nautilus* passed near the Russian coastline on its second voyage to the Arctic near Alaska, flaunting its reactor in the face of the Soviets, who had yet to deploy their first nuclear submarine. Not long after this trek, the U.S. Navy's second nuclear submarine, the USS *Seawolf* (SSN-575), departed for North Atlantic waters.

In July 1962, following in the footsteps of the *Nautilus*, the USS *Skate* (SSN-578) logged the first surfacing through Arctic ice when it popped up at the North Pole. The risky maneuver, if done incorrectly, could have damaged systems or caused severe flooding. The *Skate*, in similar fashion to the *Nautilus*, faced several near-fatal scenarios while operating in northern regions. The crew quickly learned that, due to abundant freshwater runoff, unique salinity gradients, massive surface ice, and a host of other challenging conditions, submerged objects operate differently in the Arctic. Sonar systems, torpedoes, communication gear, and navigation equipment transported to this northern "Bermuda Triangle" often became problem children when temperatures dropped below zero and ice entered the equation. These revelations spurred hundreds of subsequent jaunts by submariners during biannual U.S. Navy Ice Exercises (ICEX), wherein two or three U.S. and NATO submarines conducted practice war games to test systems and hone Arctic tactics.

"Thanks to Waldo Lyon and other pioneers, U.S. submarines have been coming to the Arctic to train for decades," says Jeff Gossett, a director at the

Arctic Submarine Lab in San Diego, California, which runs ICEX in concert with the Applied Research Lab. "Without ICEX, fast attack submariners operating up here don't stand a chance against the elements or the enemy."

In 1963, THE ARCTIC REMAINED one of the most dangerous places on earth to operate a submarine. To help solve this problem, the USS *Skate* and USS *Seadragon* (SSN-584) made the first rendezvous at the North Pole for ICEX. In 1969, the USS *Whale* (SSN-638) surfaced at the North Pole, sixty years to the day after Admiral Robert Peary planted the first flag there. The USS *Pargo* (SSN-650) and USS *Skate* completed joint ICEX operations in 1969, and despite the fact that more than a dozen submarines had crisscrossed the Arctic over the previous two decades, the Navy had yet to conduct any surveys or complete bottom contours or shelf maps. This lack of knowledge created a high risk for boats operating in the area.

The year 1970 was a difficult one for America. Vietnam protestors lined the streets, and Russia kept escalating tensions with aggressive political and military moves. The U.S. Navy suspected the Soviets were building new ballistic-missile submarines with greater launch ranges so they could hide under the Arctic ice until it was time to lob missiles at America. For U.S. submariners, the difficulty of finding and sinking those subs was already a tough task; now it would be even harder. To help mitigate this problem, the navy tapped Commander Fred McLaren, CO of the second USS *Queenfish* (SSN-651), to skirt the Siberian coastline, navigate around hazardous sea ice, and complete an extensive survey. Shifting ice floes, deep ice keels extending down to one hundred feet or more, and tumultuous sea conditions made this mission one of the most dangerous conducted during the Cold War.

The *Queenfish*'s first jaunt retraced much of the 1958 *Nautilus* track, starting in the Bering Strait near Big Diomede where Harry Hall on the first *Queenfish* had almost met his demise in 1947. The second excursion began 240 nautical miles past the North Pole down to the Laptev Sea to complete a detailed survey of the Siberian shelf. The crew endured several close calls as the sub dodged enormous icebergs, scraped its hull across massive ice keels, and more than once almost collided with the bottom.

The *Queenfish* inched across three seas at less than seven knots and covered 3,100 miles in less than a month. What ice warriors fear the most in the Arctic is getting wedged into an "ice garage" in shallow water—meaning stuck in between deep ice keels with no way out. Backing a three-hundred-foot-long submarine out of an ice garage using a single propeller is nearly impossible. But that's exactly what McLaren and his crew had to do while surveying a Siberian shelf. When they reversed the prop, it threw the stern down and to port. Going forward was not an option. Only through perseverance and blind luck did McLaren and his crew finally maneuver out of harm's way by backing up and going forward—in similar fashion to dislodging a large truck from a mudhole.

This dangerous mission, and many others, set the stage for U.S. fast attack submarines to become the espionage workhorses of the Cold War by conducting top-secret excursions deep inside enemy waters. The most daring, dangerous, and decorated operations were codenamed Ivy Bells.

CHAPTER 3

IVY BELLS

"To air is human. To HeO$_2$ is divine."

—DAVID LEJUENE, Saturation diver

In February 1968, the Soviet submarine K-129 was lost with all hands in the Northern Pacific. Years later, the CIA asked billionaire Howard Hughes to find and raise the sunken sub so they could pilfer its military secrets. The project was codenamed Azorian and became one of the most amazing technological feats in history. Josh Dean has written an excellent book titled *The Taking of K-129* that explores this project in detail.

To locate the K-129, the nuclear submarine USS *Halibut* (SSN-587) used an advanced underwater drone mounted with high-resolution cameras. A few years later, a Navy captain named James Bradley determined that the drone, nicknamed "The Fish," could also be used to find Soviet communications cables in the Sea of Okhotsk at a depth of four hundred feet.

The Soviets frequently sent unencoded top-secret messages through their Ministry of Communications cables that connected the Vladivostok and Petropavlovsk naval bases. Given the depth of the cable and the complexity of such a task, they thought it was impossible for the U.S. to tap the signals. The U.S. Navy thought otherwise. It decided the cables *could* be tapped by using a sophisticated wiretapping and recording device placed by deep-sea divers. If successful, U.S. intelligence agencies could gain access to the Soviet Union's private military conversations. Bradley created a plan to have the *Halibut* sneak in, attach the recording devices to the cables, and later return to extract the recordings, which would contain weeks of communication traffic. Russian-speaking analysts could then transcribe the unencrypted tapes and deliver the information to the U.S. Navy's intelligence headquarters at Suitland, Maryland.

Bradley convinced the Navy brass that captured communications might include Soviet military plans, details of maneuvers, unguarded conversations between key military and political figures, and other intelligence information. Soviet naval officers might openly reveal the location of practice missiles that had landed near the Kamchatka Peninsula, or perhaps plans for future ballistic-missile tests. Provided with foreknowledge of exercises, U.S. subs could be deployed on espionage missions to photograph and monitor the tests. The National Security Agency (NSA) could also be alerted to upcoming exercises by the Navy's monitoring of increases in military communications traffic. Before any of these benefits could be realized, however, the Navy needed to climb one tall technical mountain.

The air humans breathe consists of 80 percent nitrogen and 20 percent oxygen. Sport divers know that inhaling compressed air from a scuba tank can kill you or cause serious injury if you go down too deep for too long and fail to properly decompress. Navy divers are taught to remain above 130 feet for most dives whenever possible, and although many dives exceed two hundred feet for various missions, divers either decompress or return to the surface within the time allotted by U.S. Navy dive tables.

Diving to 350 feet compresses air so much that a single lungful has an order of magnitude more nitrogen than humans breathe on dry land. Concentrations this high can result in nitrogen narcosis, which can turn a diver into the town drunk, complete with slurred speech, crazed thoughts, and blurred vision. To overcome nitrogen narcosis, Sealab underwater habitats experimented with a diving mixture that used helium instead of nitrogen. Divers acclimated to the pressure by remaining inside a hyperbaric chamber for days or even weeks at a time. They would often complain about the cramped environment and the helium-induced Donald Duck voices and would wonder if the process was safe.

The death of one diver, caused by a diving accident, ended the Sealab experiments, but helium–oxygen diving experiments continued in other labs. Saturation diving was still nascent and experimental during the early seventies, and planned missions to deploy saturation divers covertly from submarines required an innovative approach. Navy scientists had created scenarios to undertake deep-diving projects, but the concepts and technologies envisioned were not yet proven. Going from drawing boards to reality forced American scientists to explore uncharted waters and required sub-mariners and divers to take extraordinary risks.

To accomplish the impossible, Captain Bradley outfitted the *Halibut* with a pressurized hyperbaric diving chamber mounted on the stern to support saturation-diving operations. The chamber resembled the Mystic Deep-Submergence Rescue Vehicle (DSRV-1) and served as the *Halibut*'s mission cover story. The fifty-foot-long, eight-foot-diameter chamber resembled a large torpedo mounted on the back of a submarine by way of metal stanchions. To enter the chamber, divers climbed up through the sub's aft escape trunk.

Almost all submarines are equipped with one or more eight-foot oval escape trunks that allow divers to exit or enter the boat while its submerged, including in the event of an emergency—provided the boat is in relatively shallow water. These trunks are adequate for standard compressed-air dives, but they are not suitable for saturation diving using helium. A hyper-baric diving chamber—which is a sealable pressure vessel with hatches large enough for divers to enter and exit, combined with a compressor to raise the internal pressure—is required for this.

There are two types of hyperbaric chambers. One is used for decom-pression and one for recompression. The former supports deep-sea diving operations, while the latter is used to treat or prevent decompression sickness. In both types, divers "press down" or "press up" by increasing or decreasing the internal pressure, respectively, which takes many long hours to complete.

The *Halibut* was upgraded to carry a stern-mounted hyperbaric chamber in October 1971. Saturation divers boarded the sub and headed toward the Soviet Union with Commander "Smiling Jack" McNish in command. Their mission entailed finding and tapping the Soviet communications cables in the Sea of Okhotsk. From the air, this ocean area resembles a large circular lake. Commander McNish and the crew of the *Halibut* covertly skirted the Russian coastline and searched for days but never found any cables. Finally, McNish noticed a sign near the shore that warned small boats in the area to avoid snagging buried cables in the sand.

To locate the cable, the *Halibut*'s crew deployed the camera-equipped minisub Fish connected to the sub via miles of cable. The tether often snagged on underwater objects, and strong ocean currents caused the cameras to jitter and go out of focus. *Halibut*'s Fish reeled off hundreds of pictures of the ocean floor but did not find the cable. Finally, after days of searching, a three-inch-diameter Soviet communications cable was spotted in one color photo.

McNish ordered the saturation divers to lock out of the submarine's diving chamber. They trudged across the ocean floor, wiretapped the cable, and collected a flurry of signals. However, the signals intelligence (SIGINT) "spooks" onboard the *Halibut* were not trained in this type of signal capture, so the recordings were of poor quality and revealed nothing. The *Halibut* made a second run on August 4, 1972 and returned with no better results. Officials at the NSA and the clandestine Naval Security Group (NSG) were disappointed but remained convinced that valuable intelligence information could be collected if skilled technicians learned how to tap the cables properly.

In the summer of 1974, the NSA asked John Arnold to solve the problem. Arnold was a Navy "mustang officer" who had come up in the ranks from seaman to lieutenant commander and gained considerable expertise in underwater espionage along the way. He had conducted several covert missions near Soviet coastlines while aboard the USS *Nautilus*. Arnold handpicked a team of spooks that included four navy communications technician chiefs, including Master Chief Malcolm "Mac" Empey, Chief Mark Rutherford, and a Russian-speaking communications tech. The chiefs boarded the *Halibut* and reported to their officer in charge (OIC), Tom Crowley, who reported to Captain Augustine "Gus" Hubel. Officially, they were all attached to the NSG.

To prepare for a planned Ivy Bells mission in enemy waters, the *Halibut* crew trained for over a year. Empey and Rutherford performed technological feats that included designing and integrating an array of advanced equipment. The *Halibut* had not had technicians with this level of expertise on the first two runs, which resulted in the poor quality of the signals collected from the cables. The previous "R-brancher" technicians had performed a "capture all" of every conversation on every wire, or channel. They had then dumped the entire mix onto a recorder. This resulted in cacophony, as if a dozen people were talking over one another in a small room. Making sense of the recorded mess was impossible. Empey and Rutherford designed a way to separate each channel, improve the signal processing, and filter the recorded conversations.

Months later, the spooks were ready for the next Ivy Bells mission. While their jobs entailed staying inside the submarine, the most dangerous part of this exercise had to be done outside the boat in dark, freezing waters. This required training dozens of additional saturation divers who were willing to risk their lives to conduct the most dangerous underwater missions in history.

In early 1975, First Class Navy diver David LeJeune walked across the brow of the USS *Halibut* and stared at the fake DSRV chamber on the deck. He shook his head and wondered if he should have declined this mission. He knew that volunteering for special projects meant living in that tiny chamber alongside three other divers for almost two months at a time. The grueling assignment required round-the-clock dives for weeks while in enemy waters. One wrong move could be fatal, not just for the divers but for the entire crew.

By then, LeJeune had years of saturation diving under his belt and had also earned his instructor's pin. He was one of the divers who set a world record for a mixed-gas dive down to one thousand feet. He'd joined the Navy out of high school and volunteered for Underwater Demolition Team (UDT) training during bootcamp. Back then, Navy SEALs and UDTs were under separate commands, and LeJeune wanted to swim, not fight in a jungle. He didn't make it on to the UDT Teams, so he decided to become a Navy Fleet Diver. LeJeune had no idea what that meant but figured it had something to do with swimming. The Navy turned him down for that billet as well, so he sent in five more requests. When finally the sixth one was accepted, he and his wife moved to Norfolk, Virginia.

After thirteen weeks of training, LeJeune earned his second class diver's pin. He later completed first class diver's school in 1970 and graduated from the Washington, D.C. navy yard in January 1971. He conducted inspection dives on the presidential yacht, the USS *Sequoia* (AG-23), before volunteering for saturation-dive training under the Navy's "Man in the Sea" program. That's when his life changed in ways he could never have imagined.

The Navy used a strange-looking craft called the *Elk River* (IX-501) to train saturation divers, which at the time was the most dangerous and advanced form of diving. Commissioned in 1945, the *Elk River* was initially designed to fire rockets but was later converted for saturation-diving operations. Early saturation divers wore one-eighth-inch-thick neoprene wetsuits, over which they pulled on a baggy canvas suit that resembled a farmer's coveralls. They attached a hose to the back of the suit to stream in hot water and prevent freezing. The heated water ran through smaller tubes that branched away from the diver's back and formed a spider's web that covered the legs, arms, and chest. The warm water coated the neoprene like a sprinkler system on a summer's day, and the skintight wetsuit prevented hot-water scalding.

The divers use full-face masks manufactured by Kirby Morgan that resemble the clear Plexiglas ones worn by firefighters. Each mask contains a speaker and microphone to allow two-way communications with the support team. Digital readouts display temperature and mixed-gas levels. A hose dangles from the Kirby Morgan to bring in helium and oxygen.

"Saturation diving uses one hell of a lot of gas," says LeJeune. "We only pump in three percent oxygen compared to almost ninety-seven percent helium, but that three percent feels like thirty to the diver."

High conductivity helium is the second lightest element known to man. The earth's atmosphere contains only five parts per million of this rare gas, which makes it very expensive. It's chemically inert and offers no color, taste or odor, making it ideal for deep-sea diving provided strict safety precautions are taken. Helium robs a diver's body of heat at a rapid pace, so staying warm can be a difficult challenge. Extended dives require large amounts of helium and place divers at great risk. The longer a diver remains down, the more depleted he becomes. That's when mistakes can happen.

"Ten- or even twelve-hour dives were not uncommon," says LeJeune. "In fact, if the job only took six, we'd stay down another two or three just to save face."

After graduating from saturation-dive training, LeJeune reported aboard the *Ortolan* diving platform, where he served from 1973 to 1975. He then joined the crew aboard the USS *Halibut*. He'd heard about the Ivy Bells missions and was intrigued. At the time, he had no idea that, given the danger, they required direct approval from the president of the United States prior to each deployment.

LeJeune learned that during the *Halibut*'s second run, one of the divers had developed kidney stones. Lieutenant Commander "Doc" Halworth had to press down, enter the dive chamber, and pump him full of Demerol. Given the *Halibut*'s slow speed, the diver had suffered for weeks before returning to port. The incident had unnerved many of the other divers, and of the twenty-two who had been aboard the *Halibut* on its first two runs, only two volunteered to go on another Ivy Bells mission.

LeJeune's new diving companions included an Asian Indian with huge Popeye forearms, nicknamed "Gunga Din." John Hunt was a smooth-talking lady's man, and Bob "Ginny" Vindetto was a cocky dark-haired Italian.

"The master diver selected the four best divers for each mission," says LeJeune. "Divers were disappointed if they didn't get picked, but we were all professional about it and worked as a team. We never forgot that we depended on each other for our survival."

The dive team conducted training runs off the coast of California near Catalina Island. The *Halibut* was designed to set down on the ocean floor using snowmobile-like skis mounted to the underside. Teams of three divers each deployed from the DSRV until each diver had been in the ocean at least once. They wore neoprene wetsuits under newer semiclosed Mark 11 saturation diving suits that cost the navy eighty-seven thousand dollars each.

Inside the chamber, divers wore dark brown fire-retardant T-shirts, pajamas, socks and boxer shorts. Bathing towels were also brown and fireproof.

"The clothing they gave us was hot and itchy and had zero absorbency," says LeJeune. "Using those towels was like drying off with sandpaper."

Scuba divers who go deep need to decompress to expel nitrogen from their bloodstreams. Likewise, helium divers must decompress to prevent decompression sickness, which is commonly referred to as "the bends." Saturation divers are also at risk for a condition known as high-pressure nervous syndrome (HPNS), which can cause nausea, dizziness, vomiting, fatigue, cramps, and decreased mental and physical performance. The condition is exacerbated by faster rates of compression or decompression, or where greater depths are required. In the early sixties, when sat diving was still new, doctors recorded several strange symptoms, including "helium tremors." The only way to prevent HPNS is to have the diver compress and then decompress slowly in a hyperbaric chamber while pausing at selected intervals to allow the diver to dissipate helium from the bloodstream.

The diving chamber mounted to the deck of the *Halibut* had two bulkheads that divided the space into three compartments. The smaller aft section housed the watch-standers—a few divers responsible for monitoring the four mission divers. The midsection hatch opened downward into a cylindrical connector attached to the escape trunk. Divers climbed up a ladder and entered the chamber through this hatch. This section also contained extra equipment and provided a pressurized entry point should Doc Halworth need rapid access to the divers.

The larger bow section of the chamber housed the four mission divers and had a life-support system like those used in spacecraft. Watch-standers funneled food, drinks, and supplies to the sat divers by way of an eighteen-inch-diameter "medical chamber" that connected to the forward pressurized section.

"Everything we ate and drank was cold," says LeJeune. "Helium doesn't just rob the body of heat; it also steals warmth from food and water. Pressure differentiation can also be challenging. Sometimes the watch-standers played jokes on us by screwing the lid down too tight on a ketchup bottle. After it's pressurized, you can't get the damn thing off. We got them back by doing the same thing in reverse. But when they opened the bottle, the ketchup exploded in their face."

Due to helium's superconductivity, the diver's forward section was heated to ninety-six degrees Fahrenheit. To the divers, however, it felt like seventy-two degrees. Humidity ran high—almost 100 percent—which caused several health concerns.

"A diver could go to sleep with a minor earache and wake up with pus dripping from his ear," says LeJeune. "Bacterial infections in that heated environment were a big problem."

The divers shared a small sink and public toilet. There was no shower, so watch-standers delivered fresh water for sponge baths through the medical chamber. When the press down started, the helium level rose and caused voices inside the chamber to sound like high-pitched cartoon characters. To compensate for the Donald Duck effect, divers used a "helium speech unscrambler." The small unit synthesized the diver's voices and lowered the pitch and tone to create almost normal-sounding speech.

Depending upon the dive depth, pressing down in the chamber often took between ten and fifteen hours. Ten hours was normal for a four-hundred-foot dive, and going any faster risked HPNS.

"If we went down too fast," says LeJeune, "every joint ached as the pressure pushed out the lubricating joint fluid. Your body needs time to adjust to a high-pressure environment. Most of us got HPNS more than once, which made us act like a drunk with a case of the DTs."

While aboard the *Halibut*, LeJeune made his first Ivy Bells training dive off the California coast in 1975. He locked into the claustrophobic hyperbaric chamber with three other divers and donned a neoprene wetsuit. Body odor filled the chamber. LeJeune sat on a small cot in the diver's section and studied various indicators. Inside the *Halibut's* diver monitoring area, master diver Al Frontz pressurized the chamber down to thirty-three feet. At this depth, the divers still breathed normal air. Frontz increased the pressure over several hours while also increasing the helium level. At 160 feet, when the percentage of oxygen in the chamber could no longer support combustion, Frontz turned off the O2 sensor alarms.

Twelve hours passed before the chamber was pressurized to four hundred feet. LeJeune stood from his cot and followed the other divers to the back hatch, which led to the diving platform. This area had been "blown down" using a small pipe with threaded ends that ran from the diver's section, through the bulkhead, and into the diving platform area. The divers blew helium through the pipe to pressurize the area. Once done, the ocean water ascended only to the bottom of the exit hole.

LeJeune stepped through the thirty-six-inch-diameter opening at the front of the chamber. He reached for the MK-11 diving rig hanging on a bulkhead. He then donned his suit and face mask. The mask was attached to a fiberglass frame that formed a hydroseal made of thin rubber. Around the rubber, a sponge-like material kept the ocean water from flooding his mask. Divers soaked the material in water to draw out the air, smeared on Vaseline, and then clamped the mask down to prevent leaks.

"One of the limiting factors on dives was that mask," LeJeune says. "After eight hours in the water, your jaw feels like you've been punched in the face by Muhammed Ali."

LeJeune pulled on his rubber boots and seated his mask. Each boot contained lead insets and a steel toecap held on with rubber straps. Gunga Din checked him to ensure he was set and ready. LeJeune sat on the edge of the diving platform and dangled his feet in the water. Adrenaline rushed through his veins as the platform was lowered into the ocean, in a similar fashion to a hydraulically operated wheelchair ramp. LeJeune saw nothing but pitch-black ocean as the platform descended.

He pushed off the platform and glided downward like a skydiver in slow motion, floating through the silent ink and descending toward the ocean floor.

"This was always my favorite part," says LeJeune. "I never knew if I was falling into a shark's mouth or what, which made the free fall that much more exciting. I used to live for that moment."

LeJeune's heavy boots landed on the murky silt. He heard only the melodic hiss of his own breathing. He switched on his light and moved toward the other divers. Given the strong currents in the area, he wore two weight belts, which slowed him to a snail's pace. Tiny fish darted past his face mask. Illuminated by his light, they looked like fireflies in an alien world. Inside his mask, near his left eye, a green indicator verified that the HeO2 mix was optimal. If the breathing mix dropped to zero, the red light would flash on. In that event, LeJeune would use a coffee-can-size bottle of mix with enough air for about three breaths. He often wondered if the small can would keep him alive long enough to get back to the sub.

Tubes snaked throughout LeJeune's MK-11 suit and sprinkled warm water across his wetsuit. A two-inch-diameter tethered cord secured him to the boat and delivered the mixed gas, warm water, two-way communications, and power for his lights. A large wire in the cable also functioned as a life-line to reel him back into the submarine in the event of an emergency.

LeJeune moved toward a line locker located on the underside of the *Halibut*. Gunga Din opened the locker and removed a cord that resembled an oversized automobile jumper cable. The cord could be reeled out to a maximum of 350 feet. "Ginny" Vindetto grabbed the cord and motioned for the team to assist. Only three divers had deployed. The fourth remained inside the sub in the event of an emergency.

The divers pulled the cord over to the three-inch-diameter communications cable running along the ocean floor. As if they were in the Sea of Okhotsk on a live mission, the three divers clamped a signal "grabber" around the cable. They covered up any evidence of the tap with a large sand-colored rubber blanket and headed back toward the *Halibut*.

Near the submarine, Vindetto started singing. At first, LeJeune thought the man was goofing around. Then Vindetto started cracking jokes like the ones he'd told on the playground in grade school. LeJeune radioed Frontz inside the sub and said Vindetto might be showing signs of HPNS. Frontz ordered the standby diver, Cleveland Smith, to prepare to reel Vindetto back inside the sub. LeJeune approached the laughing Italian and reached for his arm. Vindetto swatted him away and told LeJeune to "leave him the hell alone." LeJeune tried again, but to no avail. Vindetto ripped down the zipper on his MK-11 and let freezing water rush into his suit. LeJeune told Vindetto to rezip, but the defiant Italian refused. Gunga Din trudged over. He and LeJeune tried to pull the zipper back up, but Vindetto fought them off.

The Italian started singing again, but no more than a few notes came out before the cold water temperature locked his jaw. His eyes rolled up into their sockets and he passed out. LeJeune radioed Smith and told him to start reeling. He clung to his friend while the unconscious diver's arms dangled and flapped in the rushing current. LeJeune's heart skipped a beat as he wondered if they were already too late.

Once inside the chamber, he pulled off Vindetto's suit while Smith grabbed a CPR kit. They pumped on Vindetto's chest and blew air into his mouth. Nothing. No life. LeJeune was certain that his friend had died, and his heart sank. Finally, Vindetto coughed and spewed out saliva.

After Vindetto's close call, other divers also showed signs of HPNS. Halworth and Frontz shortened the dives and rotated the divers to see if physical conditioning might be the cause. Then John Hunt, one of the best-conditioned divers, started acting up after only six hours down. Halworth and Frontz decided they likely had equipment issues.

Several divers, including LeJeune, flew to Panama City, Florida. They spent months in simulated environments testing the MK-11 suits until a suspect finally emerged. Each suit came with a CO_2 scrubber in the backpack that "burped off" one-fifth of the expelled gas. The scrubber used baralyme chemicals to remove CO_2 and recycle fresh HeO_2 back to the diver. This process also evaporated air bubbles to ensure none reached the surface, where they could be seen. The scrubbers had not been heated during the dives, so they were subjected to freezing temperatures at saturation depths. The low temperature prevented the baralyme from scrubbing effectively and caused CO_2 build up. The team redesigned the system and replaced the baralyme with lithium hydroxide—the same chemical used by submariners to scrub CO_2. One of the drawbacks included the possibility of chemical burns, but as far as the divers were concerned, remaining sane took precedence.

In June 1975, loaded with safer equipment and trained sat divers, the *Halibut* made its third voyage to the Sea of Okhotsk. The trek to the Western Pacific took almost a month—twice the normal time due to the *Halibut*'s aging reactor. The geriatric sub could hit no more than thirteen knots. After sneaking past the Soviet fleet near the Kamchatka Peninsula, Commander McNish told the crew their mission would be one of the most dangerous in naval history. They'd be well within Soviet territorial waters, and if caught, they might not survive. Explosive charges had been placed throughout the sub to prevent equipment or survivors from being captured. McNish did not inform the entire crew about the top-secret cable-tapping mission. Only he, his officers, the sat divers, and the spooks knew the full details of their mission.

The *Halibut*'s crew relocated the cable and used a set of anchors and a winch system to settle the submarine onto the ocean floor. Sitting atop the two skis, the boat was anchored near the communications cable. The divers suited up and locked out of the diving chamber. One diver remained inside while three divers walked in moon-like fashion. The HeO_2 mix made the back of their tongues dry, while reflective plankton clouds obstructed their vision.

The divers opened the sealed compartment on the *Halibut*'s hull and removed the electrical cord. They dragged it over to the Russian cable and located the repeater—a large metallic cylinder used to amplify the signals and join sections of the cable every thirty miles. Unlike the previously failed missions, two sets of signals were recorded from the cable. One was a "capture all" containing all the signals, and the other separated each channel so clear conversations could be heard. The team took this function seriously, as hundreds of lives were at risk to gather the signals and they had only one chance to get it right.

Technicians Empey and Rutherford collected the information and validated parameters while a Russian-speaking spook strapped on a set of headphones and listened. To his amazement, clear, unencrypted Russian voices filled his ears. He handed a set of phones to one of the spook chiefs, grinned, and said, "I've got a Soviet admiral talking to his wife on one line... while his mistress is on hold on the other line."

Empey said, "So we just spent tens of millions and years in training to listen to a cheating naval officer?"

The spook smiled and shrugged.

The *Halibut* remained on station for another two weeks, filling reels of tape with recordings. Near their departure time, a flooding alarm sounded. A diesel engine pipe had ruptured, sending a geyser of ocean water into the boat. The divers were still outside and unaware of the situation. The *Halibut*'s crew raced to stop the leak, but freezing water numbed their fingers as they worked. The extra ocean water made the submarine heavier, and Commander McNish knew he'd soon have to "emergency blow" to head toward the surface and save his crew. He ordered the divers back into the chamber but feared they might not make it in time.

As the water rushed in, McNish had only minutes to make the most difficult decision of his career: blow to the surface to save the sub or wait for the divers to return and risk the lives of the entire crew. Moments before he ordered the blow, the damage-control team managed to fix the leak. McNish breathed a sigh of relief as the divers scrambled back inside.

The *Halibut* returned home after a short stop in Guam for repairs, and the dated sub was replaced by the *Seawolf*, which was relieved by the *Parche* in 1978. David LeJeune reported aboard that sub and joined the crew to make several more dives, some in the Barents Sea at depths to seven hundred feet. Submariners on these boats referred to LeJeune and the other navy saturation divers who undertook harrowing Ivy Bells missions by a special name.

They called them heroes of the deep.

These unsung heroes set the bar and stage for numerous saturation dives to follow, and many experts agree that Ivy Bells missions played a significant role in allowing the U.S. to "win" the Cold War. However, after the Cold War, military sat diving waned. Most divers accepted positions with commercial oil and gas companies to conduct deep-sea excursions in remote locations to construct and repair diving rigs and platforms. Given the dramatic decline of the Russian Navy post-1991, the loss of qualified divers in Russia was even more acute. So much so that saturation diving was abandoned altogether. This decision set up a domino effect that later became both fateful and fatal.

CHAPTER 4

WHEN ENEMIES COLLIDE

*"We knew that if [we were] caught, the Russians would show us
no mercy. We had entered their territorial waters
and rammed one of their boats...."*

—WILLIAM REED, Petty Officer, USS *Drum*

During the Cold War years, collisions between U.S. and Russian submarines became almost commonplace. President Nixon at one point placed a temporary hiatus on Holy Stone espionage operations until a serious sonar problem that had caused some of the scrapes could be solved. Unfortunately, when these missions finally resumed, so did the smacks. To understand what really happened in August 2000 to the *Kursk*, how a U.S. attack submarine might have been involved, and how such a tragedy could be covered up for almost two decades, I will now reveal details about a similar collision that occurred during the Cold War. I know this story is true, because I was personally involved.

Near the end of the Cold War, at the request of Submarine Group (SUBGRU) 5, I received a transfer from the USS *Haddo* (SSN-604) to the *Drum* (SSN-677), a newer *Sturgeon*-class submarine. The crew on the *Drum* numbered under one hundred. Our CO, Commander Michael Oliver, was an experienced and proficient leader. Also on board was Lieutenant Robert Kamensky, who many years later was promoted to Rear Admiral in charge of all submarine operations for NATO.

By that time, Soviet tactics had changed dramatically. The Russian Navy had decided to focus on protecting its ballistic-missile submarines (SSBNs) by finding and destroying U.S. submarines and antisubmarine warfare (ASW) ships. The *Victor III* attack submarine had been constructed to perform these missions and was thought to be on a par with U.S. *Sturgeon*-class boats. The NSA also harbored serious concerns about the purpose and capability of a strange object mounted on the rudder of the *Victor III*.

The object resembled a large egg about twenty feet in length and eight feet in diameter, and the NSA had no idea what it might be. Some said it was a new magnetoelectric propulsion system, an innovative weapon, or an advanced towed sonar array. Not knowing the answer sparked fear and urgency at the NSG and NSA.

SUBGRU 5 had seen several photographs I'd taken of *Victor IIIs* while on my previous boat. They wanted more—but closer and clearer. Commander Oliver called a meeting with a handful of the crew. He informed us that we'd been selected to help obtain photos of the odd pod during upcoming Western Pacific (WestPac) Holy Stone missions. Over the next few months, we trained and prepared for the run. Since I'd taken and developed more *Victor III* shots than almost anyone in the fleet, and had also received advanced photographic training, I was asked to assist with the photographic operations.

I completed a few more classes in recon photography and some on-the-job training during local at-sea exercises, and then received orders to report to the diving tower at the Navy SEAL training facility on Coronado Island. Oliver requested that I spend time conducting photographic reconnaissance training with SEAL Team 1. These types of missions were not new and had been commonplace during the Vietnam War. Navy diver photographers like Steve Waterman, author of *Just a Sailor*, completed such operations frequently. Navy divers and photographers sometimes accompanied SEAL teams to locales near beaches, foreign vessels, or shore-based facilities to take reconnaissance photos for upcoming operations.

Months later, we left San Diego Harbor and headed toward Russia. We spent weeks in the Arctic near the Petropavlovsk naval base on the Kamchatka Peninsula before heading south toward Vladivostok inside the Sea of Japan. Despite our proximity to one of the Soviet Union's largest submarine ports, we experienced several uneventful weeks. I wondered if we'd come up dry and head back without any *Victor III* odd-pod photos.

Just over two months into our run, we finally found a *Victor III*. In the reddened "rig for dark" control room, cigarette smoke swirled into the stale air and danced with the steam from a half-dozen coffee cups. The chief of the watch (COW) sat on the port side of the boat. He faced a gray structure filled with black panels and covered with an array of switches, dials, and gauges. His large left arm hid the low-pressure blow panel, and his right shoulder all but covered the square snorkel control area. Just above his head, a horizontal row of red indicators validated that there were no hull openings exposed to the sea.

To the COW's right, a helmsman and planesman slouched in bucket seats, hands resting at the ten and two o'clock positions on two half-oval steering wheels. Cigarettes dangled from their lips as they talked in hushed tones. Each focused on two large dials at eye level that indicated the boat's depth. These two seamen were responsible for maintaining depth control and steering the boat on the ordered course. When trailing a Soviet submarine, which we did frequently, we would often close to within a few dozen yards to record various machinery and propeller noises. One wrong move by either of these sailors could cause a serious collision and send one or both subs to the bottom.

Above and in between these two, dials depicted rudder, fairwater, and stern plane angles, along with gyro course, speed, and dive bubble—the latter indicating the level of the boat in similar fashion to a carpenter's level. Just behind the planesman and helmsman, a burly diving officer puffed on a pipe. The sweet tobacco fumes drifted about the control room like smoke from a chimney.

To the right of the diving control area, just in front of the MK-113 fire control panels, a large gray navigation and plot table, covered with a chart of the area near Vladivostok, kept two people occupied: the quartermaster of the watch and the junior officer of the deck (JOOD).

A panel flanking the left side of the table had recessed buttons to control various functions and a navigation ruler rested on the glass top. The plot served a dual role: one, to plot the course to our next destination, and two, to manually keep track of nearby contacts in relation to our track. Making sure we knew where the other guys were could be critical in preventing a smack. One wrong calculation or assumption could spell disaster.

That night, just over two months into the Holy Stone special operation (SpecOp), a technical spook in the radio room got a distant sniff on the BRD-7 electronics surveillance system. The signal from a MRK-50 series Topol radar, codenamed Snoop Tray 2 by NATO, was faint at first. So faint that the spook almost missed it. As he analyzed the signal captured by the

BRD-7, his eyes lit up. At that time, only *Victor III*s and a few *Delta*-class submarines used MRK-50s.

Commander Oliver smiled in the corridor outside the radio room when he heard the news. However, the spooks had reported both good *and* bad news. The good news: the Snoop Tray 2 signal was not moving, indicating that the *Victor* might be resting at night on the surface, something Soviet subs did occasionally before an exercise. The bad news: the sub was deep inside Peter the Great Bay near Vladivostok, which meant a possible traffic jam of lethal Soviet warships.

Oliver decided to take the risk. If we could get some close-up shots of the *Victor III*'s mysterious odd pod and under-hull pictures of her sleek frame, there'd be big medals and promotions waiting at home. On the other hand, one small miscalculation could result in catastrophe.

Oliver hadn't slept in a while, so he ordered our executive officer (XO) to take the Conn and follow the radar signal, then wake him when we drew close enough for periscope photos and an under-hull photographic run. The *Victor III* wasn't moving, but dozens of other contacts in the area, including several surface ships, were going to and fro at fast clips. Since our fire control system could plot only four targets simultaneously, we dialed Master Two, our *Victor III* submarine contact designation, into one of the digital computer displays, and three other contacts, representing the closest warships, into the other consoles.

We dodged the warships by running slowly while weaving our way into Peter the Great Bay. As we neared our contact, just off Popov Island outside Vladivostok's harbor, and the signal strength on the Snoop Tray 2 radar increased, the XO had someone wake up Oliver. He strode into the control room a few minutes later. He smelled like Old Spice aftershave as he approached the periscope stand.

Oliver rested a hand on my shoulder. "Ready the thirty-five."

"Yes, sir." I opened a locker, removed the thirty-five-millimeter camera, checked the film status, and waited.

Oliver relieved the XO of the Conn and called the under-hull photographic operations party to the control room. He brought the *Drum* to periscope depth and raised the number-two periscope, spun the metal cylinder back and forth, and then stopped. "There she is," he said. "Bearing to Master Two on my mark...mark! Range...nine hundred yards."

Our WLR-9 electronic surveillance measures (ESM) warning indicator started beeping, signaling that enemy radar had gotten a whiff of our extended mast. Through the small PeriViz video display, mounted in the overhead near the periscope stand, we could see what Oliver saw in full color. Streaks of purple-orange clung to a barrage of gray clouds on the horizon as dawn crept toward sunrise.

Against the gray, the dark silhouette of the *Victor III*'s sloping conning tower and extended masts seemed surreal, as if only a picture out of the pages of *Jane's Fighting Ships*. Certainly, the real thing could not be less than a half mile away. Lights blinked onshore behind the Soviet submarine, as Russian families prepared for their day. I wondered who they were, what they were like, if they loved, laughed, and cried like we did. I wondered what they would think if they knew we were hiding in their front yard.

Oliver pushed the small red button on the scope's right handle. A half-second soft whir could be heard as he snapped a seventy-millimeter photo with each button push. He unglued his eye and stepped back from the scope.

He looked my way and asked if I was ready.

I swallowed a lump and nodded.

"You've got two minutes," Oliver said as the WLR-9 chirped away in the background.

I moved over to the scope well and snapped the thirty-five-millimeter into position, then settled my eye onto the back of the camera and squinted. Morning light crept across the ocean as the sun peeked above the snow-capped Sikhote-Alin mountain range on the horizon. With moist palms, I gripped the scope handles tighter and tried to slow down my breathing. On low power, the Soviet submarine filled my view. By feel, I adjusted the camera's focus and f-stop setting and lined up the crosshairs on the odd pod.

The control room settled into silence, save for the manual snapping of the camera shutter. I snapped a dozen photos, then switched to the highest power setting. The oval pod took up the entire cross-haired circle through which I gazed. The WLR-9 beeped again in my left ear, now delivering an almost steady procession of tones.

"Thirty seconds," Oliver said.

The CO's deep baritone pushed my pulse up a notch. My fingers twitched as I swung the view over to the masts and snapped a few more pictures. Moving at what felt like light speed, I detached the thirty-five-millimeter camera and flipped up the scope handles to the vertical position.

"Down scope!" The oily mast lowered into the scope well. Around me the world turned crimson again. I squinted as my eyes readjusted to the dim red light.

Dark circles underscored the CO's brown eyes as he asked about the quality of the shots. I reported that with the lighting angle at this distance, I didn't think they were good enough. I recommended we move to the other side, draw in closer, and get the light behind us.

Nine hundred yards off our port bow sat one of the best attack subs in the Soviet Navy. In almost every way, it was comparable to our *Sturgeon*-class submarine. Yet I had just recommended that we move in closer to take more shots.

Oliver later requested I prepare to egress from the sub and, if needed, take close-up photos of the pod unfettered by the periscope optics. That meant donning a Draeger rebreather, that did not emit any bubbles, and locking out of the escape trunk in a Soviet harbor. Then, swimming to the surface while tethered to a line and taking photographs of a Soviet submarine just a few hundred yards away. Even though I had trained for such a mission, I knew he was asking me to volunteer. I also knew that if I did wind up taking those photos, I could never talk about the ordeal with anyone, not even most of the crew, for decades to come.

Once inside the bow compartment, I opened the bottom hatch to the eight-foot-diameter escape trunk. With the help of a seaman trained in escape- trunk operation, I climbed up the ladder and squeezed inside the oval. I closed the hatch below my knees and fought the fear that filled my chest. A small, dim light cast strange shadows about the tiny metal dungeon filled with gauges and valves. I readied my gear, sat on the bottom of the cold trunk, and shivered. My eyes focused on the small metal communications box mounted on the bulkhead. I prayed that I'd never hear the order to egress come out of that speaker.

While I was in the trunk, I later learned that the XO had taken the boat deeper to maneuver to the other side of the *Victor* so we could get shots with the sun behind us. With the *Victor III* sitting still, sonar remained useless, and our ESM's Snoop Tray 2 radar hits were the only means to determine the target's approximate range and bearing. That information provided only a rough idea of the Russian sub's location, despite the previous periscope fix.

The XO ordered JOOD Nick Flacco to maneuver the *Drum* to a point opposite our previous location, then bring the boat to periscope depth again. Knowing that doing an under-hull photographic operation might be next, Flacco ran through a mental checklist. As he did, a silent alarm went off in his head. They had not yet reeled in the VLF radio wire.

Flacco called for a radioman, who sprinted into the control room. The petty officer opened a door at the front and stepped inside the tiny area that led up to the bridge. He undogged the lower hatch, climbed up the ladder, and started reeling in the wire. Meanwhile, Oliver returned to the Conn and once again took command. He approached the number-two periscope and waited until Flacco confirmed that the *Drum* had almost reached periscope depth. Oliver wrapped his hand around the orange metal hoop encircling the scope well and then pulled the round bar clockwise. "Up scope."

With his hands gripping the scope handles, Oliver seated his eyes into the rubber socket and waited for his prize to come into focus. As the *Drum* neared the surface, Oliver frantically lowered the scope and yelled, "Emergency dive!"

Too late.

A thunderous boom shook the boat.

The radioman who'd been reeling in the wire tumbled down the ladder and slammed onto the deck. Blood oozed from his head. The frightening sound of metal screeching across metal filled ears in the control room. The boat lurched forward and angled down at the bow by ten degrees. Flacco glanced at the unconscious radioman, then at the door leading to the bridge. His heart raced. The lower hatch was still open. If the sail started to flood...

Down in the bow compartment, shoved into the escape trunk, I heard a deafening clap above my head, followed by an earsplitting metal shriek. The dim light in the trunk blinked out, leaving pitch black in its wake. The force shoved me headfirst into a valve handle. My jaw hit the metal wheel. A stinging pain rippled across my face, and the salty taste of blood filled my mouth. I cupped my palm across my bleeding lip and felt for the communications unit in the dark. My fingers found the square box. I depressed the key. I spat out a clump of blood and blabbered something unintelligible. Nothing but silence. I keyed the box again. Still nothing. I tried opening the bottom hatch to the trunk using every bit of muscle I could muster, but the wheel would not turn.

Alone in the dark, I wondered if we had suffered a major casualty; wondered if we were on a death spiral toward the bottom. For a moment, I contemplated flooding the trunk and escaping through the upper hatch. Then I remembered that we were deep in Soviet territorial waters. I decided we must have collided with the *Victor* and the force of the impact near the escape trunk had knocked out the bow compartment communications circuit. My chest heaved as I realized that the oxygen flow to the trunk had also been shut off. A shock wave must have hit oxygen bank number one and ruptured the O2 valve. The collision must have also caused a pressure imbalance in the trunk, making it impossible for me to open the hatch from the inside. I spat out some more blood and bit on my Draeger's mouthpiece. The throbbing pain around my bottom lip made we wince as I sucked in a breath of air from my rebreather.

I was now living on borrowed time.

Up in the Conn, Flacco had ordered a sailor to drag the radioman away from the bridge door and shut the lower hatch. The quartermaster called for the doc. Commander Oliver demanded to know why the sub wasn't diving. Flacco glanced at the depth gauge. Still at sixty feet.

"Chief of the watch," Flacco said. "Flood forward trim tanks."

The boat surged forward a few feet. It angled down even more but did not go deep. More screeching and grinding rippled through the control room, followed by several loud thuds. Flacco figured the *Drum* had likely impaled the *Victor's* ballast tank and informed Oliver, who ordered all back full.

Metal crunched as the *Drum* moved back several feet. The bow dropped by a few degrees. Oliver ordered all-ahead flank. The boat shot forward and downward. The depth gauge registered a hundred feet and descending. Then the flooding started. Rain poured from the overhead and drenched the scope well.

Flacco looked up. One of the scope seals had ruptured in the collision. Cold saltwater rained onto the deck and splattered shoes. The flooding alarm sounded.

Oliver clicked the 1MC main communication circuit. "Now flooding in the control room."

The XO called for a damage-control party. Auxiliarymen came running with tools and patches. Taking on water, the *Drum* shot toward test depth, 1,300 feet down. Freezing ocean water sprayed out of the scope well. Flacco knew they had to get the flooding under control soon or vital equipment might short out and systems might shut down, which could send the *Drum* to the bottom.

As the "A-gangers" worked on the scope well leak, Oliver ordered a course change south toward Korea. Flacco heard the nearby pings of Soviet fifty-kilohertz active sonar through the hull. He knew Russian ASW forces were now determined to catch the *Drum* red-handed.

In the escape trunk, I heard Oliver's flooding report over the 1MC.

The announcement meant someone was still alive, but the flooding verified we had serious problems. Regardless, I had to get out of the trunk. The air in my Draeger would not last forever. I took out my diver's knife and started tapping Morse code on the metal hatch. My dad had taught me the entire alphabet when I was a kid, and at one point I could even keep up with a Continuous Wave (CW) transmission. Now, however, all I could remember were a few letters. It didn't matter; the seaman on the other side of the hatch probably knew less than I did.

I tapped "SOS."

No response.

I tapped again, louder. Still nothing.

Panic threatened to block what little air I had left from reaching my lungs. I remembered my navy diver training, during which I'd been harassed in the water for hours. The trainers had pulled out my regulator, spun me in circles, and tried to make me panic. The training had taught me a valuable lesson: how to control my fear. Now, thousands of miles away from that training facility, I closed my eyes and said a quick prayer. Then I sucked in a few breaths and tapped again.

Finally, the lower hatch opened and fresh air rushed in.

Back in the control room, the "A-gangers" managed to stop the flooding and fix the leak, while the corpsman patched up the radioman. He'd sustained a concussion and a deep cut to his forehead. Flacco watched the doc help the petty officer hobble out of the control room.

Above us, Soviet helicopters dropped sonobuoys that bombarded the ocean with active sonar pings. ASW destroyers and fast gunboats came out of Vlad and started chasing the *Drum* southward. Dozens of propellers chopped at the Sea of Japan, and our sonar jockeys couldn't keep up with all the contacts. Oliver ordered a thirty-degree course change—a zig to remain undetected. Flacco figured the Soviets knew what Oliver knew: the *Drum* could only head south through a narrow passageway to escape. If they threw enough ships and planes at us, the odds of getting away would be dismal.

While Flacco contemplated his odds of survival, a depth charge exploded.

By now I had scrambled out of the escape trunk and sprinted to my rack to pull on my coveralls. I shuddered as an explosion shook the boat, and then climbed up the ladder to the crew's mess to find the doc and get a patch for my bleeding lip. I scrambled up to the control room and slid onto the bench next to a half-dozen officers and sailors in front of the fire control equipment. The weapons officer (weaps) glanced at the bandage on my face and gave me a look that said, "What the hell happened to you?"

I didn't bother to explain.

Another depth charge exploded, and all eyes glanced upward. All lips muttered silent prayers. Weaps informed me that we'd rammed into the *Victor III* and probably smashed the entire front end of our sail. The ESM antenna was gone, and both periscopes were useless, not that we needed them now anyway. The flooding had been contained, but now every Russian ship, plane, and submarine in the Far East wanted us dead.

I wondered if I should have stayed in the escape trunk.

Sonar reported that our closest pursuers were two *Kresta I*–class guided missile destroyers. They carried two twin-missile launchers and a Ka-25 Hormone ASW helicopter on the after deck, complete with sonobuoys. ASW ships and planes pinged nonstop. We hugged the ocean floor for the next two days while explosions shattered the silence, some far away, others so close they rattled dishes. Sonar reported high-speed screws in the water more than once, signaling that the Russians were blindly shooting torpedoes at us and hoping one would land.

We knew that if we were caught, the Russians would show us no mercy. We had entered their territorial waters and rammed one of their boats. Oliver would take us below crush depth before he'd surrender. All of us understood well the consequences should we fail to escape, yet everyone controlled their fear and did his job. During those few days of hell, I gained a new understanding of what it meant to be a submariner.

We managed to escape and crawl back to Apra Harbor, Guam for repairs. We pulled in at night so Soviet satellites would not see the damage. When we slid next to the pier and climbed up through the hatch, I caught a glimpse of the sail before the crew covered it with a tarp. It looked like a crushed beer can. My throat tightened at the memory of the explosions, and to this day, I still occasionally have nightmares about those three days in hell.

The collision was never reported to the press. When the Russians claimed that an American submarine had collided with and severely damaged their K-324 *Victor III* submarine, the U.S. Navy denied any involvement. In fact, the incident was covered up by the U.S. for decades. In August 2000, when I heard the news that the *Kursk* had gone down, a chill ran down my spine. Tears filled my eyes as I watched the horror unfold and imagined what those twenty-three survivors must be enduring. Memories of the collision on the USS *Drum* left me sleepless for weeks.

Later, when the news broke that the survivors had died and Russia claimed that the USS *Memphis* or *Toledo* had collided with and sunk the *Kursk*, my heart rocketed into my throat. Could it be that the U.S. was covering up another collision? One that had caused the death of 118 submariners? If so, why?

Years later, I discovered the shocking answer to that question.

CHAPTER 5

THE SPY'S ARREST

"[Pope]...was involved in a dangerous situation,
but they didn't warn him."

—U.S. SECRET OPERATIVE

During the latter part of the Cold War and well into the 1990s, the U.S. Navy harbored deep concerns about Russian underwater weapons development. By the mid-nineties, U.S. intelligence networks confirmed that some of Russia's *Oscar*-class boats, like the *Kursk*, had been modified to fire Shkval rocket torpedoes capable of hitting speeds of up to two hundred knots underwater. Soviet Research Institute NII-24 had started working on this advanced design back in the 1960s and merged with the GSKB-47 in 1969 to create the Research Institute of Applied Hydromechanics in Kiev, Ukraine. Out of that merger came the first Shkval.

A decade passed before the first rocket torpedo became operational, an event that sent a shudder down the spine of U.S. Navy admirals who'd been briefed. If a Soviet sub fired one of these things at you, there might not be enough time to escape. Also, if a U.S. boat fired a MK-48 ADCAP torpedo at a Russian sub, and the Russians shot a Shkval in reply, the U.S. crew might be forced to evade and cut the guidance wire on the MK-48 before it exploded.

Dubbed the VA-111, the Shkval is one of the fastest and deadliest torpedoes in the world. While bragging about the design in an essay, a Russian submarine designer described the weapon as having "the lightning stab of a dagger."

To understand how the Shkval achieves its mind-boggling speed, I met with Chuck Brickell, one of the directors at the Advanced Research Laboratory (ARL) located on the Pennsylvania State University campus in University Park. The spry seventy-two-year-old former submarine commander took me on a tour of the lab, which included the facility's famous water tunnel, where the latest torpedo designs have been tested since ARL's inception.

Originally launched by the U.S. Navy in 1945, the ARL technology think tank is one of the world's best-kept secrets. It has connections to the Office of Naval Research (ONR) and is operated by Penn State. ARL has been at the forefront of numerous technological advancements for underwater systems, including breakthroughs in torpedo, sonar, propulsion, navigation, and other technology disciplines. Today, the lab is involved in several secret projects, including supercavitating weapons, Advanced SEAL Delivery Systems for clandestine operations, underwater "jet engine" propulsion systems, *Star Wars*-style laser weapons, *Star Trek*-like command centers featuring holographic systems, and much more.

During the Cold War, and later, submerged frontline heroes barely made it home alive due to technological limitations and problems. ARL is committed to solving these real-world issues with inventions that demonstrate how American ingenuity is still very much alive and well. While standing in a back room at the lab, Brickell explained how supercavitation allows the Shkval torpedo to run faster than a track star.

The twenty-seven-foot-long Shkval isn't a rocket torpedo, per se. It uses a rocket engine to boost the projectile up to cavitation speed, whereupon a hydrojet takes over and burns a magnesium fuel that employs seawater as the oxidizer. By supercavitating, the torpedo forms something akin to a force field around the tip of the projectile that allows for ultrahigh speeds.

Shkvals are launched from 533-millimeter torpedo tubes at fifty knots— around the top-end speed for a MK-48 torpedo—whereupon the liquid-fuel rocket propels the cylinder to a speed of two hundred knots. Propellant tanks on the Shkval contain one and a half tons of $H2O2$ and five hundred kilograms of kerosene. When the two are combined, ignition happens.

The rocket uses four fins that skim the inner surface of the supercavitation "force field" to control the direction in the water. To make a course correction, a fin on the inside is extended while a fin on the opposite side is retracted. For whip-fast turns, there's a push plate on the nose that controls the cavitating bubble shape, which in turn modifies the direction.

Initial Soviet designs called for nuclear warheads, but most Shkvals carry conventional explosives. Brickell mentioned that the Russians had since developed a next-generation version of the Shkval called the Predator, which could achieve a speed of more than three hundred knots underwater.

Pope's Prison

By the late nineties, the NSG and NSA had placed "Shkval intelligence-gathering" at the top of their espionage list. Given the threat posed by this new type of weapon, understanding its capabilities and limitations became a high priority. To capture the information needed, they enlisted the services of a retired U.S. Navy captain named Edmond Pope. When Pope accepted the clandestine mission, he understood the risks, but he had no idea just how dangerous and terrifying his journey into the unknown would become.

Pope had been chosen for the mission because he was the founder and director of the U.S. Navy's Foreign Science and Technologies Program, which promoted the exchange of scientific information between former Soviet nations and the U.S. This gave him access to military facilities in Russia. He was also an expert on submarine and torpedo technologies.

Pope grew up as an all-American boy in a small Oregon town. Friends described him as a driven and devoted patriot. He joined the Navy in 1969 and became an intelligence officer specializing in Soviet weapons. His role required him to work closely with ONR, and his official title, according to federal staff directories, was "intelligence adviser and director of security."

Pope retired as a Navy captain in 1994 and accepted a position with ARL at Penn State. His job included initiating collaborative efforts between Russian and U.S. engineers to research various technologies and weapons. He left the lab in 1997 but remained on the books as a consultant. The collapse of communism in 1991 left Russian labs and factories desperate for business. During the late 1990s, Pope undertook dozens of trips to Russia, where he used this fact to convince Russian engineers and plant directors to divulge details about sensitive technologies.

"Ed would have a meeting with a group of engineers, and five others would show up for a show-and-tell, and others would line up out the door," says one of Pope's colleagues. "Ed was trying to get as much exposure to the technology as possible. His message was, 'You lift your skirt, and I'll lift mine.'"

Pope became successful in gaining intelligence nuggets, but he also sparked consternation among Russian businesspeople. According to colleagues, he would promise the world, including lucrative U.S. Navy contracts, but rarely delivered more than empty words. One witness reported that a lot of Russians got mad at Pope because he was a big talker and waved money around, but then wouldn't deliver.

One Russian defense lab, called Region, had distributed glossy marketing brochures about the new Shkval rocket torpedo. Region was based in Moscow but had built a testing and fabrication facility near a large lake in Kyrgyzstan, an impoverished nation that had gained independence from Russia after the end of the Cold War.

Frequently unable to make payroll, Region was hungry for business and therefore an easy target for Pope. While it could publicly promote the Shkval's capabilities, Region was not authorized to sell any technical specifications to foreign nations. Russia's arms export agency, Rosvooruzhenie, retained control over most arms sales and weapons information.

In 1999, Pope signed a contract with Region to commercialize some of the technologies used in the Shkval. A Russian government export agency called Russian Technologies was also involved in the deal. Under the guise of studying the Shkval's technology for use in the commercial ferry industry, Pope had secured a one-hundred-and-eighty-thousand-dollar contract paid for by ONR. To obtain additional information for ONR and ARL, Pope paid thirty thousand dollars to Anatoliy Babkin, a Moscow academic and engineer who had once worked on the Shkval. The former employee, who had rarely been paid by the Russians, offered details about the torpedo's new variants and fuel, which was partially made from a powdered metallic substance.

To study the technology and create countermeasures, and potentially reverse-engineer a similar torpedo, officials at the NSA, NSG, and Pentagon had been trying for years to get their hands on a Shkval. Their attempts had always failed. Russia had deported several British arms experts for doing nothing more than inquiring about the technology. Although the rocket torpedo had been publicly touted at defense expositions and in magazines and books, only the Chinese had been allowed to purchase forty of the torpedoes in the mid-nineties.

In 1998, a group working for the Canadians—and indirectly and discreetly for the U.S.—had offered the Region weapons facility up to ten million dollars to buy five Shkval torpedoes and testing equipment. In March 2000, the sale was about to close. Due to Pope's likely involvement with the deal, the Russian Federal Security Service (FSB)—the replacement agency for the infamous KGB—had placed him on a short list of a dozen foreign defense experts they were targeting for possible criminal charges.

During some of his visits to Russia to meet with Region, Pope more than once detected undercover agents following him. His heartbeat accelerated at the thought of being arrested or potentially even killed for his involvement in the operation. On one occasion, men with dark faces and suits cornered Pope and demanded a cut of the proceeds. He never knew if they were FSB or Russian mobsters, but he did know that his life had been threatened if he did not comply. Despite the risks, he refused to pay.

Days before the fifty-four-year-old Pope had bought the plans and his Canadian partners had secured the purchase of the Shkval torpedoes from Region, the FSB and Rosvooruzhenie rushed in and halted the sale. Because Region's headquarters were in Moscow, the facility fell under Russian restrictions for weapons sales to foreign nations.

On March 26, 2000, Vladimir Putin was elected president of Russia. Eight days later, brandishing guns and badges, Russian security agents slammed open the door to Pope's hotel room in Moscow, manhandled him into subservience, slapped his wrists with handcuffs, and shoved him into a black government vehicle. The KGB also arrested Anatoliy Babkin, the former Shkval engineer, and Daniel Kiely, a U.S. underwater propulsion expert from ARL. They forced those two men to sign confessions admitting to an attempt to steal state secrets. Kiely was eventually released, but Pope was thrown into a tiny cell, where he paced back and forth and did push-ups to remain active and sane. He suffered from frequent dizziness and blinding headaches, and his wife harbored concerns that the ailments were caused by Pope's thyroid problems or a resurgence of a previous bout with bone cancer.

During the ordeal, one intelligence source commented that Pope "was involved in a dangerous situation, but they didn't warn him." He said that Canadian and U.S. operatives "should have said to Pope, 'Things are too hot right now, so stay away from Shkval.'"

As expected, U.S. Navy spokesperson Admiral Stephen Pietropaoli said, "To our knowledge, Ed Pope was a businessman who occasionally did work on a contract basis with our Navy research lab." The government's position was that Pope was not a spy and therefore did not need a warning.

Nikolai Patrushev, the FSB director at the time, said the Pope incident demonstrated that "in Russia's murky waters, foreign businessmen-spies have worked freely, buying technologies created by thousands of people for mere kopeks. With Pope, Russia showed this has ended."

In early April, Mark Medish, the thirty-seven-year-old special assistant to President Clinton, received an urgent call. As the senior director for Russian affairs on the National Security Council, Medish was no stranger to stressful situations or the U.S.'s ever-rocky relationship with Russia. He had studied Russian relations at Georgetown, Harvard, and Oxford. Although he had grown up in the D.C. area, he was the son of a Russian emigrant. His father had served in the Soviet Army during World War II and had been captured by the Germans while fighting near Stalingrad. Medish's father later died in captivity, but Medish managed to find his way to America. His expertise in Russian affairs propelled him toward a career with the U.S. government and into his role as the primary expert on what the Russians were thinking, doing, or planning to do in the future.

Medish was tasked by Clinton with finding a way to free Pope from his prison cell. He knew how Russians thought and acted. He was also experienced in difficult negotiations with Russian government officials, and informed Pope's family that he would do everything possible to secure Pope's release. He also devised a strategy to continuously place the matter on Clinton's desk to keep the balls rolling forward.

"Negotiating Pope's release required balancing on a tightrope," says Medish. "We had to give the case enough attention to secure his release, but not so much as to make the Russians think he was an asset. Doing that would have heightened suspicions that he was guilty and reduce the chances of bringing him home."

After Pope's arrest, the NSA and NSG now also needed to balance on a tightrope. The former naval officer had failed to secure information about the Shkval, and gaining acoustic, photographic, and electronic intelligence on this dangerous new weapon became an even higher priority. In April 2000, the COs of two U.S. espionage submarines were given orders to obtain that intelligence on upcoming missions, regardless of the risks involved.

CHAPTER 6

PRELUDE TO A TRAGEDY

"[I]t was very dicey at times when we had to weave around obsta-cles or dive quickly to avoid slamming into an iceberg."

—TOM KUNZ, Petty Officer, USS *Memphis*

Vladimir Putin was never destined to be a ruthless world leader. He was born into the Leningrad home of Vladimir Spiridonovich Putin and Maria Ivanovna Putina on October 7, 1952. Maria worked in a factory, and Vlad Sr. was a diesel submariner in the Soviet Navy. Putin Jr. was by no means a silver-spooner, and endured a humble and difficult life in a communal apartment in Leningrad. Putin's meager beginnings allowed him to understand well what it means to lack life's basic necessities, including adequate food, water, shelter, and gas for heat.

Young Putin was a strong-headed and rowdy boy. By the time he reached the fifth grade, his defiant behavior denied him membership into the coveted Pioneers organization at his school. He found a release for his anger by learning how to take down opponents in the boxing ring. He then traded his gloves for judo and karate belts, and eventually won his city's sambo championship by beating the reigning world judo champ.

When Putin turned sixteen, he imagined himself as a KGB officer on exciting undercover assignments. He set up a meeting with the KGB directorate to find out what it might take to join their ranks, and was told to get a law degree and never call them again. He acted on the advice, signed up for law school in Leningrad in 1970, and graduated five years later. He did not contact the KGB. Instead, they recruited him in 1975, and at the age of twenty-two, he was finally living his boyhood dream.

Putin completed his training as a KGB officer and was eventually recruited by the first chief directorate to monitor U.S. and other foreigners in Leningrad. He later accepted an undercover assignment as a translator and an interpreter at the KGB station in Germany. Part of his job entailed recruiting other undercover agents to become spies stationed in the United States.

Putin ended his KGB career in 1991 after attaining the rank of lieutenant colonel. He was then selected as the head of the Committee for External Relations in Saint Petersburg, where he was responsible for promoting international relations and foreign investments. During that time, he became embroiled in a ninety-three-million-dollar foreign aid scandal, but his cunning allowed him to avoid losing his job. Instead, he effectively got a raise by employing strong negotiating skills to maneuver his way into various promotions within the government at Saint Petersburg.

President Boris Yeltsin appointed Putin deputy chief of presidential staff in March 1997. Yeltsin later made him head of the FSB. In 1999, a decade had passed since the collapse of the Berlin Wall, but that historic event had done little to dampen global fear and paranoia. That same year, Putin watched the wind fall from Russia's sails as Yeltsin was embarrassed on the world stage by NATO. Objections voiced by the ailing president over the U.S.-instigated bombing of Yugoslavia in March 1999 had been brushed aside like the buzzing of an insignificant fly. Defense ministry general Leonid Ivashov uttered what every Russian believed: "NATO is an agent of war, not peace. It is a criminal organization that does not have the right to exist."

Having served as a KGB colonel, Putin used the public anger over Russia's fall from grace to propel his rise to power. He campaigned as a pro-military leader with a plan to breathe new life into Russia's withering war machine. As the son of a proud Soviet submariner, Putin proclaimed that the Navy should not be treated "like a poor relative."

Yeltsin's health and public image continued to decline as the president engaged equally with vodka and corruption. He propelled Putin into the position of acting prime minister of the government of the Russian Federation and announced that he wanted the former KGB officer to be his successor. Putin then declared his decision to run for the presidency. His odds of winning did not look good. On August 16, 1999, the State Duma approved Putin as the prime minister of Russia, but an election poll taken that month gave him less than 2 percent of the votes for president. Little did he know that the captain of a Russian submarine would change the course of history by helping to propel him to power.

In late August 1999, Captain Gennady Lyachin and his crew aboard the *Kursk* embarked on a two-and-a-half-month voyage to secretly traverse the coastlines near England and Norway and glide undetected through the Strait of Gibraltar. The *Kursk*—an *Oscar II*–class killer submarine—was longer than a football stadium and taller than an eight-story building. The massive behemoth was one of ten submarines of the *Ante*-class and carried twenty-four Granit nuclear missiles, each with warheads containing forty times the explosive power of the bombs dropped on Japan during World War II. The sub's double hull made the vessel nearly impossible to sink, even after a direct hit by a U.S. MK-48 ADCAP torpedo.

During his mission, Lyachin inched up the attack periscope to spy on ships traversing the Mediterranean. An anxious circle of officers crowded around the periscope stand as their captain turned the metal cylinder left and right and flipped from low to high power. Lyachin removed his eye, smiled, and cupped his hands near the eyepiece to reflect golden sunlight off a nearby fire control panel. The officers let out a chorus of oohs and aahs at the sight. Later that day, in the Adriatic Sea near Yugoslavia, with a tense hush permeating the GKP, Lyachin ordered his crew to close in tight on the aircraft carrier USS *Theodore Roosevelt*. The space was rigged for ultraquiet, and with all unnecessary systems turned down or off, all clanking and chatting ceased. With orders issued in hushed whispers, the *Kursk*'s fire control party gained an accurate firing solution for its Shipwreck missiles.

Lyachin swiveled the periscope cameras upward and beamed the images via closed-circuit video to televisions in the GKP and crew's mess. The crew gasped as images of the aircraft carrier's massive hull came into view. The ship's huge propellers pounded the ocean with fury as its aircraft screamed from the deck to complete missions over Yugoslavia.

In the control room of the *Roosevelt*, officers were alerted by sonar operators that a predator had been detected. Nine P-3 Orion ASW aircraft were spun up and sent on the hunt. They occasionally got a sniff of the *Kursk* but could not keep an accurate track. When they were finally able to close in, Lyachin reluctantly ordered his sub to leave the area. Filled with mixed emotions, he both fretted and smiled. He was disappointed he'd been chased away, but he was ecstatic he'd proven to the West that the Russian Navy was still a formidable adversary. NATO had been sent a sobering message: a Russian submarine had easily slipped through its defenses and obtained a firing solution. At any time, the *Kursk* could have launched its missiles and obliterated the *Roosevelt*.

With his chest full of pride and confidence, Lyachin led the *Kursk* on another mission to the North Atlantic in the fall of 1999, again to spy on and harass the American fleet. He and his crew also accomplished this task with flying colors, but the deployment was not without peril. A fire broke out in a turbine compartment and filled the area with heavy smoke. Some of the crew were rendered unconscious, and tensions ran high. Aided by his damage-control team, Lyachin displayed a calm demeanor and ordered the crew to do as they had learned through countless drills. They quelled the fire, evacuated the unconscious sailors, and rose to periscope depth to ventilate the boat.

Having survived a near catastrophe while completing another successful run, the crew pulled up next to a Northern Fleet pier on October 19, 1999. They were met by smiling senior officers, a brass band, and the scent of roast pig steaming in a large vat. To a man, they felt lucky to have been selected to serve aboard the best submarine in the Russian Navy.

Later that month, during congressional testimony, U.S. Sixth Fleet vice admiral Daniel J. Murphy Jr. revealed that the USS *Roosevelt* had been harassed by a Russian *Oscar* submarine. He said the sub had demonstrated "the very best technology" and offered "the highest difficulty in tracking and locating." He went on to explain that the *Oscar* had caused NATO aircraft to continue "looking for a tank one day and then looking for a submarine on the following day."

During a subsequent interview about the affair with a Russian newspaper, Lyachin bragged about the mission by saying, "We did not give the adversary's forces any rest." Prime Minister Putin read the article and invited Lyachin to Moscow to debrief his military advisors. He then leveraged the *Kursk*'s mission successes to announce his plans to upgrade the country's naval forces—especially the submarine Navy—so Russia could continue to challenge NATO forces in the Mediterranean and elsewhere. Naval officers and sailors breathed a sigh of relief. Perhaps the decade-long naval neglect was finally over. Although most of the country was still impoverished, many citizens viewed plans for expanded military construction as hope that more jobs were on the horizon.

On December 31, 1999, a withering Boris Yeltsin helped usher Putin to power by naming him acting president. Navy commanders displayed their elation by inviting Putin to visit the naval base on the Kola Peninsula and spend an evening aboard a nuclear sub. Putin accepted and that night participated in a centuries-old ceremony. He became an honorary sailor by descending into the torpedo room to kiss a grease-lined hammer and drink a cup of ocean water. The following day, while bundled in a navy greatcoat and cap, he observed the launch of an unarmed ballistic missile, fired from a submarine, as it streaked across a gray Arctic sky and shot toward the Kamchatka Peninsula.

Later, to a cheering crowd huddled on a Northern Fleet pier covered in frosty white, Putin spoke about the *Kursk*'s mission success and his ten-year plan to upgrade the Russian Navy. A key part of that plan was a massive exercise scheduled for early August 2000, featuring the *Kursk*, followed by a display of might and power in the Mediterranean later that fall. An article in the *Rossiiskaya Gazeta* echoed the majority sentiments of the entire nation: "Yes, we know how to make war. Yes, we no longer want to hear Tomahawk missiles on the heads of the Serbs, the Iraqis, and the Arabs."

Three days later, Vice Admiral Nikolay Mikheev stoked the fire by stating, "This time, our presence will be even higher than it was in Soviet times."

Thanks to his tough war policies in Chechnya and his promises to build more submarines like the *Kursk*, Putin soared in popularity, earning 53 percent of the votes (a surge from the previous 2 percent) and winning the presidency in March 2000. Russia's Military News Agency provided details about the announced three-day-long naval exercise on May 11, 2000, which sent the NSA and NSG into a frenzied spin. Three espionage ships and two submarines were put on high alert and tasked with preparing for the most important covert operation in the past decade. Naval officers with a need to know exchanged nervous banter as their eyes sparkled with anticipation. They were tired of a decade of decay brought about by a bevy of less-than-important missions. Now, finally, they were about to earn their sea pay as spies of the deep.

The USS *Memphis* Prepares for the Hunt

Dozens of ships and submarines were scheduled to participate in the unprecedented display of Russia's military might. Eyebrows at the NSA shot upward when intelligence sources reported that the *Kursk* was not only carrying several Shkval rocket torpedoes, but planned to test-fire the weapons during the upcoming Russian naval exercise. Naval intelligence officers rushed down to piers in Groton, Connecticut, where the USS *Memphis* and USS *Toledo* were moored. They shimmied down ladders, cornered the COs of both submarines, and updated them on their top-secret orders: prepare for a critical Holy Stone operation to maneuver in close to the *Kursk* and monitor the Shkval test-firings.

Both COs were painfully aware that their crews, as good as they were, might not be as honed for this mission as desired. During the Cold War, most fast attack submarines had spent over 90 percent of their mission time trailing Soviet ships, SSBNs, and attack submarines. They had gained key knowledge and experience on how to sneak in close—sometimes to within less than five hundred yards—and follow the enemy for days or even weeks at a time. Prior to 1991, crews aboard U.S. subs gained thousands of hours of on-the-job training to hone their espionage skills to a fine point.

When the Cold War ended, there were far fewer Russian submarines to trail. Fast attack crews spent less than 20 percent of their time conducting these missions and over 80 percent on drug interdiction or other mundane assignments. Instead of being on-the-job, most training was conducted on dry land in simulation training facilities. As a result, most submariners and COs had lost their edge. Their ability to operate effectively in hostile environments that required "up close and personal" surveillance had waned. During the Cold War, submarine crews conducted these dangerous missions like well-oiled machines. By May 2000, they were far less proficient, trained, and alert.

During May and June 2000, crews aboard both boats knew they were preparing for a deployment that was far from ordinary. Although most were not briefed on all the details, they were seasoned enough to know that this was not a typical run into "Ivan's" backyard. Excitement and fear ran high. Nonqualified sailors paced the deck on watch or tapped nervous fingers on keyboards to test systems or tossed sleeplessly in bunks in anticipation of the unknown. Qualified and experienced petty officers, chiefs, and officers pretended like it was just another mundane excursion while secretly wondering if they'd make it back home.

WHEN CHIEF YEOMAN (YNC) TOM KUNZ WALKED across the brow to board the USS *Memphis* in May 2000, he knew something was different. Being chief yeoman entailed shuffling papers, managing personnel files, and typing up mission reports. The position gave him access to top-secret information not divulged to most of the crew, but he had not been briefed on the nature of their upcoming SpecOp. His fingertips tingled with anticipation as he thought about the unknown dangers that lay ahead.

Kunz had grown up in snowy Lancaster, a community near Buffalo, New York. He bypassed college and instead chose a career in the Navy after graduating from high school in 1983. He served on a ship for a few years before volunteering for submarine duty, whereupon he reported aboard the USS *Cavalla* (SSN-684) in 1991. Kunz was no stranger to Holy Stone and other harrowing missions. During one deployment, he watched in awe as a SEAL team completed operational training by locking out of the forward escape trunk to inflate Zodiac rubber boats and motor toward a simulated shore-based facility to complete a clandestine mission.

Kunz transferred to the USS *Helena* (SSN-725) in 1997 and then to the *Memphis* in 1999. When he first met the sub's CO, Commander Mark Breor, he found him to be quite different than either of his previous commanding officers. Breor was a "digithead" with a degree in physics and mathematics from The Citadel, in South Carolina. He had also earned an MBA in logistics from the University of New Haven, Connecticut. Breor had a medium build, an affable smile, and dark brown hair and eyes. He also preferred a minimalist communication style.

"Breor was more reserved and quieter than other COs I'd served with," Kunz says. "Tactically, he was outstanding. He was smart, efficient, and knew the boat well. He was not a micromanager and preferred to be more hands-off, but that made him less involved with the crew's welfare. He could be a bit impersonal at times and rarely inquired about or visited anyone who was sick or injured."

Kunz noted that rather than allowing an OOD in the control room to work his way out of a difficult situation, as a baseball team's manager might let a pitcher throw his way out of a rough inning, Breor preferred the safer and more secure path. He had no problem "walking onto the mound" to immediately relieve an OOD if any operational issues arose.

"If we saw a vessel coming out of port," Kunz says, "Breor often dove from periscope depth down to at least one hundred feet while going in the opposite direction."

The XO on the *Memphis* had been the weaps on the *Cavalla* when Kunz was on that boat. He was a bit rough around the edges and stern with the crew, but that was often commonplace for an XO.

"For the most part, we had a tight crew," Kunz says. "The chiefs got along well, which is really important to maintaining efficiency and morale."

In early 1999, Kunz had completed the paperwork to welcome Lieutenant Michael Chin and Yeoman Petty Officer Joseph Ferretta aboard the *Memphis*. Less than a month later, on April 9, 1999, the sub left Groton for a thirty-one-day Arctic excursion to participate in ICEX. Kunz recalled the crew's unease during these exercises, as operating under the polar ice cap is wrought with risk.

"We had cameras pointed up at the ice pack and sonar systems to detect ice keels, but it was very dicey at times when we had to weave around obstacles or dive quickly to avoid slamming into an iceberg," he says.

At the time, Kunz questioned the need for ICEX, as the *Memphis* rarely cruised that far north or operated under the ice. A year later, while preparing for a northern run, he was grateful the crew had honed their skills in frigid waters where sounds and systems operate differently, and where one wrong move could spell disaster.

During May and June, the crew drilled and trained for the upcoming excursion. They loaded stores and made repairs and exchanged excited whispers about where they might be heading. They lay awake at night and wondered if they'd get lucky enough to reel off juicy photos of Ivan or record new sounds or capture interesting signals. They hugged their children and wives and promised them a safe return. All of them hoped their promises did not turn out to be lies.

LIEUTENANT MIKE CHIN RECEIVED ORDERS to report to the USS *Memphis* in March 1999. His father had served as a U.S. Marine and encouraged Chin to get a degree in electrical engineering. The Navy recruited him into nuclear power school, and after graduating, he got excited about serving on a fast attack submarine stationed in Hawaii. Instead, he was sent to a boat in Groton, Connecticut—a long way from any palm trees or pineapple farms.

Chin had a different opinion of Commander Breor. He found his new CO to be firm but fair, caring about the crew, and more hands-on. He did concur that Breor was an engineering-oriented tactical math major who did not micromanage. When someone failed, Breor did not lose his cool, and when someone succeeded, he gave the person credit.

"Breor trusted his guys," Chin says. "He was personable, approachable, and a good father to his children. He was also an old-school leader that used printed family grams instead of emails to communicate with the crew. He did a great job of delegating and trusting and was one of the best COs I have ever served with."

It's not uncommon for enlisted personnel to have a different opinion of their CO as compared to the officers, but commonalities in description indicate that Breor was an analytical, logical, cautious, and delegating type.

Chin was transferred off the *Memphis* in late June, just prior to the SpecOp run. Six months later, when his former CO returned to port, he could not help but notice that the man was dramatically changed.

"He had obviously been shaken by something that had happened on that northern run," Chin says. "He looked distraught and upset. He had also lost a lot of weight. Most people gain weight on a six-month SpecOp. Other members of the crew were also somber and changed. I had heard about what happened when the *Memphis* was on station. I could only imagine how that might have affected me had I been there with the crew."

The USS *Toledo* Heads Toward Russia

Rays of flickering light danced across oily water as it lapped against the hull of the USS *Toledo*. A harsh summer sun baked the backs of blue-clad sailors lined up along the deck. Standing on the pier, Torpedoman Third Class Todd Grace stared at the metal gangway connecting the shore to the hardened HY-80 deck of the black submarine. He glanced over his shoulder. Behind him an array of gray Navy buildings lay scattered across the Groton Naval Base. Beyond the run-down monoliths, eastern hemlock and sugar maple trees dotted the Connecticut countryside.

Grace's shirt fluttered with each heartbeat. At the young age of eighteen, he was a long way from Kansas—or, more accurately, from Massachusetts. He looked again at the pier, back at the forest, and then back at the sailors atop the sub. The topside watch motioned for Grace to board. He placed an unsteady foot onto the gangway and began his journey into the unknown.

The topside watch checked his ID and file and pointed toward the hatch. Grace descended into the belly of the beast. He had been instructed to report to the chief's quarters for assignment, but he had no idea where it was. One petty officer pointed toward the bow, while another pointed toward the stern. Twenty minutes later, Grace finally stumbled into the "goat locker."

A small table took up most of the room in the chief's quarters. Above the table, a line of unwashed coffee cups hung like stockings on the night before Christmas. Grace had heard that "old goat" chiefs rarely washed out their cups. They all swore it enhanced the flavor of a strong cup of Navy black. Grace cringed, thinking of the bitter taste.

The door to the goat locker slammed open, and a giant entered. Grace raised an unsteady chin and looked into the stern eyes of the COB. The man stood six foot seven and did not smile. The name tag on his uniform read "Atkinson." The chief motioned for Grace to sit. He introduced himself as Big Al and grabbed the personnel file from Grace. While rifling through the contents, Big Al said the gang topside was loading stores, as the *Toledo* was heading out on a secret northern run within a few days.

Fifteen minutes later, Big Al shoved Grace toward the yeoman's shack. An hour after that, Grace met his boss, Chief Lawrence, who advised him to pack for a six-month deployment. Lawrence suggested packing light, as bunk space was limited and until he had completed his submarine qualifications, Grace would be cordially compelled to "hot rack."

Grace soon learned what all green "nonqualified pukes" discover in their first few weeks aboard a *Los Angeles*–class submarine: while these boats typically had a complement of 110 to 115, they usually went to sea with around 105. There were not enough bunks for the entire crew, so the more senior and qualified sailors or chiefs got their own rack. Everyone else hot racked by sharing a single bunk between three sailors on a rotating basis.

On a WestPac or northern run, subs might be required to remain "on station" for ninety days or more. Older-class boats, like the *Sturgeon* class, had been designed to do runs this long, but *Los Angeles* subs were not quite as efficient with space. To hold enough food and stores for that length of time, some decks were lined with cardboard boxes full of canned flour, sugar, coffee, and so on. The boxes were stacked a foot and a half high, and sailors often slipped and fell or smashed a foot through the cardboard. Anything fresh disappeared within a few weeks, and toward the end of long runs, cold stores and selections ran thin. By day eighty, sailors started complaining about having only peanut butter and canned corn for almost every meal.

While trying to find his shared bunk, Grace watched in silent fascination as sailors loaded stores through the midsection hatch and filled passageways with boxes. In the head, a petty officer used a screwdriver to remove the doors off the stalls. The A-ganger explained that once on station, while the sub was rigged for ultraquiet, one sound—like a dropped tool or stall door whack—could alert the enemy and reveal their position.

Grace had been trained on underwater sound characteristics and shuddered at the thought of just how close they'd need to be before the enemy could hear a stall door clack.

FIRE CONTROL TECHNICIAN FIRST CLASS PAT MOORE TAPPED on the screen of a BSY MK-1 CCS panel. On submarines, "fire control" refers to the firing of weapons and not necessarily fires as in smoke and flames. Unless, of course, something goes wrong. His job was to ensure nothing did. Moore had been running a series of maintenance tests when one of the panels started acting up. The BSY MK-1 was a newer digital system that had replaced the MK-117 and provided the boat with the ability to fire Tomahawk cruise missiles from bow-mounted tubes.

Moore had enlisted in the Navy while still a junior in high school, with aspirations to be a Navy pilot. He had been mesmerized by the movie *Top Gun* starring Tom Cruise. He changed his mind after graduation based on advice from a friend, who said submarines would be more interesting and offer the thrills seen in the movie *The Hunt for Red October*.

His friend had been right.

Moore's heart had pounded almost nonstop during his first northern run aboard the USS *Hammerhead* while "chasing the Russkies." He later transferred to the *Santa Fe* and did a few more runs before joining the crew on the *Toledo* in 1999. Unlike the *Hammerhead*, the *Toledo* did not have fairwater planes on the conning tower. Most submarines have "planes," not too unlike airplanes, which are large flat "wings" that tilt up or down to allow the boat to go up or down in the water. Older *Los Angeles*-class subs, like the USS *Memphis*, have forward planes mounted on either side of the conning tower. On newer 688-I (Improved) boats, the fairwater planes were placed on the bow, below the waterline and just aft of the Tomahawk cruise missile tubes. These bow planes were retractable and pulled in when the sub neared a pier or ship. Moore had heard war stories from sailors serving aboard this class of sub wherein they'd come too close to a Russian boat and almost scraped the other guy with a bow plane. He hoped his new CO would be cautious enough to never let that happen.

Moore had mixed emotions about the *Toledo*'s next mission. He was excited about going to sea and standing watches in the control room while tracking Russian ships and subs. Nothing compared to the adrenaline rush of sneaking into Putin's backyard and spying on the enemy through a periscope. On the other hand, he'd be leaving his wife and four-year-old daughter at home. Spending six months away from his family was a hardship he wished had not been a part of his job description.

Moore made a few tweaks to the BSY and again tapped on the screen. He smiled. The system was now working properly and was ready to create a firing solution. This entailed playing the cat chasing the mouse by getting close enough to determine the range and bearing to a tracked ship or sub, then creating an accurate solution to program a weapon—whether a torpedo or missile—to destroy the target. While nearly every encounter with the Russian fleet required going through the motions to obtain such a solution, Moore knew they'd never actually fire. Not unless they were fired upon first, or the two countries officially declared a war. He was not too concerned about the latter. After all, the Cold War was over. However, he *was* concerned about the former. If they were caught prowling Russian territorial waters or accidentally ran into one of Ivan's ships or subs, all bets were off. Instead of playing the cat, they'd quickly become the mouse.

BLEARY-EYED AND DROWSY, Electrician's Mate Petty Officer First Class Steve Montafia sauntered onto the deck of the USS *Toledo* at eleven p.m. on a warm night in late June. He climbed down the midsection hatch, found a cup of coffee in the crew's mess, and ambled aft into the engineering spaces. There he met a swarm of nuclear-trained crew members ("nukes") and spent the next eight hours starting up the reactor and preparing to get underway.

Commander James Nault, the boat's CO, had ordered a maneuvering watch set for eight a.m. the following day. Nault liked to cast off early, not long after sunrise. Montafia preferred a later start, as an earlier one meant spending all night getting ready. The nukes aboard the *Toledo* were painfully aware that Nault demanded perfection, which required checking, double-checking, and sometimes triple-checking each detail of the start-up process.

Nault was an average-looking, average-height, jovial-faced guy with blue eyes and an above-average mind. He had graduated from the U.S. Naval Academy with a bachelor's degree in mechanical science and held a master's degree from the Naval Postgraduate School. That combination made him technical, detailed, and brainy. It also made him observant and demanding. He did not tolerate mistakes, especially when dealing with nuclear power.

At around seven a.m., tugboats pulled alongside the three-hundred-sixty-five-foot-long *Los Angeles*–class fast attack submarine. Their diesel engines thrummed and exuded a pungent odor as they neared the sub. Lines were thrown and cinched, and blue-clad sailors waved in anticipation of casting off. Below deck, a team started testing the secondary propulsion motor, aka the outboard, which was a small auxiliary thruster that extended below the ship's hull and allowed the submarine to maneuver inside the harbor. The breaker kept tripping, indicating an electrical fault. Nault's jaw tightened. He asked Montafia how long the repair might take. Montafia replied that he had a spare breaker, but it would take three hours to make the change and do all the paperwork.

Nault fumed. He wanted to know if they could speed up the work. Montafia said yes, he could do it in less than an hour, but it would require bypassing the paperwork. Nault nodded and gave his authorization.

Montafia made the repair and learned an important lesson about Nault: he was impatient and at times might bypass protocols and caution to avoid being delayed in achieving a goal. That character trait might be advantageous in some situations but could be dangerous in others.

Still a first class petty officer, with aspirations to make chief within a year, Montafia had been around the proverbial submarine block. He'd joined the Navy in 1988, completed nuclear power school, and initially deployed on the USS *Albuquerque* (SSN-706). He did several northern runs up near Murmansk, Russia, during the nineties and spent a few years in Groton on shore duty before reporting aboard the *Toledo* in December 1999. Although he had not served much during the Cold War, he knew several chiefs who had, and most harbored the same opinion: the submarine Navy had grown rusty over the past decade.

Montafia had seen indications of this while observing the training procedures during his time at the sub base in Groton. The Fleet Readiness Training Plan (FRTP) outlined specific requirements to ensure submarine crews maintained their edge, but most of the training occurred in shore-based trainers and not at sea. When the Russian Navy had become a mild threat in 1991, fast attacks shifted their roles dramatically. Montafia had also noticed that subs previously spent most of their time trailing Soviet subs and ships and collecting acoustic, photographic, and electronic signals intelligence, but now those runs were far and few between.

During SpecOps in 1990, Montafia's boat had been required to sneak in close and use stealth tactics on Holy Stone intelligence, surveillance and reconnaissance (ISR) missions. By 1992, most of their assignments had shifted to drug interdiction or other mundane deployments. In Montafia's opinion, these runs were "kind of boring."

To adapt to these missions, routines and training changed dramatically. The stealth mindset started to fade as the submarine force diminished its ability to sneak into the baffle area behind an enemy submarine and trail the sub for days or weeks at a time. While sub crews still trained diligently, most of this now occurred onshore in training facilities. These trainers came fully equipped and provided a degree of realism, but they could never duplicate the learning that occurred while on an actual mission. According to Montafia, with more diversified mission assignments, crews became "jacks of all trades and masters of none."

That morning, in late June 2000, when the hatches were shut on the USS *Toledo* and the boat slid beneath the waves, fingers and noses twitched as the crew contemplated future encounters with the Russian Navy. Montafia and his shipmates would soon be headed north to test their stealth skills on a real enemy and not on a fake one in a trainer.

Few journeys begin without delays, and such was the case for the *Toledo*. They received orders to head south to Port Canaveral, Florida, before heading north toward the Barents Sea. They were tasked with spending a week in warm waters testing the navy's newest Submarine Escape Immersion Equipment (SEIE) suits. Orange and bulky, the suits are designed to keep a crew alive in the event of a collision or other mishap that might put them on the bottom. SEIEs replaced the older Steinke hoods and allow around eight sailors per hour to lock out of a pressurized escape trunk and ascend to the surface without running out of air. Most sailors on the *Toledo* never imagined they'd need or want to use one where they were headed. The suits were good down to only six hundred feet, and the average depth in the Barents Sea was 750 feet. Moreover, if they did escape, they'd likely be captured by the Russians and subjected to a fate worse than drowning.

As the *Toledo* increased speed to full and headed toward enemy waters, one salty chief, a communications tech spook who could speak Russian, joked with a green sailor by advising him to learn enough Russian to say, "Don't shoot; I know secrets."

The *Kursk* Readies for War

In early July 2000, President Vladimir Putin and Russia's naval brass paced nervously in front of ocean maps and war plans. An armada of unprecedented size had left port and was now headed toward the Barents Sea in preparation for the largest naval exercise since the end of the Cold War. Putin had been in office only a few months, and these war games represented more than just random tests of the latest technology and platforms. With the nation still suffering from a severe economic decline, success was paramount. Failure could tarnish Putin's reputation and his ability to push agendas forward.

The odds were not in his favor. Most of the warships that had once spearheaded the majestic Northern Fleet sat empty next to untended piers. Oil slicks surrounded their gray and rusting sides. Convinced that Russian military leaders might threaten his presidency, Putin's predecessor, Boris Yeltsin, had slashed spending to only 5 percent of the amount at its former Cold War peak. The Russian Navy had suffered gaping wounds from these cuts. By mid-2000, the once proud submarine force had shrunk from 114 boats to only thirty-four. Lacking proper maintenance and trained crews, many of these were not seaworthy. Decommissioned nuclear subs had been mothballed and left for dead. Scavengers bribed guards to look the other way while they descended on these metal cadavers to steal parts for resale on the black market.

Calling the decaying 130 nuclear submarines "floating Chernobyls," environmentalists demanded that the Russian Navy clean up the radioactive mess, but their pleas fell on deaf ears. To keep local citizens informed about pollution hazards in the Kola Peninsula waterways, radio station operators in Murmansk monitored the radiation leakage and provided daily updates.

Russian submarine rescue capabilities, never world class even during their heyday, had declined to the point of being almost nonexistent. The *Mir-1* and *Mir-2* deep-diving submersibles, which could be used to examine a downed submarine in the event of a catastrophe, had been converted into recreational vehicles to ferry tourists on underwater excursions to view the wreckage of the *Titanic*. Left with only a few older-model deep-submergence rescue vehicles (DSRVs) with ill-equipped and poorly trained crews, the Russian Navy had little chance of rescuing a cat in a tree, let alone sailors in a downed sub on the ocean floor. Even worse, deep-sea saturation divers, trained to use helium-oxygen at depths below a few hundred feet, had become distant memories. Lacking the funding to maintain decompression chambers or keep trained divers from taking lucrative contracts with foreign oil and gas companies, the Russians had all but written off their sat-diving program.

Russian submariners were painfully aware that should they ever need rescuing, they were damned no matter what. If in shallow water, the antiquated DSRVs might not be able to dock. Qualified divers know that every thirty-three feet of descent below the surface adds one atmosphere of pressure to the equation. For a DSRV to maintain a tight enough seal around an escape trunk hatch, it needs roughly ten atmospheres of ocean pressure, which equates to 330 feet (ten times thirty-three feet per atmosphere). It's not too unlike trying to push a basketball filled with air down below a few feet in a pool. Near the surface, there's not enough water pressure to help keep the ball down. If the sub was below 330 feet, the DSRV could more easily dock, but without saturation divers, the crew would have difficulty assessing the sub's condition to direct the submersible, clear debris, assist with docking, or whatever else might be needed. When reminded of this potentially disastrous shortcoming, most Russian submariners offered an unconcerned shrug. Some subs, like those in the newer *Oscar*-class, had large rescue chambers built into the sail that could carry the crew to safety.

A few weeks after the naval exercise in July had concluded, the Russian Navy planned to run some drills to test these systems and train rescue crews, even though few believed the DSRVs would ever be used in real life.

Sailors on older subs that did not have this fail-safe rescue module only smiled and shook their heads. If they were ever unlucky enough to go down, it would most likely be in waters too deep for a rescue. They'd have only a few minutes to utter a final prayer before the boat hit crush depth and imploded.

While the Russian Navy prepared to play war, its opponents on the other side of the fence prepared to observe and record. A half-dozen NATO ships steamed toward the Barents Sea and Russia's thirty-six-ship armada. Under the waves, three NATO subs—the USS *Memphis* and *Toledo* and the HMS *Splendid* snuck into the area, while four Russian submarines cocked ears and prowled near the fleet to keep the enemy at bay. The largest and most modern of these submarines was the *Kursk*.

Next to a dilapidated pier in the Zapadnaya Litsa fjord, floating near chunks of Arctic sea ice, the nearly fifteen-thousand-ton *Kursk* bobbed up and down as cold water slapped against its sides. From a distance, the long black object looked like a massive whale atop which sat a conning tower in place of a blow hole. The sixty-foot-wide cylinder contained ten compartments separated by round hatches. A slew of twenty-eight torpedoes occupied compartment one, controlled by the latest fire control systems in the compartment-two GKP. Compartment three held the combat stations and radio room, while compartment four carried enough supplies to feed a crew of 118 for three months. Two compartment fives housed two modern nuclear reactors, and compartment six contained a coffee shop and a small swimming pool and sauna. The main propulsion turbines could be found in compartments seven and eight. Two long shafts ran through compartment nine and spun twin propellers that could push the *Kursk* to speeds exceeding thirty knots.

A thick inner hull wrapped all nine compartments in a metal shield. A second hull, twelve feet outside the first, made the *Kursk* almost unsinkable even with a direct missile or torpedo hit. Between the inner and outer hull sat twenty-four tubes that tilted forward and housed the lethal Granit cruise missiles. Armed with conventional warheads, each one could sink a ship. When tipped with nuclear warheads, they could annihilate an entire city.

Trim and tall, Lieutenant-Captain Dmitri Kolesnikov stood on the pier next to the *Kursk* and watched bundled sailors load stores and weapons. Massive cylinders of various shapes and sizes—the practice torpedoes the

Kursk would fire during the exercise—were gently lowered by crane into the bow-located torpedo room. One of these was quite different from the others. Thinner, sleeker, and sporting a spear-like point, it looked more like a green javelin than a torpedo. The tip had a silver cap that resembled three cones atop one another, and the aft had no propeller. Instead, it contained a rocket engine. Kolesnikov had been told they were firing a few Granit missiles and some older-model torpedoes, but he had also heard rumors about the new Shkval rocket torpedoes and wondered if this might be one. He grinned. If the *Kursk* was going to fire this new weapon, that would be spectacular indeed.

Aboard the *Kursk*, Kolesnikov commanded the team responsible for the turbines in the seventh compartment, which were spun by the ship's twin nuclear reactors. The tall and lanky Lieutenant-Captain Rashid Aryapov oversaw the sailors in the sixth compartment, which housed the sub's propulsion train and main engines. Although they had been close friends for a decade, Kolesnikov reported to Aryapov. According to both, their relationship never interfered with their duties.

Twenty-two other crewmen served alongside Kolesnikov and Aryapov in the aft compartments six through nine, and over the course of many months or years, they had all become like brothers—ready and willing to die for one another, should a tragedy call for such a sacrifice.

While the *Kursk's* crew readied systems to play war, Russian officials and citizens hoped the pending naval exercise would help propel their country out of one of the worst recessions in its long and storied history.

Putin Prepares for Battle

On the dusty streets of Moscow and dozens of other Russian cities, starving families reached toward strangers for food or money. The communist way of life, while harsh and meager, had at least ensured basic subsistence. After the demise of the Soviet Union, that was no longer the case. Citizens had become disgruntled and restless. Not long before the scheduled naval exercise, several Russians had been killed by bombings in Moscow. The Kremlin blamed it on Chechen terrorists, but skeptical reporters intimated that the attacks had been perpetrated by Putin's new regime to justify the controversial war in Chechnya.

For Putin, the August naval exercise was more than just a show of might, more than just a sharpening of swords. As Russia's newly elected president and the protector of his people, he was motivated to improve the standard of living and place his country back on the map. The Cold War had been a costly one, both monetarily and psychologically. By the year 2000, Russia topped the list for violent deaths. In terms of gross domestic product, it had fallen financially to the status of a third-world country. Russia had one of the worst life expectancies of any nation in the world. A Russian man was considered lucky to reach the age of sixty.

A small number of ruthless and powerful oligarchs controlled most of the wealth, including vast oil and gas resources. Many of these depraved individuals were involved in illegal human trade, including the sale of babies to childless Westerners, mail-order companions to lonely men, and sex slaves to monsters. To shift the spotlight away from their nefarious activities, they bribed the media to blast Putin for his KGB history and inability to run the country.

On the eve of the exercise, Putin and his new administration battled a host of demons. Western journalists questioned his motives and plans. That Thursday, he spent two hours meeting with Mikhail Gorbachev to ensure a smooth transition of power. On Friday morning, he met with Yasser Arafat to discuss national cooperation, and that evening he acted as a referee between two of his top-ranking military officials, including Defense Minister Marshal Igor Sergeyev. In that squabble, he was caught between spending more precious rubles on nuclear defenses and spending them on conventional weapons to support the war in Chechnya. Either way he leaned, he would lose a political ally.

Putin needed the naval exercise in the Barents Sea to be a resounding success. Not only would it celebrate his initial one hundred days as the country's new president, but it also offered a path toward renewed power and economic growth—a way to catapult Russia toward a brighter future. Putin had planned to monitor the booming cannons and streaking missiles while with his family during their visit to the Black Sea's sandy beaches on Monday, August 14.

That weekend, his plans changed in ways he never could have imagined.

CHAPTER 7

THE COLLISION

*"After the incident, we were waiting for the Russians
to shoot something at us."*

—PETTY OFFICER, USS *Toledo*

The Barents Sea is one of the most dangerous ocean areas in the world. It spans 540,000 square miles and skirts the coastlines of Russia and Norway. During the Middle Ages, the Russians called it the Murman Sea, but the formal name came from Dutch navigator Willem Barentsz. In August 2000, high above the choppy waves of the Barents Sea, silver satellites kept a watchful eye on gray-painted ships coming out of Murmansk and other Russian naval bases. Cameras in the satellites were programmed to snap photos and beam them back to NSG analysts at Fort George G. Meade in Maryland and others in Norfolk, Virginia.

Radar dishes had been placed in strategic locations and spun nonstop to capture signal intelligence from Russian emitters and antennae jutting from ships and subs. The dishes were augmented by various spy ships, such as the Norwegian *Marjatta* and USNS *Loyal*, which were disguised to look like ordinary vessels but fooled no one. Both sniffed the air for voice and electronic signals and towed mile-long sonar arrays that passively detected underwater noise.

The Beginning of the End

Aboard the Russian flagship *Peter the Great*, Northern Fleet Commander Admiral Vyacheslav Popov adjusted his uniform and dusted off his medals. The staunch and loyal Soviet-era admiral had been placed in command of the naval exercise. His sea-weathered face, now more than five decades old, was accented by a bright red mustache tinged with splashes of gray. Popov was known for his ability to play politics. He could easily switch gears from rubbing elbows with officials in the Kremlin to cavorting with his NATO counterparts in Norway.

Sunrise on Saturday morning, August 12, painted the Arctic sky with brushstrokes of bright orange and crimson. Popov glanced out a glass window on the bridge of the Russian cruiser and wondered if the old sailor's adage might be true: *Red sky at night, sailors take delight. Red sky in the morning, sailors take warning.*

Deep beneath the surface of the Barents, the U.S. NR-1 minisub, manned by twelve highly trained espionage experts, remained on high alert. The spy sub was supported by a surface ship, *Caroline Chouest*, and its mission included diving deep and using high-resolution cameras to locate enemy missiles, torpedoes, or other items that might otherwise become "lost" during the exercise. A set of external mechanical arms could retrieve the objects and place them into a storage bin. Like a trained bloodhound, the NR-1 could then deliver them back to its NSG master. The crew hoped that one of the subs, most likely the *Kursk*, would fire a Shkval torpedo. If the NR-1 could grab it before the Russians, they'd all get shiny medals. The Russians would search in vain for days and finally give up. They might harbor suspicions that a lurking U.S. sub had snatched their prize, but without proof, they'd be like an annoying dog barking up an empty tree.

Not far from the NR-1, in the sonar shack of the *Memphis*, Petty Officer Joe Ferretta narrowed his gaze as he monitored displays and remained focused on the hydrospace encircling the boat. With thirty-six ships in the vicinity, one mistake at the wrong time could end their mission in a bad way. He was not officially a sonarman but had been asked to stand an occasional watch to allow some of the techs more time to tweak the new A-RCI system, which had been installed a few months earlier. Pronounced "arkee," A-RCI stands for Acoustics-Rapid COTS Insertion (COTS stands for "commercial-off-the-shelf"); the system was a part of the sub's ultrasensitive BQQ 5D bow-mounted passive and wide-aperture flank arrays. The 5D handed captured sounds off to the BQQ-10 sonar processing system, which crunched them through a massive database of cataloged squeaks, whines, and hisses to figure out the *what* and the *who*, such as an *Oscar*-class submarine with twin screws. Complementing the BQQ-10, twin mile-long towed arrays, strung from the aft of the sub, listened for more distant tones created by spinning propellers or pulsating propulsion systems. Now wishing he hadn't volunteered for sonar duty, Ferretta watched waterfall lines paint a sonar display like a stylus gone mad on an Etch A Sketch. The dark lines represented noise, such as a ship's screw, while the blank ones displayed silence. Given the number of vessels in the area, there were now very few blank lines, and Ferretta hoped none of those warships would start racing toward them with guns blazing.

TOM KUNZ LIGHTLY STEPPED ACROSS THE TILED DECK of the *Memphis*. With the sub rigged for quiet, all planned maintenance had ceased. Garbage piled up in the crew's mess freezer, as nothing could be ejected through the trash-disposal unit (TDU). Heaven forbid a cook should drop a frying pan that might be heard through the hull by nearby Russian ships, subs, or ASW planes. Kunz popped into the control room to deliver Commander Breor a report. The air was so thick, it felt like an upstate New York fog. He glanced about the somber space and noticed watch-standers wiping away beads of nervous sweat. Panel lights flickered and cooling fans hummed, but no one joked or told stories or uttered a single word, except to whisper command acknowledgments. Breor read the report and handed Kunz a handwritten set of notes. The CO then buzzed between the navigation table and the fire control panels, his eyes darting back and forth as he absorbed the plethora of information displayed.

Kunz tiptoed back down to the yeoman's shack, where a sign hung that warned anyone without a secret clearance and access permission to stay out. He stepped inside and opened a safe on one bulkhead. He grabbed a special removable hard drive and slid it into a slot on a ruggedized laptop computer. He then took his CO's handwritten notes and typed them into the PC. He had to be creative to decode Breor's cryptic scribbles, which at times were worse than those written by a doctor. Kunz's eyes widened as he read the last few lines in Breor's report. He now knew the primary reason they were on station and what was about to happen during the Russian naval exercise. He wondered if this day would go down in history as the turning point that ignited a new cold war. One that might become far worse than the last one.

COMMANDER BREOR SLAPPED UP THE HANDLES on the number-two scope and lowered it into the well. The *Memphis* had participated in ICEX the year before, and the training and tactics learned by the crew had come in handy while they were sneaking up on the *Kursk* in quiet Arctic waters. Unfortunately, ICEX had lasted only a few weeks—not nearly long enough to scrape off the rust that had built up over the past decade due to a large decline in SpecOps.

The previous day, using digital photographic and video cameras inside the Type 18 periscope, Breor had captured some excellent photos and footage of the *Kursk* launching a Shipwreck Granit missile. He had anticipated another firing, but the *Oscar* did not comply. If a malfunction had prevented the Russian Navy from executing a second launch, it wasn't untypical, and Breor had witnessed many such mishaps over the years.

He'd taken command of the *Memphis* two years earlier after a stint as a senior submarine school instructor. Books and simulators are never a match for the real thing, and most submariners long for a dose of adrenaline, even if they won't admit it. One of the best locations on the map to find a good thrill ride is in the Barents Sea. The average depth in this region is about twice the length of the *Memphis*. Although not covered with ice during the time of year when the naval exercise was taking place, the Barents is nevertheless located in the Arctic. Ocean characteristics and surface refractions are unpredictable and treacherous. And, as they had since the days of the *Queenfish* and *Nautilus*, ever-changing and challenging sound layers made sonar classifications, range, and bearing calculations far more difficult. Breor knew that a miscalculation in the Barents could end a career, if not a life. He had so far avoided a collision with an adversary, but he also knew there had been a dozen recorded submarine smacks since 1967, including eight in northern waters. Several had been serious.

If Breor believed the rumors, the accident between the USS *Drum* and the Soviet K-324 *Victor III* topped the list. Like any good submarine skipper, he was highly motivated to ensure his submarine never slammed into another vessel, and that his crew never had to endure seventy-two hours of living hell like they had aboard the *Drum*....

SEVERAL THOUSAND YARDS AWAY, aboard the *Toledo*, Commander Nault studied the naval chart atop the quartermaster's table in the control room. Nault knew the USS *Memphis* and HMS *Splendid* were also on station nearby. They had all been tasked with monitoring the largest Russian naval exercise in a decade, but the *Toledo* had been given the most important assignment: to capture critical intel on the *Kursk*'s firing of the new Shkval rocket torpedo.

Sonar reported that the *Kursk* had just opened an outer torpedo tube door. Nault's adrenaline surged. If the Russians were about to fire the Shkval, he wanted to be near enough to record every nuance of the event. At the risk of being heard, but motivated by scant time before the *Kursk* fired, Nault increased speed.

Sonar maintained a constant stream of reports from the shack. The tinted voice of a petty officer piped in every few seconds with bearing, range, and speed information. In the control room, Nault peered over the shoulder of a petty officer. A color monitor on a fire control system panel displayed the *Toledo*'s relative position to the *Kursk*, indicated by a small triangle inching its way toward the target. Nault had no intention of firing at the *Oscar*, but he knew there were digital recorders in the sonar shack that were collecting every noise the Russian submarine made. Still, he wasn't quite close enough to grab the important launch sounds.

An agitated voice from the sonar shack reported a sudden course change by Master Two. The *Kursk* was now headed right at the *Toledo*. Nault had seconds to react. He could not order a deep dive as the ocean was too shallow. All he could do was order a slight downward angle and a hard-right turn to avoid the impending collision. The diving officer quickly relayed the order. The helmsman and planesman struggled to obey. Their hands gripped two half-circle steering wheels. One cranked to the right and the other pushed slightly downward. The boat angled toward the bottom. A coffee cup crashed to the deck.

Commander Nault ordered all-ahead full and a course change away from Master Two. Once at a safe distance, he decided to bring the boat to periscope depth to assess the situation. The *Toledo* angled upward. Seconds before it reached periscope depth, a muffled clap rocked the boat from side to side. Nault called sonar for an explanation. A petty officer reported an explosion from the direction of Master Two, now less than one thousand yards away. Nault raised the scope and swung the metal cylinder from side to side. He called off bearings to targets. The fire control team punched in the bearings and updated firing solutions. If the Russians turned hostile, the four MK-48 warshots in the tubes were ready to retaliate.

Two minutes after the initial explosion, a sonarman in the shack heard Master Two slam into the ocean floor. He clicked his comm to inform Nault, but before he could speak, he was forced to rip off his headphones.

An earsplitting explosion, hundreds of times louder than the first, shattered the silence in the control room. The *Toledo* rocked from side to side, like a bottle tossed about on a rough sea. Nault lowered the attack scope and ordered a shallow dive and all-ahead full. As a trained submarine commander, he could not feel anything but shock and dismay. The strong smell of navy coffee in the control room served as a morbid reminder that he was still alive, and the crew of the *Kursk* might not be.

"After the incident, we were waiting for the Russians to shoot something at us," says a petty officer first class who was aboard the *Toledo*. "We went up to periscope depth and wondered if Master Two was going to flood down and equalize their torpedo tubes. Then we heard this massive explosion. Our boat shook like a truck in a tornado. We all looked at each other with our eyes wide and mouths open. Nobody wanted to say it, but we all knew what had just happened. Then Nault started yelling orders, our training kicked in, and we sprinted to a safe distance away."

"I was in a middle rack," says a *Memphis* petty officer. "The explosion damn near threw me out. When you feel something like that, with that much force, alarms go off and everyone starts scurrying about and asking what's going on. You don't expect something to shake the boat that much when you're submerged. Something that violent knocks stuff around. Everyone assumed damage-control stations and started checking for damage, leaks, and broken mounts. We inspected everything three times within fifteen minutes. Fortunately, we didn't find anything, but it felt like we were in a movie like *Das Boot*."

THIRTY-TWO MILES TO THE NORTHWEST, the Russian submarine *Karelia* also heard the blast. Sailors gave one another questioning looks. Thirty-seven-year-old Captain Andrey Korablev wondered if there might have been a collision, or worse, if someone had fired a real weapon by mistake. He consulted with his ride-along exercise observer—a fleet admiral—who shrugged and said if anything was wrong, they'd be informed by command. After all, there were thirty-five other vessels in the area.

Fifteen miles closer to the *Kursk*, the crew of the *Leopard*, an *Akula*-class submarine, felt a mild shudder. Their mission was to covertly search for unwanted NATO subs that might be trying to observe the exercise. Although the *Leopard*'s sonar systems were some of the most advanced in the Russian navy at the time, they failed to detect the nearby *Memphis* or *Toledo*. With the *Leopard*'s bow facing away from the *Kursk*, the blast occurred in the sub's baffle area and was only peripherally detected by Acoustic Cutting operators. The captain was made aware of what appeared to be a minor disturbance, but he did not record this in his log.

Aboard the flagship, *Peter the Great*, almost thirty miles away from the *Kursk*, the bridge officers and crew barely noticed a slight jolt. However, in Acoustic Cutting, Senior Lieutenant Andrey Lavriniuk's wide eyes resembled radar dishes as his passive sonar system registered a large anomaly. He keyed his mic, contacted the bridge, and reported the incident. The collected data, including the bearing to the blast, was relayed to the fire control systems in the combat information center (CIC). The Northern Fleet admirals, now gathered on the bridge in anticipation of witnessing the launch of a secret new weapon, were informed that something strange had occurred, but as yet, no one had any answers.

Vice Admiral Boyarkin and Admiral Popov maintained their cool exteriors. They acknowledged the report but issued no orders to the junior officers on the bridge. Despite the apparent size of the blast and subsequent shock wave, the two admirals dismissed the news and considered it an ordinary part of a large naval exercise.

Hell Freezes Over

Aboard the *Kursk*, hell became an agonizing mixture of freezing cold and blazing heat as the rushing sea failed to quell the flames. The bulkhead separating compartments one and two broke loose from its welds and slammed into pipes and valves and an array of electronic systems. Crimson blood and white bone splattered across wrinkled decks and coated smashed equipment. A tall cylindrical periscope and other masts twisted and crumpled as the malevolent fire bellowed like the breath of a dragon, enveloping everything in its path. The third and fourth compartments succumbed to the blast and turned into a charred jumble of unrecognizable shapes. The GKP, medical center, crew's quarters, and crew's mess transformed into an underwater inferno as pipes burst and oxygen lines erupted and fanned the superheated flames.

Senior Warrant Officer Igor Yerasov died instantly while still standing next to his shipmates. In his hands he clutched a top-secret box that held Russian communication codes. Forty more sailors barely had time to don emergency breathing apparatuses and escape suits in the hope of fleeing the doomed sub, via the sail-mounted escape pod. None of them survived more than a few minutes.

The steel hull covering the starboard side of the torpedo room blew outward as a result of the enormous rise in pressure. Frigid ocean water filled the void between the first and fourth compartments and rushed toward the fifty-millimeter-thick bulkhead standing guard in front of the fifth compartment. Behind the still-intact hatch, in the vicinity of one of the *Kursk's* reactors, Sergey Lubushkin must have heard the explosive horror unfolding in the forward section. He could do nothing more than his training and instinct allowed. Likewise, his comrades could only stare in amazement as the heavily shielded bulkhead bent inward but miraculously held.

The *Kursk* rolled slightly to one side and remained at a modest downward angle as the aft section settled in the sand 380 feet below the surface. What was left of the bow pointed northwest at about 288 degrees. The raging fire, still fueled by propellant and ruptured oxygen tanks, heated the thirty-eight-degree-Fahrenheit ocean to almost boiling as the rumbling and popping continued unabated.

Hundreds of yards away, aboard the *Toledo*, sonarmen cupped hands over headphones and listened to the tragedy unfold. Helpless and shocked, they dutifully recorded the incident and relayed reports to the control room. Maintaining ordered radio silence, Nault executed a slow and silent crawl away from the scene while ensuring that the sounds of the dying *Kursk* did not fade into the sub's baffle area.

Aboard the *Peter the Great*, several junior officers monitored the distant rumbles and wondered why the senior officers were neither fazed nor responsive. Many of them scanned the horizon in search of any signs of attacks or accidents. They saw nothing but a calm, cold sea. The flagship maintained its original course and speed while Fleet Commander Popov acted as if nothing had happened. As if the exercise was still proceeding as planned. As if the *Kursk* would fire its new torpedo at any moment.

Four thousand miles away, on the other side of the Atlantic Ocean, a team of communications techs at the NSA in Fort Meade, Maryland, perked up. Clocks on walls read three thirty a.m. Monitors displayed data spikes emanating from the Barents Sea. The USNS *Loyal* reported acoustic anomalies and an increase in Russian ship-to-ship chatter. Analysts studied the data intently due to its relevance to the Russian naval exercise. They contacted counterparts at other stations and at the NATO submarine command in the U.K. Once they had ruled out the probability of a brewing hostile attack, they explored the possibility of a downed sub. As communications with the *Memphis* or *Toledo* could not yet be established, the Undersea Rescue Command (URC) in San Diego, California, went on alert.

Aboard the *Kursk*, following instinct and training, the twenty-three survivors in compartments five through nine called out for one another. All but one verified they were still alive and conscious. Dim lights flickered and buzzed, and the waterfall sound of ocean water hissed as it continued to cascade into the forward section. As it would for any sailor in this situation, fear gripped the men as they concluded that the hatch between compartments six and five-bis (variant B) could not be opened. This hatch represented their only way to reach the escape module in the sail above the fourth compartment. The backup escape route was through a ten-foot oval escape trunk in compartment nine, but only if a rescue vehicle docked with the *Kursk*. Otherwise, the remaining option called for donning emergency escape suits and climbing, two men at a time, into the trunk.

After shutting the lower hatch and pressurizing the escape trunk, the survivors could open the upper hatch and ascend to the surface while wearing escape suits. They knew the depth of the ocean in their operating area; knew they were at more than 350 feet deep; knew that even in the unlikely event they survived the ascent, they'd die within fifteen minutes in the freezing water. No doubt they ruled out this fate and concluded that the best option was to wait for a rescue vehicle to dock and open the hatch.

The senior officers did as trained and ordered their men to don emergency air breathers (EABs) and man emergency stations. Despite repeated tries, no answers came from superiors in the forward compartments. Once communication could be established between the aft compartments, Aryapov assumed command and issued orders to quell flooding wherever possible. Most of the water now leaking into the aft section came from loose seals surrounding the propeller shafts. When the shafts were spinning, the leakage was minimal, but while the sub was at rest and at depth, the trickle turned into a rivulet. Water also rose in the bilges, but not enough to cause panic. At least not yet.

As a trained officer, Aryapov knew that compartment nine, where the water was coming in past the shaft seals, had 19,420 cubic feet of space. Compartment eight did not taper like compartment nine, so it was almost twice the size. Compartment seven was a bit smaller than eight, and six was much smaller. Two more compartments, five and five-bis, which held the nuclear reactors, were about the same size as compartment seven. Unfortunately, these two compartments were now inaccessible, as the hatches had been sealed to prevent contamination leaks. The bulkhead to compartment six was still warm from the reactors, and even with the sub at a slight downward angle, not much water had filled this area.

In the sixth compartment, Aryapov verified that both reactors had shut down automatically during the incident. He found the reactor manuals and followed procedures to prevent any temperature spikes or potential radiation contamination—inside or outside the boat. In the sixth and seventh compartments, Kolesnikov supervised the gathering of supplies, including rations, water bottles, oxygen masks, and regeneration cartridges. He also tested the emergency buoy lever to verify if it had deployed to signal the fleet and provide their location, but there was no indication either way. He could only hope that at least one of the other two buoys forward had deployed, but he knew they may have been welded to the hull to prevent accidental release.

Seasoned and trained, both officers certainly discussed and confirmed the obvious: due to the possibility of hypothermia or embolism, ascent to the surface through the compartment-nine escape trunk might be suicidal. That left escape via a DSRV through the compartment-nine trunk, provided the rescue sub arrived in time and it could dock with the upper hatch. At a depth of less than four hundred feet, Russia's antiquated rescue vehicles might have difficulty keeping a tight seal. Without that seal, a rescue would be impossible.

With water coming in past the shaft seals, compartment nine would fill up first. The overflow would then come through the compartment-nine hatch into compartment eight and so on. As the temperature continued to drop, and given that the most amount of heat was near the reactor bulkhead in compartment six, the best decision was obvious. They would later congregate in compartment nine in the hopes of a rescue through the trunk, but for now, it would be best to remain less compacted in one area while continuing to monitor for leaks in all compartments. This would also help reduce the CO_2 buildup in any one area. All hatches remained open for the same reason. If anyone started to suffer from hypothermia, he could take a turn flattening against the compartment-six bulkhead, which might remain heated for several hours. Any other course of action would be counterintuitive for trained and experienced submarine officers to take.

ON THE BRIDGE OF THE FLAGSHIP, *Peter the Great*, Admiral Popov assumed the explosion heard by Acoustic was actually the hard-splashing sound of a fired missile plunging into the ocean near its target. He also assumed that the *Kursk* was experiencing a communications failure or that Lyachin was maintaining radio silence as part of his evasive maneuvers while remaining undetected. His theories were plausible, but the lookouts had yet to spot the weapon fired from the *Kursk*. Conditioned by years in a system that avoided facing truths that might be frowned upon by superiors, Popov did not at the time voice suspicions that catastrophe might have befallen the *Kursk*. If he harbored such thoughts, they remained private.

Publicly, he completed a taped interview conducted by a government-controlled media team embedded with the crew of the flagship. The recorded broadcast was scheduled for release the following day. Popov said the Northern Fleet exercises were about to conclude successfully and without incident. After the interview, still smiling as if everything was fine, Popov boarded a helicopter and flew over to the aircraft carrier *Admiral Kuznetsov*.

The weather turned sour as Vice Admirals Boyarkin and Burtsev, still aboard the *Peter the Great*, watched Popov leave. Following standing fleet orders, they remained on station. The flagship was not allowed to depart the exercise area in the event of a misfire or missing submarine. For now, both applied. It had been over an hour since the explosion, which should have triggered a fleet-wide alarm and search efforts, but neither admiral wanted to be the harbinger of bad news.

Admiral Popov squinted through the bridge windows of the *Admiral Kuznetsov* carrier as a sixteen-knot wind ushered in a gale from the northwest and dropped the cloud cover down to 1,400 feet. The darkened skies and chilled air heightened his apprehension and nudged him to return to the *Peter the Great* flagship. He decided against this course, as landing a helicopter aboard a rocking ship carried far too much risk. Instead, he flew in the opposite direction and returned to the Northern Fleet headquarters at Severomorsk. Upon landing, he received word that the admirals aboard the *Peter the Great* had decided to leave the exercise area. This was a direct violation of protocol, but Popov did not countermand the order. Instead, he again acted unconcerned on the surface, even though he harbored fears of a worst-case scenario.

Aboard the *Peter the Great*, as the massive warship turned away from the designated firing range, a seaman recorded a log entry: "At thirteen fifty we start to operate on the worst variant."

ON THE SUNKEN SUBMARINE *KURSK*, Captain-Lieutenant Dmitri Kolesnikov studied the names of the survivors. He began at the top of each line, called out names, and waited for a reply. This allowed him to determine each man's condition based on the tone of the response. He started with the men from compartment six and worked his way aft. He found a scrap of lined paper and wrote the names on separate lines to ensure readability, and then placed a status mark next to each name. Of the twenty-three survivors, including himself, there were only four commissioned officers. The rest were warrant officers or below—some still teenagers. None had been injured, indicating minimal damage to the aft compartments. All were consumed by fear but remained alert and in control. Some checked and readied oxygen masks, supplies, or escape suits. Several took turns to bang out an SOS distress signal on pipes or on the escape trunk hatch with a wrench.

A few hours later, at 15:15, Dmitri wrote a dated and timed message to his wife. "Olichka, I love you. Don't suffer too much. My regards to GV and regards to mine."

"GV" stood for Galina Vasiliena, his mother-in-law, and "to mine" was obviously meant for his own mother. He signed the note "Mitya," the Russian diminutive for Dmitri.

FIVE HOURS AFTER THE SECOND EXPLOSION, Putin was at the Kremlin. His meeting had started at two p.m. that Saturday, and the main topic centered on the Moscow bombings. The incident had delayed his vacation, and investigators had yet to uncover evidence of Chechen involvement.

On the other side of the globe, in the Pentagon, the sun crested above the eastern horizon. At eight thirty a.m. Eastern time, U.S. Marine colonel Roy Byrd placed an urgent call to Robert Tyrer, chief of staff to Defense Secretary William Cohen. Byrd reported on the situation in the Barents, including the possibility that the Russian submarine *Kursk* might have been lost during the naval exercise. Tyrer dropped his putter onto the ninth-hole green of the Burning Tree Club's golf course in Bethesda, Maryland. He told Byrd to immediately call Cohen and brief the secretary.

In his home in the Washington, D.C. suburbs, Cohen took the call from Byrd but did not recommend any actions beyond continued observation, vigilance, and prayer—not only for the lost submariners but for the entire world. Cohen was certainly aware that situations of this magnitude were fraught with risk. One misunderstanding or one stroke of bad luck could easily lead to a skirmish or even a full-scale war.

CHAPTER 8

THE AFTERMATH

*"There are reasons to believe
there has been a big and serious collision."*

—ADMIRAL VLADIMIR KUROYEDOV,
Commander-in-Chief, Russian Navy

On August 12, at nine-thirty a.m. Eastern time, six hours after the loss of the *Kursk*, Mark Medish wiped a bead of sweat from his forehead and swatted at a tennis ball. His mobile phone chimed in the middle of a match at Rock Creek Park. He sat down his racket and reached for his phone. An eyebrow raised as he listened to the voice from the White House Situation Room. "We're following reports of a large underwater explosion in the Barents," the attendant said, "possibly involving a Russian submarine exercise." Medish learned that top Pentagon officials had been informed about the situation and instructed the caller to ensure that Sandy Berger, Bill Clinton's national security advisor, also got the word.

While attending the National Democratic Convention with President Clinton in Los Angeles, Berger received a call from Medish, at 6:35 a.m. Pacific time. He was briefed on the situation and forced to make a difficult decision. He decided not to wake the president and instead waited to see if the Russians made a public announcement about the situation in the Barents. If history held any portent, they would not. By chance if the Russians did do the unexpected and asked NATO for assistance, Berger would recommend to Clinton that the U.S. Navy activate the URC in San Diego.

Clinton had previously indicated a desire to nudge Russia toward a more amiable posture with the U.S. The last thing anyone wanted was another cold war, or even worse, a hot one.

Since Putin's election, the new president had consistently resisted any handshakes from the West. When Clinton administration officials had made proposals or offered help in any way, Putin had displayed a stoic demeanor and offered a noncommittal response followed by no action. The stonewalling had become so frequent that many on Clinton's staff had started calling Putin "Mr. Nyet," which translates to "Mr. No" in English.

After breakfast, Berger called Medish and instructed him to dig for more details on the incident and have the White House staff determine how he might best reach Security Council secretary Sergei Ivanov—Berger's counterpart in Russia. Medish said details were still sketchy and they were also trying to determine if, or how, any American fast attack subs might have been involved. Berger said he hoped they were not, as that could cause an escalation neither country wanted. The two men agreed that, for now, no more than a small handful of senior officials should be briefed, at least not until the picture transitioned away from blurry.

Six hours after the explosion in the Barents Sea, at 4:35 p.m. local time, no communication from the *Kursk* had been received by any Russian ships or planes. On the bridge of the *Peter the Great*, Vice Admiral Boyarkin ordered his crew to send a message to the submarine by way of the underwater communications system that transmitted voice via hydrophone. The system had a short range, and the flagship was still quite a few miles away, so Boyarkin did not expect a response. He followed protocol all the same. Fleet rules dictated that all vessels participating in the exercise were required to report in every four hours. The *Kursk* was now two hours overdue.

The hydrophone system operator sent the *Kursk*'s codename, Vintik, but did not receive a reply. Boyarkin relayed the bad news to Popov, who was still in Severomorsk. Popov said he was preparing to return to the *Peter the Great* via helicopter once the weather cleared. He then contacted his chief deputy, Vice Admiral Mikhail Motsak, and authorized him to alert the fleet's rescue forces without also informing any news media. At 5:20 p.m., Motsak concluded his call with Popov and ordered officer Alexey Palkin to ensure that the rescue ship, *Mikhail Rudnitsky*, was placed on a one-hour readiness status.

By 5:40 p.m., the fleet's rescue chief, Captain First Rank Alexander Teslenko, finally reached the *Rudnitsky*'s commanding officer, Yuri Kostin, at his home in Severomorsk. Teslenko relayed Palkin's order to place his ship on hot standby in the event a rescue was initiated. Kostin acknowledged the order and used the local grapevine, via calls and messengers, to locate his crew and have them report to the ship. Most were startled, as they had recently completed exercises using three DSRVs and, given a shortage of naval funds, had not expected another test quite this soon.

Aboard the *Peter the Great*, dozens of binoculars scanned the horizon for any sign of the *Kursk*, such as a spent practice torpedo, a distress buoy, flotsam, trash, oil, or bodies. Vice Admirals Boyarkin and Burtsev maintained the search from the bridge while displaying calm poker faces. They divulged no information to the crew about the explosion, although most had heard the news from others on the ship. Gray clouds hung low against the darkening sky, and despite a biting breeze that buffeted the cold sea, visibility remained high.

At 6:14 p.m., Vice Admiral Motsak decided to wait no longer. He ordered the search-and-rescue team, including the ship *Mikhail Rudnitsky* and five Il-38 aircraft, to deploy. By 6:52, six helicopters, twenty-one rescue vessels, twelve warships, and two diving ships had joined the hunt. The armada began a methodical search within a twenty-mile radius. During the search, a radio operator at a shore station reported a weak signal coming from a vessel that used the *Kursk*'s codename of Vintik. Motsak hoped the *Kursk* had surfaced but was having radio transmit issues.

Rescue ships and planes raced toward the signal. Heartbeats increased as they drew near. At fleet headquarters, Popov was about to inform his superiors, but upon hearing the Vintik radio transmit report, he delayed. Instead, he ordered Boyarkin to increase the search efforts and keep him informed should the Vintik signal pan out.

Seven hours after the explosion, the Vintik signal proved to be a false alarm. No sign of the *Kursk* was found, and no vessels could be identified as the source of the transmission. Boyarkin contacted Popov by radio and gave him the bad news. Popov lowered his head and paced in front of the radio, painfully aware that he could no longer keep the situation under wraps. He had to inform his superiors and deal with the fallout.

U.S. Officials Discuss Options

Mark Medish arrived at the Situation Room, located in the West Wing of the White House, at ten thirty a.m. Eastern time. Still sweaty in his tennis attire, he rifled through a stack of briefing papers but found nothing he didn't already know. What he did know was that Russia's leadership was either uninformed or unconcerned. Putin had left the Kremlin after his meeting to start his vacation in Sochi. If a crisis was brewing, or Russia was gearing up for an attack, the Russians were doing an excellent job of disguising their moves. Satellites and on-station assets reported that the Russian fleet had concluded the exercise but now appeared to be conducting a massive search. They were communicating on open channels, an indication of some type of emergency, most likely a lost submarine.

The USS *Memphis* had left its station and was en route to Norway. The USS *Toledo* and HMS *Splendid* were still in the area and monitoring the Russians but had not broken radio silence. Medish connected with colleagues at the State Department and Pentagon, as well as Berger in Los Angeles. Frank Miller, senior Pentagon policy official, voiced his concerns that should the U.S. ask the Russians if they needed help to find a downed sub, it might compromise NATO intelligence sources. He also said the Russians would certainly be reluctant to admit the need for help from a former enemy.

Debra Cagan, director of the Office for Security Affairs at the State Department, sided with Miller, as she typically did. She recommended staying out of the mess, as any overture at this juncture could be perceived as either too forward or too contrived. The Russians would likely view any gestures as a ploy for intelligence-gathering, which would not be too far from the truth. She also suggested that given the Russian Navy's propensity to hide bad news from their superiors, full details about the incident had probably not been given to officials in Moscow, up to and including Putin. Any overture at this juncture from the U.S. would likely be answered by a typical nonplussed response from Mr. Nyet. Even if the Russians did accept help, the odds that any NATO rescue teams would receive accurate or necessary details to execute a successful rescue were slim.

Medish and Berger concurred with the team and elected not to contact the Russians, at least not yet. Medish then continued his attempts to reach Russian security chief Ivanov, but he knew this might be difficult given that most Russians and Europeans took extended vacations in mid to late August. Nevertheless, he asked the Situation Room operatives to get in touch with their counterparts in Moscow and "do a full court press" to find the man.

Medish soon learned that Ivanov would be joining Putin on vacation in Sochi and would not be available to speak until Monday. Medish decided to call Berger. The two men concluded that, seven hours after the blasts, Ivanov had to be fully aware of the situation in the Barents Sea. He was therefore purposely avoiding contact with the U.S. He obviously did not want to divulge any information or confirm there was a crisis, but more important, he had likely not informed Putin. If he had, the Russian president would not be going on vacation. Perhaps Ivanov had not yet delivered the bad news to his boss because he and the Russian Navy still clung to the hope that the situation might magically resolve itself. Perhaps the missing submarine might suddenly pop to the surface and its captain might sheepishly apologize for seven hours of radio silence.

Medish concluded his call with Berger and found Captain Phillip Cullom, a naval officer attached to the NSC staff. He asked him to contact the URC in San Diego and gather details on the assets the U.S. might deploy to assist with a rescue of a downed sub. Also, to contact their NATO counterparts and do the same. Cullom nodded, spun on a heel, and disappeared. Medish then reconnected with Cagan and Miller and discussed plans to inform the press, when the time came. For now, they needed to exercise great caution in not letting any cats out of any bags too soon. Such an announcement was way above their pay grade anyway and would likely be initiated by the secretary of state or the president. They agreed to call it a day and meet again first thing in the morning. In the meantime, from his home in the Palisades along the Potomac, Medish planned for a long night of calls and keyboard-tapping as reports flowed in from Captain Cullom and the rest of the White House team.

Unfortunately, his evening remained surprisingly quiet. He made some calls and determined that no one was doing anything. Captain Cullom had not contacted Commander William Orr at the URC in San Diego as requested. Instead, he had obtained information on the URC's rescue capabilities from other sources—reliable but not direct. Furthermore, the URC team had not been put on alert. Those in charge had concluded, with a minimum of seventy-two hours needed to spin up the team and be onsite, any rescue attempt might be too late. Moreover, it might take twice that long to get the technical specs from the Russians. Still, Medish wished they had at least started preparations so as not to appear unconcerned about the situation.

Medish also discovered that none of the "inner circle" contacts he and his colleagues had informed had reached out to their contacts in Russia. No one at the U.S. embassy in Moscow had been alerted or questioned. Even the British Ministry of Defence (MOD), typically informed about most U.S. intelligence tidbits, had been left out of the loop. Medish knew the Brits had a sub in the area and were certainly keeping a watchful eye on the Russian rescue operation, but they had remained strangely quiet. Even stranger, the British LR5 submarine rescue platform, referred to as the "underwater helicopter," had not diverted course. It was still headed toward Turkey to complete a scheduled "Sorbet Royale" rescue exercise in the Mediterranean. The LR5's commander, Royal Navy commodore David Russell, had not been instructed to head toward the Barents. Medish frowned. No one was talking to anyone, as if there were no crisis brewing in the Barents Sea at all. What if a U.S. sub had been involved in a serious collision with a Russian sub? What if one of them had also gone down? How long could those brave souls survive on the ocean floor while the world did nothing?

EIGHT HOURS AFTER THE LOSS OF THE *KURSK*, at 7:28 p.m. Moscow time, Putin's presidential jet roared off the runway and banked toward the Black Sea and sandy beaches at Bocharov Ruchei. Ivanov, still unresponsive to U.S. overtures, accompanied the Russian president. In three hours, he would begin his vacation instead of dealing with the brewing incident. Hundreds of miles away, as the sun set on the Barents Sea, dozens of ships and planes continued to search in vain.

At the fleet headquarters in Severomorsk, Admiral Popov entered the command post. He scanned the room and ordered reports from the operators. One of the operators contacted the *Akula*-class attack sub *Leopard*, and requested an update. The *Leopard* had been nearest the *Kursk* when the explosions were recorded. The sub's commander replied with a truncated report. "We did not observe K-141's work."

Other ships involved in the exercise offered similar reports, but the submarine *Karelia* had not yet responded. Popov contacted Boyarkin aboard the *Peter the Great* and ordered him to have ASW planes drop a series of light grenades to signal the *Kursk* to surface. Boyarkin acknowledged, and the first explosion lit off at 8:27 p.m. and continued in succession for ten minutes. No response was received, and no submarine came to the surface. With the sun fading on the horizon, the Il-38 aircraft were ordered to break off and return to base. The planes landed at ten p.m., twenty minutes after sunset. From his office, Admiral Popov checked on the status of the rescue ship, *Mikhail Rudnitsky*. He learned it was still tied to the pier and not yet ready to cast off. If the *Kursk* was on the bottom of the sea, as was likely the case, Popov wondered how much longer any survivors could remain alive.

Captain Korablev, commander of the submarine *Karelia*, finally checked in and said they had felt the boat rock from an underwater explosion at approximately eleven thirty a.m. but assumed it was part of the exercise. He asked his Acoustic Cutting operators for a rough bearing and relayed this to Popov, who contacted Boyarkin aboard the *Peter the Great* and told him to speed down the bearing line.

Boyarkin ordered all-ahead flank. By using the intersected bearings reported by the *Karelia* and the *Peter the Great*, the navigator created a rough search grid. As any range data was lacking, the grid was not small. Boyarkin ordered a zigzag search course across the grid while Acoustic Cutting operators saturated the ocean with active sonar pings.

At eleven p.m., almost twelve hours had passed since the Russian Navy had lost contact with the *Kursk*. Boyarkin obtained permission from Popov to broadcast a fleet-wide report to coordinate the search. Over an open communications channel, the *Peter the Great* sent the radio message: "At 1130, at a bearing of zero-nine-six from location 69.40 north and 36.24 east, an impact blow was heard...."

At the risk of ending his career, Popov decided to make an official announcement with a formal fleet alarm at eleven thirty p.m.

Through a light rain, with the wind speed at ten knots and nighttime visibility at eighteen miles, Boyarkin watched the lights of a seagoing tug comb the site for any sign of flotsam—or floating crewmen. Fifteen minutes before midnight, Popov inquired about the progress of the *Mikhail Rudnitsky* rescue vessel. He curled his fingers into fists when he learned that it still hadn't left the dock. Frustrated, he placed a call to Moscow and asked for the Russian Navy's commander-in-chief, Vladimir Kuroyedov. When Kuroyedov came on the line, Popov let out a long breath and told him the *Kursk* was still missing and the rescue ship had not yet left port.

In turn, Kuroyedov updated his staff and Minister of Defense Marshal Igor Sergeyev. He then recommended informing President Putin. Sergeyev waved him off and decided not to disturb the president on vacation until the Navy could gather more information.

To ensure that a tight lid remained atop the situation, the Northern Fleet's alarm was shared discreetly with a small number of commands near the Kola Peninsula, a few key officials in Severomorsk, and a select number of individuals at the *Kursk*'s home port in Vidyayevo. These updates did not inform family members but instead requested that senior officers from the *Voronezh*, a sister sub to the *Kursk*, prepare to assist in any rescue effort.

Captain Third Rank Evgeny Zubkov, a senior officer aboard the *Voronezh*, received an urgent call in his apartment that afternoon. He was ordered to report to the dock to ready the submarine for immediate deployment. He was not told why, but he harbored suspicions. Originally, the *Voronezh* had been selected to participate in the summer naval exercises, but due to a spate of operational issues, the honor had been transferred to the *Kursk*. To that end, due to a spare-parts shortage, the Russian Navy cannibalized the

Voronezh to ensure that the *Kursk* could deploy. The submarine community is a tight knit one, and Zubkov had befriended several of the *Kursk's* officers, including Aryapov, Kolesnikov, and Lubushkin. Now he wondered if something disastrous had happened and if he'd ever see his friends again.

Sounds of Life

Thirteen hours and thirty minutes after the incident, Captain First Rank Alexander Teslenko, the Northern Fleet rescue chief, stood on the bridge of the *Mikhail Rudnitsky* as the crew finally cast lines and pulled away from the Severomorsk dock. He ordered Captain Kostin to increase speed to flank on a course toward the Kildin Island rendezvous point, east of the Murmansk fjord. There, the rescue ship was scheduled to meet the salvage tug *Altay* and then proceed to the *Kursk's* last known location in the Barents Sea. Teslenko had not given the crew details about the rescue operation, but nearly all had heard about the missing *Kursk* and made the connection.

With a maximum speed of only sixteen knots, the *Rudnitsky* would take almost twelve hours to reach the search area. Even so, the fleet had yet to locate the downed *Kursk*. Until they did, there could be no rescue mission. A few hours later, Teslenko received the news. The chief navigator aboard the *Peter the Great*, Captain Third Rank Evgeny Golodenko, had noticed a distinct sound pattern forming on the Acoustic audio monitors on the bridge starting at 2:28 a.m. The light pings appeared to create a uniform series of seven beats.

Golodenko had grabbed the comm and called Andrey Lavriniuk in Acoustic Cutting. The seaman confirmed the pattern and said it sounded like repeated SOS signals. Golodenko informed Boyarkin, who ordered the *Peter the Great* to close in on the signals. The massive warship turned toward the sound of hope while the signals increased in strength on a bearing of 281. The sound intensified and was joined by a second noise resembling metal grinding on metal. By 3:15 a.m., as a dull red sun peeked through the morning clouds, the flagship's Acoustic Cutting operators reported five rhythmic taps across an eight-second period beginning at 2:57 a.m.

Nearby ships, including the destroyers *Admiral Chabanenko* and *Admiral Kharlamov*, joined the search. A sailor aboard one of the ships spotted a blue-and-green object—perhaps a distress buoy—just below the surface of the ocean. The ships closed the gap. A small launch was lowered into the water, and its crew tried to grapple the object. They finally gave up, but rumors circulated that it might have been a buoy from a foreign sub, as

Russian buoys were red and white, not blue and green. In truth, due to light refraction through murky waters, colors can appear distorted. Also, buoys on U.S. subs are not blue and green.

By 4:13 a.m., with most of the officers suspecting the buoy was a sea creature, a sailor aboard the *Peter the Great* pointed at a bright orange object floating on the surface nearby. They drew closer and identified it as a glove, and concluded it was likely common debris lost from another ship, as no other flotsam was seen in the area. In Acoustic Cutting, operator officer Lavriniuk reported continued signal-tapping that sounded like an SOS. He was hopeful that his conclusion was correct, as he had attended naval college with some of the *Kursk*'s officers, and they remained close friends.

Other ships in the area confirmed Lavriniuk's conclusions that the tapping, heard again at 4:03 a.m., indeed sounded like an SOS, although Vice Admiral Burtsev voiced his doubts. He was not a trained Acoustic operator but concluded that the tapping was just "the sound of a perishing ship."

Deep beneath the waves, aboard the USS *Toledo*, trained sonar operators heard what their Russian counterparts did—SOS tapping coming from the bearing of the explosions. As they sat helplessly with headphones glued to their ears, they could not feel anything except a deep sense of remorse and prayerful hope that the Russians would eventually rescue the *Kursk*'s survivors.

In Moscow, naval commander-in-chief Admiral Vladimir Kuroyedov received an update from the fleet. SOS signals might have been detected but had not yet been verified. The analog clock on his wall ticked past five a.m. as he frowned and ordered a crew to ready a plane for a flight to the fleet headquarters in Severomorsk. Defense Minister Sergeyev countermanded the order, as he wanted Kuroyedov to remain at his post in Moscow. By 5:05, Acoustic Cutting operators aboard several fleet ships had reported "wailing and grinding" noises near the bearing of the SOS tapping—perhaps the sound of a dying submarine. Sailors with binoculars sighted oil slicks on the water at 6:24 and relayed this to officers on the bridge of the *Peter the Great*. Admiral Popov called Moscow to voice his opinion: the *Kursk* had likely been found. However, none of the ships in the area had deep-diving DSRVs or submersible camera equipment, so they could not yet verify anything. The rescue ship, *Mikhail Rudnitsky*, did have two DSRVs, but it was still over five hours away.

By 7:15, Defense Minister Sergeyev finally had decided to inform Putin. During the tense conversation, he heard several seconds of awkward silence from the president followed by two questions, the order of which clearly indicated Putin's priorities. The first question was, "What is the situation with the reactors?" The second, asked a few minutes later: "What is being done to save the people onboard?"

Sergeyev gave vague answers to both questions, as no clear ones could yet be given. Putin offered to fly to the Northern Fleet headquarters in Severomorsk, but Sergeyev advised against this, as doing so would have "no practical effect." Sergeyev also ensured Putin that the Northern Fleet rescue command had everything under control, and they would handle the situation efficiently and quickly. Putin obviously believed his defense minister, as he did not cut his vacation short. This later proved to be a fateful decision, severely damaging the president's reputation.

On the Barents Sea, the rescue ship *Rudnitsky* finally neared Kildin Island, where it was scheduled to meet with the tug *Altay*. Unfortunately, Teslenko's navigator made an error on the coordinates, causing a ninety-minute delay. Meanwhile, the CO_2 inside the *Kursk* continued to increase while the survivors shivered in the cold and dark and prayed for a rescue.

A day and a half after the incident, the USS *Toledo* remained on station in the Barents Sea to monitor the situation. The crew did not break radio silence but stayed at periscope depth to visually track the warships involved in the rescue attempt and ensure their VLF wire could receive transmissions. They did not raise the BRA-34 antenna as it was a large radar target that could be detected by the Russians. The VLF had limited bandwidth, but enough to pick up a few news reports about the situation, wherein the Russians were blaming an American submarine, perhaps the USS *Memphis*, for colliding with the *Kursk*. The *Toledo's* sonar operators heard active sonar pings and underwater voice transmissions coming from several Russian warships as they searched for the lost sub. They also continued to hear SOS tapping signals coming from the location where the *Kursk* had disappeared.

"We suspected there were survivors aboard the *Kursk*," says a petty officer on the *Toledo*. "Sonar heard tapping, and we knew they were alive. We couldn't understand why the Russians were waiting so long to rescue them, and there was nothing we could do to help."

Russia's Run-Down *Rudnitsky*

Cruising across the dark blue waters of the Barents Sea, the *Peter the Great* continued to circle the area where the *Kursk* might be at rest on the ocean floor. At 8:17 a.m. on Sunday, Captain-Lieutenant Yuri Ostryanin and seaman Oleg Zyryanov continued to monitor the SOS and code-tapping coming from what they believed to be survivors aboard the downed sub.

The rescue ship *Mikhail Rudnitsky* arrived on the edge of the search area at 8:39 and reported an estimated on-location time of twelve p.m. The delay spurred the officers aboard the *Peter the Great* to contact Russia's main intelligence department in Moscow and ask permission to redirect the top-secret AS-15. The small spy sub was around two hundred feet long and carried a crew of thirty-six officers. It had been laid down in 1983 and commissioned eight years later. The sub's unique side thrusters gave it dynamic maneuverability to support its primary missions, which included espionage-gathering, sabotage operations, and disruption of NATO's underwater hydrophone listening systems. It was not equipped to dock with a downed submarine for rescue operations, but hopefully its crew could at least get eyes on the *Kursk* to assess the situation in preparation for the DSRVs.

The main intelligence department approved the request, and the AS-15 sped toward the *Kursk*. Hours later, its high-resolution cameras verified the Russian Navy's worst nightmare. The AS-15 inched forward, and the black hull of the *Kursk* came into view. The minisub's camera broadcast startling images of shredded and bent metal on the seabed. Officers and crew aboard the *Peter the Great* gasped as they spied the gaping hole where the torpedo room compartment had once been.

The crew on the AS-15 gathered useful intelligence, including the *Kursk*'s lie on a heading of 285 degrees, visibility of about ten feet, and minimal sea currents of less than 1.5 knots. They saw no bodies and reported no damage to the compartment-nine escape trunk upper hatch that might prevent a rescue. All this information was relayed to the *Rudnitsky* rescue ship at 9:20 a.m., and at 9:39, while the AS-15 was still down, watch-standers on the *Peter the Great* made a log entry reporting one long and seven short taps heard from the wreck site.

On the *Toledo*, sonar operators heard the sounds made by a small submarine in the area near the *Kursk*. They ran the tones through their database and concluded that the minisub was likely the AS-15. Commander Nault ordered his sub to close the gap while the sonar jockeys recorded the AS-15 and added the additional sounds to the database. Given the shallow depth and the need to stay far enough above the downed Russian sub, the *Toledo* was forced to run shallow, which left it vulnerable to detection.

On the *Peter the Great*, sailors manning the deck pointed at a dark green obelisk just beneath the surface. They thought it was another buoy sighting, as the object appeared to be a few feet in width and several feet long.

They launched another small boat, but the object disappeared before they could get near. On the bridge, operators reported that the ship's fathometer had just detected an abrupt "shallowing" of the ocean's depth near the object's location. Officers wondered if a second submarine was in the area and they'd just spotted the top of the conning tower. They knew it could not be Russian, and so decided it had to be American or British. The AS-15 was ordered to investigate but found nothing.

The Survivors Cling to Life

Aboard the *Kursk*, still less than one day after the explosions, the fifty-two-millimeter-thick internal bulkheads held firm, but the gurgle of water seeping into compartment nine escalated. This increased the pressure and CO_2 buildup. By now, freezing and wheezing, the survivors knew they could not last more than a few more days. Based on communications likely received from the AS-15, they also knew any rescue attempt was still many hours away.

The eighth-compartment commander, Captain-Lieutenant Sergei Sadilenko, conserved air by lying in a bunk on the upper level. He struggled to breathe as the air thinned and turned sour. Earlier, he had helped collect oxygen plates from other compartments. The survivors tore open the sealed packages to expose the chemicals. The brick-size wafers helped scrub CO_2 from the air, and the crew had enough of them to survive in the cramped space for more than a week. However, the plates were highly dangerous. They were not designed for stand-alone use, but instead were normally used inside an air-regeneration system. If accidentally exposed to oil or seawater, they could ignite and cause a fire. This danger was heightened by the increasing pressure inside the disabled sub.

As the water level increased, so did the pressure, which significantly increased the percentage of nitrogen seeping into each man's bloodstream. Once it reached ten times the normal rate of saturation, it would not take long to cause nitrogen narcosis. The men would at first feel lightheaded, numb, and somewhat drunk—as if they'd consumed a pint of vodka. They'd soon become delirious, frightened, and confused. Then, as death neared, they would have convulsions, tremors, and blackouts.

Even if they managed to survive the increased nitrogen buildup, the leakage past the shaft seals would eventually bring the water level up so high that it would cover their feet and ankles and drop their ambient body temperature. They'd succumb to hypothermia and freeze to death. With time running out, each man could only sit or lie in silence and listen to the bell chime of the wrench as it banged out a desperate cry for help.

Due to the CO_2 buildup, the survivors aboard the *Kursk* eventually felt nauseous and left many of the food packages unopened. The officers relied on training to time the use of the limited supply of oxygen plates in relation to an estimated rescue time. Across the hours, the number of plates dwindled. The men were unaware that several unopened packages lay unseen behind and under various pieces of equipment in the aft compartments.

Captain-Lieutenant Sergei Sadilenko, while lying in an upper bunk, scribbled an update on a small piece of paper. He wrote, "Twenty-three men in ninth compartment. Poor health. Weakened by effects of carbon monoxide during damage control. Pressure in compartment increasing. Running out of V-64 [oxygen plates]. We will not endure compression during an escape to the surface. Not enough brass belts for personal breathing devices. Missing clasps for safety cords. Need to fasten the buoy cable reel assembly [by pulling it in]."

Collision Questions

Early Sunday morning, on the naval base in Norfolk, Virginia, the phone rang in Admiral Harold Gehman's home office. The fifty-eight-year-old naval officer was responsible for all NATO submarine operations and had earned a high degree of respect across his thirty-five years of distinguished service. The voice on the line, calling from the other side of the base, was Commander, Submarine Force Atlantic (COMSUBLANT) Vice Admiral John Grossenbacher. He asked for an immediate face-to-face meeting with Gehman, as he did not want to talk on an unsecured line. The two men agreed to meet in an area along a sidewalk that separated their two homes.

Several minutes later, as they stood toe-to-toe, Grossenbacher informed Gehman that the USS *Memphis* had just transmitted a secret report from the Barents Sea. Commander Breor, the sub's CO, believed an explosion aboard the *Kursk* had sent the submarine to the bottom. Grossenbacher said the report validated other signals intelligence data collected by additional platforms in the area.

Gehman raised both eyebrows. Grossenbacher held up his hands, palms out, as he clarified that Breor swore the *Memphis* was not involved; however, the *Toledo* had not yet broken radio silence. The crew was still on station and observing the situation. Gehman shook his head from side to side. He knew better than to trust or believe any reports from anyone until verified. Even trusted COs occasionally distorted or obfuscated the truth to avoid serious consequences. If there had been a smack between one of his boats and a Russian sub, which had occurred many times over the past few decades, he might not be able to uncover the truth for months—if ever.

Measuring his response with caution, Gehman said, "This is going to be blamed on us, and we're going to have to prove a negative." He advised Grossenbacher to step lightly and meter any responses. Also, to gather data on the precise locations of all submarines in the area, including the U.K. boat. He went on to say, "Tell the defense secretary not to go too far out on that limb before I get back to you."

Grossenbacher agreed and said his staff would move quickly but not compromise U.S. sub missions, positions, or crews. He would not force the *Toledo* to take undue risks by breaking radio silence, and besides, it was important to have the crew remain in the area to gather intelligence. The two men settled on a course of action, which involved stepping on a large pile of eggshells, and turned to walk in opposite directions down the sidewalk.

Rescue Failure

Twenty-six hours after the explosions, the tug *Altay* swept back and forth across the area where 350 feet down the *Kursk* had come to rest. The tug's crew gathered flotsam and debris, including garbage and clothing. The *Rudnitsky* finally arrived on station at 1:27 p.m. and, while anchoring, reported the slick presence of oil coating the surface of the ocean. Russian IL-38s flew over the area and dropped two buoys on the edges of the thousand-foot-long slick.

Just after two p.m., Admiral Popov's helicopter set down on the *Peter the Great* flagship. He again assumed command and was told that the crew aboard the *Rudnitsky* now had also heard the SOS tapping and marked the bearing. Popov was convinced the sounds were coming from survivors. He also believed the sailors aboard the *Kursk* were using designated code tables to report flood levels in the sub.

Acoustic Cutting operators on the *Admiral Kharlamov* recorded repetitive rounds of twenty consecutive rhythmic taps on a bearing of 129 degrees. Spurred by this news, the crew aboard the *Rudnitsky* hurried to ready the deep-diving AS-34 *Priz*-class DSRV, but they were delayed by gusting thirty-knot winds that batted the small submersible about like a piñata. The AS-34 minisub was thirty feet long and twelve feet wide and packed an array of technology into a small space. Battery-powered motors allowed a top speed of three knots submerged. The maximum range was twenty-one miles at a moderate speed of 2.3 knots. Manipulator arms allowed the AS-34 to lift and carry objects or vessels weighing up to sixty tons. The DSRV could dive to a maximum depth of just over three thousand feet and remain submerged for several hours before the batteries ran out.

Captain Alexander Maisak and chief pilot Sergei Pertsev on the AS-34 flipped switches, checked gauges, and waited. Behind them, trained divers Andrei Sholokhov and Sergei Butskikh readied gear, including full-face masks attached by hoses to an air manifold. The DSRV was not equipped for deep-water saturation diving.

The crew aboard the *Rudnitsky* lowered the AS-34 into the water at 4:14 p.m. The DSRV whirred and hummed as it descended into the abyss. Maisak's and Pertsev's breathing accelerated while bubbles coated the small round windows in the submersible. They saw nothing but murky dark water. Six minutes later, the DSRV's active sonar reflected off an anomaly on the ocean floor. The echoing pings confirmed that the object was indeed the sunken *Kursk*.

The pilots estimated the sub was 1.3 nautical miles distant and steered toward the pings. Old and slow, the AS-34 took almost ninety minutes to reach the *Kursk*. Just after six p.m., now thirty-one hours after the explosions, Maisak saw the fuzzy outline of the sub on his Acoustic sonar screen. It took Pertsev another fifteen minutes to close the distance. Both men pointed as the outline of the *Kursk* came into view.

Even in the gloomy darkness, the two men could see how the entire bow of the sub had been shredded by a massive explosion. The sail was mostly intact, and the operators knew there was an escape trunk above the fourth compartment, but they had little time to do a complete examination to confirm there were no survivors forward. As such, they maneuvered immediately toward compartment nine.

Pertsev used a steady hand to guide the AS-34 toward the aft section of the *Kursk*. He slowed as the massive twin screws came into view. Maisak pointed at the large round seating ring surrounding the compartment-nine hatch. Knowing they might soon be called upon to assist with opening the hatches, the DSRV's divers pulled on hose-attached breathing masks and waited near the docking section. Pertsev slowly lowered the AS-34 toward the *Kursk*'s fluorescent docking ring.

Pertsev glanced at the digital clock on the control panel. It read 18:20. He gently guided the AS-34 over the aft hatch. With Maisak offering guidance instructions, Pertsev descended, inch by inch, until the small DSRV rested atop the hardened steel of the *Kursk*. The divers verified a mating between the two vessels, but it was tenuous at best. At only 350 feet, there might not be enough ocean pressure to allow the DSRV to maintain an adequate seal for an extended period, or at all, if they experienced a sudden pressure change when they opened the *Kursk*'s escape-trunk pressurization valve. They could be blown off during the rescue op, and if that happened while the upper and lower hatches of the escape trunk were open, it would kill all the survivors inside.

The divers would need to work quickly to equalize the pressure in the escape trunk, open the upper hatch, and then tap on the bottom hatch to let the survivors know it was safe to egress. Unfortunately, before completing these tasks, the unthinkable happened.

The AS-34 lost its mating connection with the *Kursk* and careened toward the massive rudder. Pertsev gripped the controls and fought to keep his craft steady while Maisak pointed and shouted.

The DSRV slammed into the *Kursk*'s rudder. The loud clang sounded like the toll of a giant bell. Maisak steered the AS-34 back toward the surface. The crew held their breath as the submersible shot upward toward safety. Finally, at 6:32, the DSRV bobbed atop the waves and waited for the crew aboard the *Rudnitsky* to haul them in.

Four hours later, the rescue team deployed the other DSRV, the AS-32, commanded by Captain Pavel Karaputa. Despite repeated attempts, Karaputa and his crew were unable to locate the *Kursk*. Fleet rescue chief Teslenko requested that a third rescue vehicle, the more modern and robust AS-36 *Bester*-class DSRV, be brought in from shore to assist in the rescue even though it lacked a viable mother ship. Admiral Popov agreed with this decision and ordered all rescue aircraft to return to base.

U.S. Officials Plan a Response

On Sunday, August 13, at eleven a.m. Eastern time, Mark Medish prepared for a team call with Strobe Talbott, Frank Miller, and Debra Cagan. A light rain tapped on his living room window while the group focused on Cagan's concerns about whether the Russian military might be obfuscating the truth and keeping the Kremlin in the dark. They questioned how much information Putin had been given and wondered if any of the submariners were still alive. The *Kursk* had been down for almost a day and a half, and Russian officials hadn't even updated the crew's families. Putin remained silent on the matter, but that seemed to be par for the course with the Russian president. In the meantime, the USS *Toledo* remained on station to monitor the situation, and NATO forces in the area had reported little to no progress made by the Russians to rescue any survivors. The group concluded that it left the U.S. between a rock and a very hard place. Clinton remained anxious to move beyond the poised daggers of the Cold War and improve the détente between the two superpowers. His administration was determined to aid the former adversary in taking steps toward democracy.

Talbott seemed to harbor this agenda more than the others, as he had previously criticized Ronald Reagan for portraying the Soviet Union as an evil empire. Cagan was less optimistic and more pragmatic about any warming relationships, and held the opinion that the Cold War was not actually over but only taking a break. She told the group that Russia, and especially Putin, had never reached a friendly hand toward the United States and likely never would. The slow-moving rescue attempts and failure by the Russians to request assistance appeared to underscore her opinion.

Miller offered a completely different point of view from the others. He was a career naval officer with submarine experience. Although he had pointed weapons at the Soviets during the Cold War, he could not help but feel a bond with the submariners trapped on the ocean floor. He wanted to find a way to offer help but agreed it was best to let the Russians make the first move. He also acknowledged that Ivanov's continued stonewalling was not a good sign.

Medish listened to everyone's opinion and then suggested, regardless of what everyone would like to do, that the U.S. had little choice but to watch and wait. The group agreed and decided to advise Berger and Clinton not to make any formal announcements about the *Kursk* incident. They also agreed to inform the URC in San Diego to remain on warm standby.

More Russian Rescue Failures

The *Rudnitsky*'s crew rushed to repair the damaged AS-34 and lower it back into the water. The DSRV's operators again located the *Kursk* but failed to dock and had to surface at four a.m. on Monday as their batteries were depleted. Normally, a full charge took about fourteen hours, but the decision was made to do a fast "hotshot" recharge despite the potential damage to the batteries. Running on borrowed time, the AS-34 submerged again at 4:55 and inched back toward the wreck. It remained down until the batteries ran dry and then surfaced at 7:48.

Details about this dive were divulged to only a few Russian naval officers, including Rear Admiral Gennady Verich, who later claimed that poor visibility, strong currents, and a high list angle had prevented a successful docking.

This was the last dive on the *Kursk* made by any of the Russian DSRVs.

The Russian Navy scrambled to deploy the newer AS-36 *Bester* model rescue vehicle, which might improve its ability to mate with the *Kursk*. This decision devolved into yet another catastrophe. The AS-36 developed an unnoticed small hydraulic leak that escalated into a thin jet. The flammable red liquid spewed across the crew compartment and eventually rendered the DSRV's controls useless. The three-man crew was forced to initiate a risky surfacing in a small area blanketed by ships. Once the AS-36 was on the surface, a tug cast a line and attempted to tow it to safety. With the hydraulic fluid now gone, there was no pressure on the DSRV's rudder and diving planes, so the minisub swerved and gyrated wildly in the rough seas. Ocean water splashed through the open hatch while the crew prayed they'd reach the *Rudnitsky* before their craft flooded and sank. Eventually they returned safely, but the *Bester* AS-36 was no longer usable.

By Monday, August 14, at nine thirty a.m. Moscow time, the *Kursk* had been down almost two full days. The Russian state-controlled radio relayed a report given by Russian Navy spokesperson Captain First Rank Igor Dygalo. He used a somber tone to inform the public that the *Kursk* had suffered a technical malfunction, but the Navy was in contact with the survivors, who had been supplied with oxygen, and rescue attempts were underway. He also said no casualties had been reported, intimating that the entire crew was still alive.

In the United Kingdom, British Navy commodore David Russell strolled into the Royal Navy headquarters at 7:45 a.m. London time. Russell served as the head of the U.K.'s submarine rescue unit. He had barely taken a seat at his desk when his phone rang. A watch officer informed him about the Russian broadcast and about an increase in rescue activity in the Barents. Russell's temples throbbed. He knew the Russian Navy had antiquated submarine rescue capability and no saturation-diving support. In contrast, the U.K. had an advanced LR5 submersible and saturation-diving chambers and personnel. The team and equipment, or "kit" as they were called, were currently divided between France and Britain while prepping for an exercise in the Mediterranean near Turkey. At 8:10, Russell made a command decision and issued an order to place the exercise on hold temporarily in the event they were called upon to assist in the Barents Sea. At 8:50, he called Admiral Sir Nigel Essenhigh, the Royal Navy's commander-in-chief, and said his team was ready to deploy on a moment's notice.

In Norway, Frode Ringdal, the scientific director for the NORSAR (Norwegian Seismic Array) seismology center in Oslo, heard the Russian news broadcast regarding the *Kursk* situation. Lightbulbs went off. He had been studying a series of strange seismic tracings on his system's print-outs indicating that a large blast had occurred in the Barents on Saturday. The explosion had been recorded by a global network created to monitor underground nuclear tests and was accurate enough to pinpoint a precise location. Ringdal had already determined that the blast was not geological or nuclear in nature but had come from what appeared to be a conventional explosion. He immediately contacted officials at the Norwegian Ministry of Defence. Admiral Einar Skorgen received the report and grabbed his red "hotline" phone to contact his Russian counterpart and longtime friend, Admiral Popov. One of Popov's senior aides answered the line and relayed a message to Popov, who was still aboard the *Peter the Great*.

Skorgen waited anxiously for several minutes before he received a reply. The response made him wrinkle his brow in confusion. Popov thanked Skorgen for his concern but said the Russian Navy had the situation under control and did not need assistance. Skorgen knew this was a lie. He knew the depth in the area was greater than three hundred feet and the Russian Navy lacked saturation divers, equipment, and modern DSRVs. He suspected Popov's hands were tied and his mouth controlled by Russian officials. Despite Popov's refusal, Skorgen alerted Norway's naval rescue services and ordered P-3 Orion ASW aircraft to patrol the area and report on the activity.

Thousands of miles away, in the U.K., Minister of State for the Armed Forces John Spellar sent a fax to Russian Defense Minister Marshal Igor Sergeyev. "I was very concerned to hear about one of your submarines currently experiencing difficulty in the Barents Sea," Spellar said in the fax. "I am sure that your own Navy is extremely capable of resolving the incident and rescuing all those involved. I would, however, like to offer assistance in the form [of] the use of our rescue vehicle LR5 and the ROV [remotely operated vehicle] 'Scorpio' and advice and assistance on the handling of casualties. The U.K. submarine rescue system is about to be transported to an exercise in the eastern Mediterranean. It would be no trouble at all to divert the equipment to assist your submarine in the Barents Sea and we would be happy to do this should you so wish. If we can be of any assistance, my Defence Attaché in Moscow stands ready to relay any messages back to London."

Meanwhile, Commodore Russell and his team ramped their preparation efforts, fully expecting the Russians to leap at the offer to have the advanced LR5 kit brought in to assist with the rescue attempt. Russell was bewildered when the Russians remained silent.

In the U.S., Medish and his team allowed Admiral Gehman, the submarine division commander in Norfolk, Virginia, to "take his gloves off" and offer NATO rescue assistance to the Russians. This offer was also met with silence. Given the situation unfolding in the Barents Sea, the refusal by the Russians to even acknowledge the offers was puzzling.

Aboard the *Rudnitsky* rescue ship, the crew prepared to once again deploy the previously damaged and sadly inadequate AS-34 DSRV. The sea state had turned rough, and the AS-34 was violently slammed against the structures supporting the two cranes. The blows reportedly damaged navigation and other systems and rendered the AS-34 useless. With the AS-36 also damaged, that left the "third-string" AS-32 as the only rescue vehicle available to the Russian Navy. However, the AS-32 remained on the sidelines and was not deployed again.

International Pressure Mounts

In Suitland, Maryland, the Office of Naval Intelligence (ONI) hammered out a secret report on August 14, 2000, titled *Russia:* Oscar II *Recoverability.* ONI experts speculated about the improbability of rescue if indeed the "acute list" of the submarine had been accurately reported by the Russians. They also estimated that the "survivability boundary [of the crew] is likely to be in the 5 to 7-day range." They commented about the probability of flooding, CO and CO_2 buildup, and whether "fires may still occur."

The ONI report said: "In the absence of a radio link, survivors in the submarine are apparently in communication with the surface by tapping on the hull." The report said the rescue ship *Mikhail Rudnitsky* was on station and had deployed two types of submersibles: the DSV AS-15 mini spy sub and the DSRV AS-34, "equipped with tunnel thrusters for maneuvering and is assessed to be capable of performing dry personnel transfers down to a depth of 600 meters."

In Russia, unable to gain any information from official sources, a *Pravda* journalist offered an eighteen-thousand-ruble bribe to a Russian naval officer in exchange for the truth about the *Kursk*'s situation. When the story broke, family members discovered what was really going on in the Barents, as well as the names of the crew members aboard.

Now forced to make a public announcement, Vice Admiral Mikhail Motsak reported publicly that due to rough sea conditions, it had taken thirty hours to find the *Kursk* on the ocean floor. Also, the steep angle of the sub, strong currents, and a damaged rear hatch had prevented the DSRVs from docking. He also informed the world that survivors aboard the Russian submarine were tapping out SOS messages against the inside of the hull, and the crew had enough oxygen to last ten more days.

Two days and six hours after the incident, U.S. National Security Advisor Sandy Berger finally reached Sergei Ivanov in Sochi on a call. He told the Russian defense minister that the URC in San Diego was standing by to help in the rescue attempt and its team could be onsite within forty-eight hours. This was a lie. He knew it would take the URC at least seventy-two hours to get there and set up. He also knew the offer was moot on two fronts—first, any survivors would likely perish before the URC could arrive, and second, Ivanov would probably refuse the help, which he did. Ivanov's answer resembled the ones he'd given Norway and the U.K.: thanks, but no thanks.

Over the next few hours, similar offers of help came from officials in Germany, France, Italy, Sweden, Israel, Japan, Canada, and the Netherlands. Like Berger, these officials probably knew their overtures would be met with polite declining.

That evening, perhaps to provide a public reason for refusing help from the West, Russian Navy commander-in-chief Admiral Vladimir Kuroyedov went on the air to again accuse the U.S. or U.K. of causing the incident. "There are reasons to believe there has been a big and serious collision," he said with a stern voice.

At the NSC, while meeting with Medish, Talbott used a New England vernacular in response to the accusation. "We are ripshit!"

Medish tried to calm him down by saying that the Russians usually have three primary reasons for lying. One, because they must. Two, because it's easier than telling the truth. And three, they need the practice.

During an afternoon White House meeting, after hearing the Russian accusation, Frank Miller from the Pentagon fumed and said, "Let's not even dignify this with a response."

Like Medish's, Berger's reaction was more analytical. He understood that the *Toledo* and *Memphis* had been in the area and that there had been numerous submarine collisions between the two superpowers in the past. The one between the USS *Drum* and the K-324 during the Cold War had almost started an international incident. Although Miller assured the group that the Russian finger-pointing was just that, Berger could not be certain. He wanted to hear firsthand from the subs' COs. The *Memphis* had previously sent a brief update and was taking a slow route to Norway, and the *Toledo* was still on station in the Barents. Both could transmit, but Miller reminded Berger that asking them to do so would be dangerous, as it risked detection.

Despite Miller's strong recommendations, Berger said the situation warranted the risk. He overruled objections from Miller and other U.S. Navy officials and ordered the *Memphis* to ascend to periscope depth and transmit. He also ordered the *Toledo* to clear the area and do the same. An official at the Pentagon called it a "Berger panic attack," but given no choice, he issued the order to Admiral Gehman.

The order was transmitted via satellite to both subs, but it would not be received until they went shallow enough to string out a VLF wire to receive the transmission.

In the Barents Sea, three full days after the *Kursk* went down, a thirty-knot wind whipped the frigid sea into a frenzy. The biting gale suspended any further rescue operations, not that it mattered. Only the limping AS-32 was currently operable. Moscow's AS-15 spy sub descended below the surface to conduct another survey, which took almost four hours. Operators reported that the *Kursk* had a slight list to starboard of about five degrees and that the shattered bow of the sub looked like a war zone. Amidst ripped ballast tanks and scattered air bottles, bent and broken pipes jutted upward and outward and occasional air bubbles rose from the wreckage. They did not report any further tapping from potential survivors. Likewise, the surface ships and ASW aircraft in the area now heard nothing but deathly silence. The Russian Navy withheld these and all other details from news reporters.

Still at his vacation dacha, Putin asked his deputy prime minister, Ilya Klebanov, to meet him in Sochi. Klebanov arrived and briefed the president, but details coming from the Russian Navy were still sketchy at best. He told Putin that assistance from the West had so far been refused, based mostly on orders from senior members of Russia's Ministry of Defense who still harbored fierce Cold War pride. Klebanov expressed his opinion, stating that these aging stalwarts would see the submariners on the *Kursk* die in agony before tarnishing Russia's reputation, by admitting defeat and accepting help from the West.

By noon Moscow time on Tuesday, however, some of the hardliners finally broke ranks. Forced into a corner by the clamoring media, who were broadcasting images of distraught and wailing relatives of the crew, they capitulated and agreed to at least explore foreign options for rescue assistance. NATO officials immediately agreed to a discussion.

The Russians tasked two Army colonels from the embassy in Brussels to speak with NATO. Five hours later, they initiated a phone conversation with British vice admiral and U.K. subrescue command chief Commodore David Russell, who was nervous, cautious, and optimistic. He gulped a glass of water and started firing questions at the colonels. He wanted to know the status of the *Kursk* and the conditions in the area, such as visibility, list angle, and current speeds, as well as any other details the DSRVs or AS-15 might have noted. He also probed for details he knew the Russians would consider secret but were vital for any rescue attempt. These included submarine technical specifications such as hatch characteristics, compartment volumes, and internal pressure estimates at depth. Also, crew complements and functions.

The Army colonels knew nothing about Russian submarines, and they had been poorly briefed. Russell was frustrated but not surprised. He expressed sincere sympathy for the crew and then covered his LR5 team's plan to assist. The colonels acknowledged Russell's input but defaulted to standard military replies, stating they would take all of this under consideration, consult with higher authorities, and respond in due time.

The call concluded with no decisions made and no action taken to rescue any submariners, who—if still alive—might have only a few precious days...or hours...before they perished.

Across the ocean, naval attaché Captain Brannon completed a preliminary offer letter from the American embassy in Moscow and sent the draft to the Pentagon. At eleven a.m. Eastern time, seven p.m. Moscow time, U.S. Defense Secretary William Cohen reviewed the document, signed an edited version, and faxed it back to the U.S. embassy. The letter stated:

> Dear Marshal Sergeyev, I must extend my deepest thoughts of concern to you and your valued crew members aboard the *Kursk*. I know I speak for the entire U.S. Department of Defense in expressing our sincerest hopes for the best possible outcome. In the meantime, our thoughts are with you and the crew's families; we wish them strength during this most troubling time. My department stands ready to provide any assistance you may need: please do not hesitate to ask. Sincerely, [signed] Bill Cohen

Brannon placed the fax into a standard diplomatic envelope and had a driver take him to the Ministry of Defense. When he arrived, he was rebuffed by the Russian lieutenant standing guard. Brannon pleaded with the man, stating there were 118 lives at stake. They were running out of air and time, and the U.S. could help save them.

Brannon's impassioned delivery finally got through, and the Russian guard's eyes filled with tears. He led Brannon to an area where Sergeyev's inner office staff were meeting. The Navy captain handed the offer to a Ministry of Defense officer and implored the group to set aside any pride or animosity toward the U.S. and accept help from the West. The group agreed to send the fax to Moscow.

When Brannon left the building, three days and ten hours had passed since the *Kursk* was lost. He had succeeded in formally handing an offer of help to the Russians, but he believed the odds of acceptance were low. Still, if it at least spurred an outreach to a more neutral country, perhaps Norway, there might be a chance to save any survivors.

While waiting for a reply, Brannon's contact in Washington took a hard line, informing the captain that the URC would not be deployed unless Russia retracted its collision statements. Brannon was certain such a condition would quell any chance of acceptance by the Russians, but he obeyed the order, contacted the defense ministry, and conveyed the requirement.

The new conditions sparked arguments between old-school Russian hardliners and new-school officials who leaned toward détente. The hardliners won, and Minister Sergeyev sent Vice Admiral Alexander Pobozhy to NATO headquarters in Belgium. His job was to maintain discussions about possible help from NATO sources but not make any commitments. Meanwhile, in the Barents, the Russian Navy publicly announced that hull inspections confirmed that the *Kursk*'s first three compartments were flooded. Also, to save face, Deputy Prime Minister Klebanov told the press that Russia's submarine rescue forces were second to none and foreign assistance was not needed.

Vice Admiral Motsak enlisted a spokesperson to falsely announce that Russian naval forces in the area could still hear tapping coming from the *Kursk*, and Navy commander-in-chief Kuroyedov went on the air to talk about the durability of Russian submarines and insist there was enough air in the massive aft compartments to sustain the survivors until Friday, August 18.

That evening, design experts provided a list of survival supplies, and Igor Baranov, chief designer at the Rubin Central Design Bureau, stated there was enough water and food and there were enough oxygen-regeneration canisters to last five or six more days.

While Putin remained strangely silent on the public stage, Israeli prime minister Ehud Barak finally managed to connect with him at the dacha vacation compound and implore him to accept foreign help. He also offered to provide Israeli submarine rescue assistance. Putin declined, stating he'd been informed by his naval leaders that the odds of rescue at this late date were "extremely small" and it was "already too late."

Oscar II-class submarine

USS *Queenfish* (SS-393)

DSRV mounted to a nuclear submarine

USS *Halibut* (SSN-587) with aft-mounted diving chamber

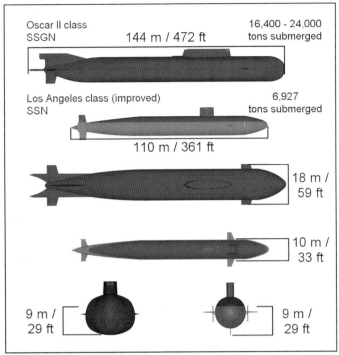

Oscar II class
SSGN
144 m / 472 ft
16,400 - 24,000
tons submerged

Los Angeles class (improved)
SSN
110 m / 361 ft
6,927
tons submerged

18 m / 59 ft

10 m / 33 ft

9 m / 29 ft

9 m / 29 ft

Russian *Oscar II* submarine comparison to U.S. Navy
Los-Angeles submarine

U.S. Navy saturation diver

USS *Drum* (SSN-677)

Russian *Victor III*-class submarine

Russian Shkval torpedo

The *Peter the Great* warship next to the submarine, *Yuriy Dolgorukiy*

The USS *Memphis* entering port

The USS *Toledo* leaving port

USS *Toledo* sonar shack

Russian *Priz*-class AS-34 DSRV

Photo courtesy of the U.S. Navy, by Shane T. McCoy

Saturation-diving chamber

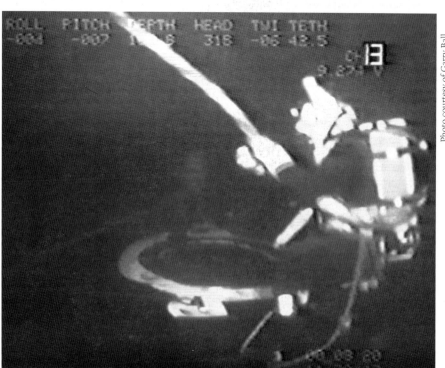

Photo courtesy of Garry Ball

Saturation diver, Tony Scott, above *Kursk* after hatch

Garry Ball (far right) with Mark Nankivell (second from left) and Russians prior to a tour of the *Orel*

Shrine to the crew of the *Kursk*

Compartment-nine hatch on Russian *Orel* submarine

Bottom escape-trunk hatch on the *Orel*

Compartment-nine upper hatch on the *Orel*

Putin addresses families of the *Kursk* crew on August 22, 2000

Photo courtesy of Kremlin.ru, by Presidential Press and Information Office

Bill Clinton and Vladimir Putin

Photo courtesy of Kremlin.ru, by Фото пресс-службы Президента России

Vladimir Putin aboard a Russian submarine in the Arctic

Mir-1 deep submersible

Photo courtesy of the U.S. Navy

USS *Queenfish* (SSN-651) at the North Pole

Photo courtesy of the author

The author in front of the USS *Connecticut* in the Arctic

Iranian *Kilo*-class submarine

Seaway Eagle construction ship

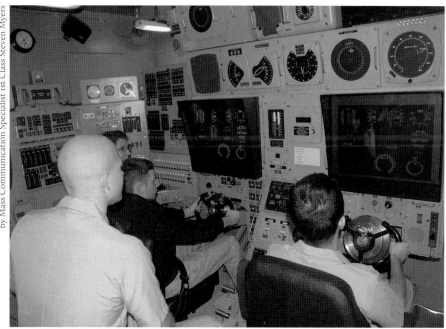

Control room on *Los Angeles*-class submarine

CHAPTER 9

FAILED RESCUE

"Our worst expectations have come true. This is the gravest disaster in the history of the Russian fleet."

—MIKHAIL MOTSAK, Vice Admiral

On Wednesday, August 16, four days after the *Kursk* had gone down, time and hope were running thin. A bevy of countries continued to flood the airwaves and phone lines with offers to help. Russian Navy spokesman Igor Dygalo maintained his defensive posture. He intimated that any effort to coordinate and manage help from other countries would take too long and perhaps lower the chances of rescue. In an apparent move to thwart further offers, he made several false statements about the *Kursk's* condition, saying that the Russian DSRVs could not mate with the sub as it was listing to port by sixty degrees, the sea currents were too strong, and visibility had dropped to only a few inches.

Russia's own media questioned the facts delivered by Dygalo. The popular daily *Komsomolskaya Pravda* called them a "chronicle of tragedies and lies." The centrist *Nezavisimaya Gazeta* said "the morally obsolete ideology of the Soviet era still dominates the mentality of the bosses." The reform activist tabloid *Segodnya* quoted an anonymous Russian Navy source who had said, "Admirals believe that if even one Russian seaman is rescued from the Russian submarine with foreign aid, this will definitely end in political disaster."

To clarify the facts reported by the media, Commodore Russell called Russian vice admiral Pobozhy, who countered most of the details given by Dygalo. He confirmed that the sea currents, list, and visibility were not issues. Russell breathed a sigh of relief. If these facts were correct, the LR5 should not have a problem mating. He confirmed that his team was standing by and the LR5 kit would soon be ready to be transported by air to Murmansk or Norway. However, they still needed a plane large enough to handle the payload. Russell sensed that Pobozhy wanted to authorize the operation but had no authority to do so. He decided to gamble and move ahead at the U.K.'s expense, hopeful that someone in power would eventually give him a green light.

The aging Russian DSRVs had logged numerous reported failures to properly mate with the *Kursk*. Admiral Popov was painfully aware, that lacking saturation divers and more modern rescue vehicles, his rescue team was not up to the task. Reluctantly, he picked up his red phone and called Admiral Skorgen in Bodo, Norway. He asked his longtime friend for help locating sat divers and a supporting cast. Popov hoped Skorgen could muster a team and be onsite before the LR5 arrived. Regardless of the situation, the Russian admiral maintained a posture of pride. He did not want Russia to suffer humiliation by allowing the Brits to become heroes on the world stage.

Half a world away, in a race against time, Russell supervised the loading of the LR5 and its support team. The submarine rescue vehicle was clamped down inside a massive cargo plane that lifted off the runway in Britain at 12:30 p.m. London time, en route to the northern Norwegian seaport of Trondheim. An oil tanker capable of handling the LR5 had been appropriated from a commercial energy firm.

While some Russian officials tried to block any help from the U.K., others softened their tone and cleared the LR5 team to land in Russia and deploy from a closer Russian seaport. They also offered to fly Russell by helicopter from Severomorsk to the Barents site. Unfortunately, shortly after takeoff, Russell received word that the Russian defense ministry had reversed its stance. The LR5 transport plane would not be allowed to land in Russia, and the oil tanker would be forced to take a much longer route from Norway. It was as if, for some unfathomable reason, the Russians did not want to rescue the survivors aboard the *Kursk*.

Or perhaps they knew for certain the entire crew was already dead.

Putin Stonewalls

In Washington, D.C., President Clinton met with Mark Medish prior to a planned call with Putin. He informed Medish that U.S. businessman

Edmond Pope, still rotting in a Russian prison after trying to obtain technical plans on the Shkval torpedo, needed to be set free as soon as possible. Clinton wanted Medish to leverage his Russian contacts and knowledge to bring Pope home. Medish nodded agreement while Clinton connected with Putin.

Medish served as Clinton's translator during the call, which was cordial but guarded. As always, Putin remained calm, but Medish sensed the Russian president was stonewalling. Still unsure how much truth the Russian Navy had divulged to Putin, Clinton proceeded cautiously. He asked Medish to convey a genuine sense of concern for the potential *Kursk* survivors and to implore Putin to accept help from the West. If not from the U.S., then at least from Commodore Russell and his LR5 team. Putin remained stoic and noncommittal. They disconnected the call, and while Medish glowered, Clinton was not quite so disappointed. He remained hopeful that Putin would capitulate.

Less than an hour later, he did. The Russian president made an unexpected about-face and ordered his naval forces to accept rescue assistance "wherever it comes from."

That evening, during a news conference in Moscow, Russian Navy spokesman Dygalo's voice quaked as he affirmed there had been no reported tapping sounds emanating from the *Kursk* for more than a day. He quickly stammered that it did not mean the survivors had perished. One of the interviewers queried Dygalo about how long the oxygen inside the *Kursk* could sustain the crew. Dygalo's voice cracked again as he held up a religious symbol and asked the Russian people to pray for the submariners.

By Thursday morning, August 17, the men aboard the *Kursk*, if still alive, had been trapped for five full days. In the NATO headquarters building in London, Admiral Gehman connected with Russian vice admiral Pobozhy in Brussels, Belgium. Their afternoon videoconference lasted four hours. During the exchange, Gehman offered the Navy's most experienced submarine rescue experts from Norfolk, the Pentagon, and the URC in San Diego. He also pumped Pobozhy for more details, but the admiral did not divulge much beyond a few sparse technical drawings. What information was obtained found its way to Commodore Russell in Norway. The LR5 team had completed loading the equipment aboard the oil tanker and would soon depart on a nine-hundred-mile trek to the Barents site.

In Norway, Admiral Skorgen also received the hand-drawn sketches of the *Kursk*'s after hatch. Angered, he grabbed the red phone and demanded to speak directly with Popov. Once connected, Skorgen asked the Russian admiral to deliver specific and detailed information about the after-hatch configuration, compartment volumes, and pressure-equalization systems. Popov at first hesitated but then eventually agreed. He promised to deliver the needed information to the dive team when they arrived onsite. Skorgen said he could not accept waiting until the team was almost ready to dive. After a long silence, Popov finally said he'd deliver the details right away. Skorgen disconnected and wondered why Popov had hesitated at all. He wondered why the admiral did not seem to have a sense of urgency while every minute, every second mattered. Skorgen could do nothing but shake his head and wonder who in Moscow was pulling Popov's strings.

Minutes later, Skorgen received an urgent call from the command post in charge of Norway's radar stations. They reported sighting a sortie of Russian fighters jetting toward the Norwegian coastline. Alarmed, Skorgen ordered F16 fighters to intercept the intruders and warn them off. He again lifted the red phone and called Popov. In a calm voice, Popov said the precaution was in response to intercepts of radio communications between a U.S. submarine and Norway. Popov said the sub, likely the USS *Memphis*, had reported an emergency and the Russian Navy firmly believed it had collided with the *Kursk*. Shocked, Skorgen drilled his friend for more details but received none.

Later that day, Skorgen learned that the *Memphis* had indeed communicated with the base at Bergen. The initial report said the sub had requested to dock for repairs, but the exchange was later corrected to "load food and water." Skorgen tapped a nervous finger on his desk. Something suspicious was happening in the Barents, and he was concerned that Norway had just been dragged into the middle of the fray.

The USS *Memphis* Nears Norway

Running slowly to avoid detection, the USS *Memphis* crept along the Russian coastline toward Norway. Days earlier, Petty Officer Tom Kunz's heart had rocketed into his chest when he'd heard the explosions in the Barents Sea. He knew something bad had happened, but until details leaked out of the sonar shack, crept along the tiled deck into the control room, and eventually found their way down the ladder into the crew's mess, he was as clueless as everyone else.

Puzzle pieces emerged along with occasional news broadcasts picked up by radio when the boat infrequently went shallow. All of them were blurry and frightening. Eventually, a picture formed. The *Memphis* had been ordered to monitor the largest naval exercise since the end of the Cold War. The most important target was the *Kursk* submarine. Few were told why, but most could guess. The Navy was concerned about Russia's new Shkval rocket torpedo, and for good reason. Every submariner shuddered at the thought of a weapon racing toward them at two hundred knots. The odds of avoiding death from such a beast were not even worth considering.

Like nearly everyone aboard the *Memphis*, Kunz struggled with mixed emotions. The crew aboard the *Kursk* had likely been test-firing a Shkval, which had only one purpose: to kill Americans. On the other hand, they were all fellow submariners. Part of a decades-old brotherhood. A fraternity of underwater bubbleheads. As such, he could not help but feel remorse and sorrow for the survivors. He could not help but pray for their rescue. He could not help but toss and turn with nightmares in his rack.

Like Kunz, Petty Officer Oscar Chaparro had a hard time sleeping. He recalled the announcement made by Commander Breor over the 1MC a day after the incident. His eyes moistened, and a knot formed in his gut. He would not hesitate to sink any Russian submarine that attacked the *Memphis*, but he would also not hesitate to risk his life to save another submariner, regardless of which flag they served.

Chaparro watched the mood aboard the *Memphis* dive toward the depths along with the sub. Light banter ceased. Joking stopped, and even movies in the crew's mess could not brighten the darkened demeanor of the crew. News flashes found their way from Radio and further stripped away any color. Faces turned gray, especially when several Russian officials started blaming the *Memphis*. The Russians claimed to have definitive proof, including video of hull scrapes and a recovered bow plane. Chaparro knew the *Memphis* was not to blame, and besides, they had fairwater planes mounted on the sail, not bow planes. However, the *Toledo* did have bow planes. They had also been operating at a closer range to the *Kursk*. Had the two subs collided?

Petty Officer Joe Ferretta had occasionally stood sonar watches aboard the *Memphis*. After the incident, he watched the sonarmen and many others exude depression, dismay, and fear. They were all saddened by what had happened but also concerned that the Russians were blaming them. What if that blame escalated into a conflict? They were not that far away from the Barents, where a large ensemble of Russia's Northern Fleet had been conducting exercises. What if all those warships and planes turned toward the *Memphis* with orders to sink on sight?

Before they'd gotten underway, Ferretta had watched Commander Breor do an occasional jig in the control room. He'd been like an excited kid who couldn't wait to race toward the enemy in the Barents. Now, he was a changed man. His smile had been replaced by a frown. His face had transitioned from beaming to bleak. He no longer made small talk but only issued orders and then disappeared into his stateroom.

The *Memphis* would soon arrive in Bergen, Norway, for a scheduled liberty stop, but few looked forward to a week of fun on shore. Instead, most wished they could stay at sea a bit longer, at least until the world knew the fate of the *Kursk* crew.

The sonar team aboard the *Memphis* had been tasked with preparing the acoustic intelligence, or ACINT, prior to arrival in Norway. All the recordings had to be cataloged and made ready for transfer. Once the sub docked, tapes, records and notes would be transferred to the Haakonsvern Naval Base north of Bergen, loaded aboard a transport plane, and flown to Fort George G. Meade in Maryland. There, a team of NSG analysts would pore through the data to determine what might have happened to the *Kursk*. They would not, unfortunately, have any ACINT on the new Shkval. As far as anyone knew, the rocket torpedo had never been fired.

The USS *Memphis* pulled into Bergen on August 18, around six days after the *Kursk*'s demise. Based on the distance between the port of Bergen and the location where the *Kursk* had gone down, the *Memphis* could not have been traveling at a speed of more than ten knots. Russian aircraft had tracked the U.S. sub and overheard the radio transmissions wherein the Norwegians confirmed the *Memphis* was pulling in "for repairs" but quickly changed the reason to "load more food and water," which made no sense. The *Memphis* carried enough food for at least ninety days and had been on station less than sixty. Also, nuclear submarines can create their own fresh water, which is needed to heat shield the reactor and create steam for the turbines.

The Call for Backup

The *Seaway Eagle*, owned by the Norwegian firm Stolt Offshore, is an odd-looking vessel with a stark white upper structure atop a bright yellow hull. Built in 1997, the modern construction ship displays an array of radar and communication antennae that sprout up from the top of the bridge area. The *Eagle* comes equipped with expensive and sophisticated systems, including a computer-controlled dynamic positioning system with thrusters and GPS links that allow it to maintain a steady "footprint" within a half meter over an exact dive location. Just forward of the bridge, a large helicopter platform supports air transports to and from the ship. The stern section houses a 150-ton yellow-and-red crane that waits for something to hoist. Also, a "Work Class" ROV rated to 6,000 feet deep with Schilling 7 function manipulators, which can mimic the seven functions of a human arm. The manipulators are sensitive enough to pick up anything from a delicate egg to a 220-pound object. A smaller "Flying Eyeball" ROV is used for visual observations. Scattered across the deck, various metal stanchions, containers, and equipment make the aft section look like a busy construction site. The most obscure of the lot is a "Flexible Lay Tower" used to install up to sixteen-inch diameter flexible pipe down to 6,000 feet.

The *Eagle* has a crew of one hundred and comes loaded with state-of-the-art diving equipment. The saturation-dive chambers, twin diving bells, and monitoring equipment are second to none, and the dive teams are some of the most experienced in the world. In 2000, the *Eagle* and its divers were leased by commercial oil firms for two hundred and fifty thousand dollars per day, but no bill would be sent to the Russians. Given the gravity of the situation unfolding in the Barents, the owners had agreed to offer the use of their vessel to the Norwegian government to assist with the crisis. It remained to be seen whether the Russians would accept an offer of help from the Norwegians.

The *Eagle* was the closest dive vessel to the Barents Sea, as her three sister ships were much further south. The crew had been working on a project for Statoil in the Åsgard fields north of Norway when the *Kursk* went down. There were two teams on the *Eagle*. The marine team, which ran the ship's functions, fell under the command of the ship's captain, and the construction team, which included the saturation divers and supervisors. The stout and soft-spoken offshore manager, Graham Mann, supervised the dive team. This typically consisted of sixteen divers and four diving supervisors, including Garry Ball, a tall and easygoing diver from Scotland; Graham Legg and Mark Nankivell from Britain, and Bob Davies, a former U.S. Navy Diver who had moved to Aberdeen, Scotland.

Only four of the divers were Norwegian, and the other twelve were British. The two lead divers were Tony Scott and Paal Dinessen. Scott was a stocky Brit with short dark hair, a round face, and a goatee. He had soft eyes and a genuine smile, and all the dive supervisors agreed that almost nothing could rattle the man. Dinessen was a tall, handsome Norwegian diver with a playful spirit. He craved the excitement of a dangerous dive and enjoyed basking in the limelight, and even though he wasn't officially part of the *Eagle*'s regular team, he had volunteered to help with the *Kursk* dive. Mann was glad to have him, as they were having difficulty rounding up the entire dive team, including a trained "gasman" who knew how to ensure the right mix of helium to oxygen. He finally located fourteen of the sixteen, the minimum needed, and they all flew to Tromsø, Norway, to meet the *Eagle* when it arrived.

The Åsgard project had not required saturation divers, so the *Eagle* was not in "diving mode." The team lacked helium gas, dive equipment, and support staff. Most important, they did not have a hyperbaric "lifeboat"—a chamber inside a lifeboat that could house all sixteen divers, used for an emergency evacuation in case the *Eagle* was in danger of sinking or had been consumed by a fire. The lifeboat had been sent to Aberdeen, Scotland, for refurbishment. Mann did not relish the thought of undertaking a dangerous dive in the Barents Sea without it, but they had no choice. The sat divers had been asked to sign an indemnity waiver to absolve Stolt from any liability related to radiation exposure or the lack of a lifeboat. Despite the dangers, all the divers signed without hesitation.

Around nine a.m. Norway time on August 18, the *Eagle* pulled into Tromsø to refuel and load up. Before the mooring ropes were secure, the cranes were already swinging crates onboard. Equipment and gas racks were loaded and welded to the deck. During a meeting with a Norwegian naval representative and a Russian delegation, the Stolt Offshore team received details about the *Kursk* incident and condition information obtained by the AS-15. They reported the depth at 110 meters and bottom currents at three knots with poor visibility. They said the sub was bow down on the seabed at an angle of twenty-five degrees with a port list of sixty degrees. The Russians further divulged that two DSRVs had tried unsuccessfully to mate with the *Kursk*. Considering the high currents and low visibility, a Stolt rep at the meeting expressed concerns about the viability of the dive. Given the angle, the rep estimated that the escape hatch would be thirty meters above the seabed, which was an important detail, as it affected the diver's mixed-gas selection.

The Russians agreed to provide updated details obtained by the DSRV crews and asked Stolt to ensure the British members of the dive team remained incognito to avoid public embarrassment. The team complied, concerned that to do otherwise might cause a delay or cancellation of the rescue mission. To that end, while news cameras pointed, Nankivell and the four Norwegian divers led the charge to board the *Eagle*. Enjoying the attention, sat diver Dinessen wore a suit and smiled and waved like a movie star on a red carpet. Following close behind, two female Russian translators from the Norwegian Navy and a team of radioactivity monitoring experts also boarded the ship. Later, after the media left, the British members of the team snuck aboard unnoticed.

Once onboard, all members of the team were required to surrender mobile phones and maintain radio silence about the mission. The primary objective of the operation was to ascertain whether there were any survivors and not to attempt a rescue. If any of the crew were still breathing, the Russian Navy would send their own DSRVs back down to bring them out.

The *Eagle* could reach the site via two different routes, both due north from Tromsø. The inner passage required skirting islands that housed small communities. This direction was shorter but also narrow and treacherous in places, and therefore required the assistance of trained local pilots to act as guides. The Norwegian government arranged for the pilots to come aboard the *Eagle* in Tromsø and also removed the usual speed restrictions past marinas, jetties, and fish farms.

The load-out in Norway took an efficient three hours and thirty minutes. The *Eagle* slid away from the dock at noon, pointed its bow toward the Barents Sea, and hit 110 percent of its top speed using forward thrusters.

Not far away, in a Norwegian hotel room, Commodore Russell threw his hands up in despair. He had been trying to convince the Russians to let him fly by helicopter out to the wreck site to do an assessment prior to the arrival of the *Normand Pioneer* support ship carrying the LR5. Repeatedly, the Russians had refused. He packed his gear, slammed his hotel room door, and met up with his translator, Captain Simon Lister. Together, they climbed aboard a helicopter and flew across Norway's coastal fjords and the Norwegian Sea to rendezvous with the *Normand Pioneer*. While gazing down at the dispassionate ocean below, Russell wondered if all his efforts might be in vain. He wondered if perhaps they were too late, if the crew aboard the *Kursk* had already perished. He also prayed the Russians would give his team the chance to find out.

The *Eagle* sped past Norway's North Cape near midnight before turning onto a southeast heading toward the Barents Sea. Graham Mann and the dive team frequently monitored the broadcasts from the BBC and CNN. The missing Russian submarine was the lead story on every channel, but the Russians had not been very forthcoming with details, so the *Eagle* team jotted down any tidbits of information that came across the airwaves. Although Mann did not expect a warm welcome from the Russians, he at least hoped their rescue personnel would be cooperative. After all, Russian lives were at stake.

While the *Eagle*'s bow carved troughs in the frigid ocean, Mann called Scott into the dive control room. They sat. Mann cleared his throat. "I need a cool head to lead the dive. I've assigned you as diver one on team one."

Normally unruffled, Scott swallowed a lump and nodded. He would be the first diver to step onto the deck of the *Kursk*. He would be the first to examine the hatch and determine if a rescue was possible. He would be the first to find out if anyone onboard was still alive.

One week after the incident, on Saturday August 19, the Russians provided an update to Stolt on the *Kursk*'s condition. They now reported an angle of only eight degrees. Either the initial report was incorrect, or the *Kursk* was suffering substantial flooding and the additional water weight had changed the angle by seventeen degrees. The *Kursk* had a submerged displacement of 18,300 tons, so the former appeared more correct than the latter. If it was the latter, the *Kursk* was probably fully flooded, making the odds of finding any survivors quite low.

That same day, the transport ship carrying Russell's LR5 reached the edge of the Barents Sea, still several hours away from the site. Commodore Russell climbed aboard a helicopter and raced toward the Norwegian *Seaway Eagle*, now slightly behind Russell's *Normand Pioneer*, to conduct the first summit meeting with the Russians. Royal Navy captain Simon Lester rode along to interpret the conversations.

Russian rescue chief Rear Admiral Gennady Verich and his entourage of five naval officers and specialists met with Russell, Mann, Nankivell, and Ball in a meeting room aboard the *Eagle*. Verich's face looked gaunt, and his eyes were red. The admiral obviously hadn't slept much over the past week. The meeting began with lengthy formalities and introductions, translated by Captain Lister, before Russell beseeched Verich to allow the LR5 team to assist. He addressed the security concerns and agreed to have Russian observers monitor the team's every move.

Verich waved a hand in the air. He did not appear anxious to launch a new rescue attempt, and intimated it was too late. They had heard no tapping from the *Kursk* since the AS-34's last dive on Monday, August 14. Verich kept shifting the conversation to a discussion about recovering bodies, not attempts to rescue the downed sailors. Russell's face turned red as he asked how Verich could be certain there were no survivors, and reminded him that if there were, the LR5 was the best option available for a rescue. The "skirt" on the bottom of the LR5 allowed for better docking with the *Kursk*, even at an acute angle. The Russian DSRVs did not have this capability.

Verich squirmed in his seat and said his DSRV teams did not need to dock, but only needed to gain access. However, they lacked the saturation divers and equipment to open the outer and inner hatches on the escape trunk and enter the sub. Russell wondered what games the Russians were playing. Verich was obviously hiding something, but what? Tensions escalated until Verich finally slapped a hand on the table. He drew in a long breath, regained his composure, and thanked Commodore Russell for offering assistance, but said it was now of no use. He said they only needed to use the *Eagle*'s saturation divers to confirm the *Kursk* was flooded and to help his rescue team gain access.

Russell shook his head in disbelief. He asked Verich to reconsider. They could not be certain there were no survivors. Verich again held up a hand to cut off the commodore. He narrowed his eyes and with a firm tone told Russell there would be no LR5 rescue. They now only needed a few sat divers on a short leash. Russell's jaw tightened. They were no longer rushing toward the site to rescue anyone, only to gain access to a graveyard.

Russell strode out to his helicopter with Captain Lister in tow. Back aboard the *Pioneer*, he heard chopper blades in the distance. He glanced up. A Russian helicopter descended toward the aft deck and landed. A portly naval officer emerged and approached. While Lister interpreted, the man introduced himself as Vice Admiral Oleg Burtsev. He said the *Kursk* was a part of his flotilla and he and Captain Gennady Lyachin, the CO of the downed sub, were old friends.

The two officers conversed while Burtsev delved into personal details about his family and the crew aboard the *Kursk*. Burtsev's eyes filled with tears as he told Russell he would do everything in his power to help the commodore deploy the LR5 to rescue any survivors. Russell assured the admiral that he and his team would do whatever they could to bring the crew home alive.

Burtsev smiled and gave Russell a Russian bear hug. He promised the commodore he would pull every string possible to gain approval from his superiors. Russell watched the admiral lumber back to his helicopter. He said a silent prayer that Burtsev's words were true, and the admiral would find a way to cut through the Russian bureaucratic red tape.

Russell had the radio operators aboard the *Normand Pioneer* contact the *Peter the Great* flagship at seven p.m. and report an onsite arrival within two hours. The reply was curt. The *Pioneer* was ordered to stand down and remain at least fifteen nautical miles away. Russell's heart sank. He had hoped Burtsev might find a way to gain approval for Western help, but the admiral had obviously not been successful. At least not yet. Russell clung to a sliver of hope but feared that if anyone was still alive aboard the *Kursk*, the Russian Navy might have just sealed their fates.

Three hours later, the Russians were still stonewalling and arguing. A few, like Vice Admiral Burtsev, still believed at least some of the crew aboard the *Kursk* might be alive. Others, like Vice Admiral Mikhail Motsak, pointed fingers at the optimistic minority and called them cruel for giving families hope. On the world stage, the pessimists prevailed. That Saturday evening, on a Russian national television broadcast from Severomorsk, Motsak pulled the rug on all hope by stating: "Our worst expectations have come true. This is the gravest disaster in the history of the Russian fleet." He informed the world that the *Kursk*'s entire front end had flooded and that most of the crew had died within minutes. He went on to say that while a few survivors in the aft section had hammered out an SOS on the hull— and had signaled a rise in pressure and water levels along with a decrease in breathable oxygen—they were certainly no longer alive. He concluded by saying, "Regrettably, in effect we have crossed the critical boundary of assuring the life of the crew."

On the *Seaway Eagle*, Graham Mann wondered how Motsak and Verich could be so certain the crew aboard the *Kursk* had died. The Russians had just told the world that none of the DSRV crews had been able to mate or attempt an entry into the escape trunk, so how did they know there were no longer any survivors? Mann was not familiar with submarines, but he did understand pressure differentials and ship compartment integrity. Given the potential leakage rate into the sub, and the consequential rise in CO_2 and pressure levels, the odds of survival were low but not impossible. Had some of the crew found a few pockets of air and used oxygen-regeneration and CO_2-scrubbing canisters, they should have enough water and supplies to last at least ten days. To dismiss the possibility of survival outright did not make sense, unless some of the Russian admirals were keeping something secret—even from many of their fellow naval officers. Apparently, the secret was bad enough to overrule the embarrassment of failing to rescue anyone.

While Mann was stewing over Motsak's announcement, the Russian Navy radioed a warning to the *Seaway Eagle* to maintain its station and not approach closer than nine nautical miles to the wreck site. Reluctantly, the *Eagle*'s captain complied. Around eleven p.m., while the night sky still clung to a glimmer of daylight, the grey hulking outline of the Russian destroyer *Admiral Chabanenko* drew closer and lowered a small launch into the water. A group of Russian officers and technicians climbed aboard and sped toward the *Eagle*. The launch cut through the bounding waves and spewed geysers of white to the left and right of its bow. Standing on the deck, Mann heard the rattle of the boat's engine as it approached and pulled alongside. He leaned over the railing and peered down. A Russian officer stared back at him. The brim of the man's uniform hat resembled a large white Frisbee. His dull yellow shirt looked like it hadn't been washed in a month.

The *Eagle*'s crew helped the officer aboard. To Mann's surprise, Admiral Verich had returned and brought with him a few Russian officers and sailors. A bright light on the ship's bridge illuminated the deck with a ghostly yellow beam that cast eerie shadows across stanchions and equipment. The night air was tainted by the dense smell of diesel fuel.

Through an interpreter, Verich asked permission to step inside and speak with the dive team supervisors. Mann nodded and guided the group through the passageways, past an array of humming and blinking systems— including dive, saturation, and ROV controls—and down three decks by way of an elevator. Along the way, the Russians gawked at the array of advanced equipment. No doubt they were in awe given the sad state of Russia's Navy and dive teams. Mann pointed here and there and by way of an interpreter explained that Russian divers, unequipped with the latest saturation-diving equipment, were forced to employ "bounce diving." At deeper depths, they had to work in short bursts and decompress frequently in pressurized chambers. In contrast, Western sat-dive teams pressed down in chambers and remained there, sometimes for up to a month. Taking shifts, they could work 24/7 for weeks on end to complete a job.

Mann finished his dissertation as they arrived at the door to the conference room. They stepped inside and sat at the table. Verich shifted in his seat while asking questions about the dive team's ability to gain access to the submarine through the aft hatch. Mann cocked his head and asked why they wanted to have the dive team get inside. He reminded Verich that doing so might seal the fate of any survivors if the lower hatch had been opened by the crew in an attempt to escape. If the men inside were unconscious, they could not be signaled to shut the lower hatch.

Verich cleared his throat and said they were certain there were no survivors, and they just wanted help gaining access to recover the bodies. Mann said the team had received a fax with only a sketch of the hatch, which did not give them many details. They would need better information. Also, they would first need to deploy an ROV, or remotely operated vehicle, mounted with a high-resolution camera. They called it a "Flying Eyeball." He explained that the *Eagle* had two types of ROVs. The smaller observation ROV (OBSROV) monitored the divers, the area, and the job. It was also used to help guide the support team when lowering equipment down to the divers. The larger work-class WOROV (designated SCV006), was fitted with a bevy of electronics, advanced sonar, and radiation monitoring gear, and was used ahead of any dives to examine the area. Mann said they needed this to monitor for radiation, check the depth of the highest obstacles, and take video of the area to safely guide the dive team.

Verich waved a hand in the air and said, "*Nyet!*" He did not want any photos or video taken of any areas beyond the vicinity of the escape trunk. He then outlined a dozen more restrictions and rules that required strict adherence or there would be no dives. Mann's mouth formed a thin line as he forced himself to remain calm. He glanced at the clock on the wall. They had started their conversation at eleven thirty p.m., and it was now almost one in the morning. Mann and Verich continued their boxing match until nearly four, whereupon Verich finally relented and said photos and video could be taken but nothing forward of compartment five, just aft of the sail. He stood from his chair and marched toward the door.

The *Eagle* finally got underway again at four thirty a.m. while Legg, Ball, Davies, and Nankivell made their way to the dive-control room to supervise the preparations. Nankivell ordered dive team one, which included Tony Scott, Paal Dinessen, and Jim Mallen, to climb into a saturation chamber at nine thirty a.m. and pressurize down to ninety meters for a dive on the *Kursk*. Dive team two also entered a chamber and pressed down to act as a backup to team one and ensure no delays between dive shifts.

CHAPTER 10

THE DIVE

"Sat diving is not for the faint of heart. It's not just physically demanding; it's also psychologically demanding."

—TONY SCOTT, Saturation Diver

When Tony Scott was only eleven, he thought he was destined to be a marine biologist. He wanted to help save the whales and play with the dolphins. He was not very interested in the academic side of the equation, so he dropped out of high school to find his fame and fortune at sea. He got as far as the submarine base at Plymouth, where he worked in construction, building various structures and working as a mechanical engineer. One day, while watching the Navy divers suit up and plunge beneath the depths, he decided to join them. He wanted to be like the famous diver Jacques Cousteau.

A variety of companies needed the services of deep-sea divers to help build and maintain oil platforms, conduct salvage operations, and build underwater structures. Many of them hired Navy divers but soon discovered they were adept at diving but not so skilled at construction or mechanical engineering. Scott was, by then, highly skilled at the latter two but was not a trained diver. He took a three-month government course to earn his certification in standard air diving and then, years later, completed deep-sea-diver training.

Scott worked for a variety of firms for about five years and then decided to learn how to breathe helium. Dive jobs were becoming more demanding and required deeper dives for longer periods of time. Saturation diving was maturing from nascent to mainstream, and there was a dearth of trained divers. The demand was high and the compensation attractive. Also, Scott relished a good thrill and wanted to dive deeper into his career, literally.

Although Scott considered himself adventurous, when it came to taking risks, he was never unsafe. He refused to work for companies or in locales where rules and precautions were ignored. This line in the sand often pushed him toward work offered by Norwegian firms. The jobs were interesting and somewhat dangerous, but the personnel were trained and cautious. Even so, underwater communications back then were patchy at best, and upon occasion, a crane operator might drop a load in a dive zone without double-checking to ensure it was clear of divers. Scott had more than once nearly been crushed to death by a mountain of steel and concrete.

"Sat diving is not for the faint of heart," Scott says. "It's not just physically demanding; it's also psychologically demanding."

A typical dive job requires climbing into a small chamber with two or three other guys, sometimes for weeks on end. "Most of the time," Scott says, "it's like camping with friends. But heaven forbid you should get paired with somebody you can't stand. Then it's like a social hand grenade."

The saturation-diving chambers on the *Eagle*, built into the structure a few decks below topside, resembled four large oval water tanks laid horizontally. Entry hatches and various controls were attached to the sides. Two of the chambers were connected to the two diving bells. As ordered, Scott joined divers Dinessen and Mallen in one of the chambers. Three other divers on team two climbed into a second chamber. They all wore flame-retardant jumpsuit pants or shorts and T-shirts. As noted earlier, helium does not conduct heat very well, so the chambers needed to remain warm. In such conditions, bacteria thrive. Precautions were taken to keep the area clean and to keep the divers from developing ear infections.

The press down took about three hours. The divers frequently equalized their ears, as one might do on an airplane, by clamping their nose and blowing out to clear. A warm stream of 95 percent helium and 5 percent oxygen rushed into the sealed chamber and turned deep male baritones into bird chirps. An electronic voice synthesizer brought the vocal frequencies back to almost normal to ensure technicians outside the chambers could communicate properly with the divers. Scott lay on a bunk and passed the time by talking with his fellow divers. They reviewed procedures and speculated on what lay ahead in the dark. To a man, they hoped their dive would not be in vain.

By Sunday, August 20, the crew had been entombed in the *Kursk* for almost eight days. The ROV team aboard the *Eagle* used a dedicated handling system to carefully lower the WOROV into the ocean. They watched as it slipped beneath the surface of the frigid sea. The WOROV looked like a small car with front-mounted cameras and six thrusters that allowed for three-dimensional rotation. Standing over Mann's shoulder in the sat-control room, his eyes glued to a video monitor, Vice Admiral Verich mumbled something in Russian. Mann pointed at the screen and explained that the WOROV was essentially an unmanned minisub with bright lights and high-resolution cameras. They were using it to do a survey prior to deploying the divers. A female translator relayed the information to Verich. Mann then rested a hand on the shoulder of an operator seated in front of the screen, and further explained how they were guiding the WOROV by way of a joystick on the panel. The operator maneuvered the WOROV using a combination of video and active sonar.

The WOROV SIT camera, which allowed for better visibility in low-light conditions, broadcasted a grainy picture that resembled a vintage black-and-white film onto a monitor in the control room. A bright yellow beam on the front illuminated the vehicle's side stanchion and a nearby school of mackerel. The sonar beam detected nothing as the WOROV sped through the ocean. Verich gasped when the outline of a massive propeller shaft suddenly came into view. The operator let out a muted yelp as the vehicle almost ran into the shaft. He jerked the control stick to the right. Verich smiled when Mann made a comment about the effectiveness of the acoustic tile on the *Kursk*. The WOROV's sonar had detected only a sight sonar bounce from the propellers, and nothing at all from the sub's hull.

The bright light on the WOROV bounced off the shiny propeller blades. Resembling massive Turkish knives, the sharp blades curved upward and outward from the shaft. The operator guided the vehicle around the port blades and then moved right to examine the starboard side. He then pushed upward and forward on the joystick to hover the WOROV atop the flat deck of the sub. Dozens of cods and pollocks danced around the hardened steel as if Mother Nature had placed the object there on a whim. No bubbles or sound emanated from the structure that lay nestled in the sand like the corpse of a giant whale.

The operator pointed the nose of the WOROV toward the back end of the sail. Verich stamped a foot on the deck and yelled something in Russian. The translator reminded Mann that photos and videos forward of the escape trunk were prohibited. Mann nodded and instructed the operator to point the WOROV toward the aft hatch. The operator tilted the vehicle downward to focus on the compartment-nine hatch.

Verich again became agitated and pointed at scratches near the hatch ring. He started squabbling something in Russian. Mann cocked an ear as the translator said that the irregularities surrounding the hatch were proof of the claims made by the DSRV teams that it was too damaged to allow a proper mating. Mann had the operator zoom in on the area with the camera lens. He and Ball studied the images and shrugged. To them, the abnormalities were nothing more than joints in the acoustic tiles. Although the seams on the rubberized outer layer appeared to be improperly joined, the anomaly should not interfere with a DSRV docking. The WOROV took water samples that would later be tested with a Geiger counter to determine if the area was radioactive, indicating a reactor leak.

At 10:35 a.m., diving operations commenced, and Mann ordered the saturation-diving bell be prepared for deployment. Now fully pressed down inside a chamber, Scott, Dinessen, and Mallen suited up and climbed into the aft bell. This was the hard part. The slow trek took thirty minutes but felt like an eternity. The divers had to sit inside a cramped oval container while wearing hot diving suits as the bell was lowered by the handling system through a moon pool on the bottom of the ship's hull.

When the bell was finally positioned just above and to the port side of the *Kursk*'s aft escape trunk, the lowering system halted. Silence filled the small container, save for a low hiss as the pressurization completed. Scott clamped on his SuperLite Kirby Morgan hard hat and stepped toward the bottom-door exit. He heard Nankivell's voice in his helmet speaker as his dive supervisor did a safety check and reviewed the instructions.

After Scott was ready and checked, his heartbeat quickened as he glided through the bottom hatch and said, "In the water." No longer adjusted by a synthesizer, his voice was high-pitched and squeaky, as the helium constricted his vocal cords. The light on his Kirby Morgan cut through the black ink surrounding the bell. With the WOROV still in its "garage" while shining a bright light on the area, and the Eyeball ROV acting as a "lighthouse" to illuminate the after hatch, Scott reported visibility of eight to ten meters. He sucked in a breath and kicked his fins to swim downward toward the sub.

On the bell, Dinessen helped reel out Scott's sixty-five-foot-long umbilical, which consisted of several bundled cables and hoses. One hose pumped in the helium-oxygen ("helox") mix, while another sucked out the used mixture, which was stripped of exhaled CO_2 and recycled back to the diver. Given the cost of helium, this was done primarily to stay within dive budgets. Warm streams of heated water were pumped in through another hose to keep Scott warm. The umbilical also allowed for a fast reel-in during an emergency. On his back, Scott carried a small cylinder of backup mix in case the primary supply shut down.

From the *Eagle*'s control room, Nankivell's voice crackled in Scott's ear. "You're going to do some tapping. Four taps, four times."

As he neared the deck of the *Kursk*, Scott acknowledged the order and removed a six-pound lump hammer from his belt. On the *Eagle*, a film crew from Russia's RTL television station barged into the control room and pointed cameras at the monitors. They watched and filmed as Scott's fins landed on the deck. He stood and glanced around. Looking forward, the massive black structure stretched longer than a football field. Aft, the beam from the Eyeball glinted off the sharp edges of the massive propeller blades. Scott's heart thudded as he realized he was standing atop a half-destroyed Russian submarine 350 feet down in the Barents Sea. Inside this giant metal container, dozens of sailors might still be alive, and they were counting on him to help save them. The enormity of the situation pressed down upon his shoulders like two heavy diving weights. His breathing accelerated.

Having noticed the spike, Nankivell clicked his mic. "Tony, you okay?"

"Diver one is fine," Scott said. He forced his breathing back to normal and knelt on the deck near a small rectangular opening in the hull. Several pipes ran through the cramped space. He raised his hammer and swung. Ocean resistance made it feel like he was swinging the hammer through a vat of liquid syrup. His arm moved in slow motion. With a loud clank, the hammer struck the side of a mooring bollard welded to the sub's hull. Scott raised the hammer and swung again. Four consecutive taps, four times in a row. The Russian code asked the question: "is water entering the submarine?" It was also an indication to any survivors to tap back a status update.

After tapping, Scott bent down and rested the side of his Kirby Morgan on the hull. He listened intently for a return tap, which he would also feel through his helmet in similar fashion to sensing an approaching train from the vibrations on a railway line. He held his breath to lower the ambient noise. The dark world around him fell silent, as if he were kneeling in a graveyard at midnight. Hoping to hear a reply, his heart skipped a few beats. He heard nothing. He tapped again and then listened. Still nothing. He tapped a third and a fourth time but heard no response. His heart sank. Although he knew the crew could be unconscious, he also knew the odds were low that any of them had lasted this long.

Nankivell's voice lit up the comm line. "No response then?"

"No response," Scott said.

Nankivell keyed his mic and asked Dinessen to push off from the diving bell and join Scott on the deck. Dinessen acknowledged and headed toward the *Kursk*. He descended through the somber darkness. The only sound he heard was the whoosh of helium as it filled his lungs. His fins brushed the metal deck. He removed a hammer from his belt, knelt, and tapped out a signal.

Nothing. No reply.

He tapped again and whispered, "Come on, boys, talk to me."

Scott drew near and signaled for Dinessen to follow him toward the hatch. While Dinessen ran a gloved hand across the scratches and scrapes, Scott unsheathed his diver's knife and probed the seams on the rubber layer near the hatch. Dinessen removed a straight edge ruler and laid it across the edges of the hatch to verify it had not been distorted during the explosion. He glanced up at Scott and shook his head. The two described what they saw to Legg, who had just relieved Nankivell as dive supervisor.

They had found no apparent issues that might prevent a DSRV docking.

Aboard the *Eagle*, Legg looked toward Verich. The Russian admiral said nothing as he lowered his head and studied his shoes. Legg asked Scott to examine the area around the hatch. Scott and Dinessen panned helmet-mounted lights and cameras in sweeping circles around the area. The yellow beams illuminated scratch marks and years of wear and tear but lit up nothing unusual until Scott held his focus on a small circle not far from the center of the hatch. Inside the circular area, something strange caught his eye.

A metal hookup pin. Resembling a towing ball mounted on the rear bumper of a pickup truck, the metal pin had been bent so badly it was almost parallel with the deck. The pin was designed to allow a DSRV to hook on with a cord to maintain a tight seal, and it normally stood vertical at a ninety-degree angle. Scott wondered how it could have been bent so badly. He captured the scene with his videocamera and then moved on to his next assignment.

He and Dinessen swam to a small opening near one edge of the hatch. There, they found the pressure-equalizing valve, or E-valve. This was designed to equalize the pressure inside the escape trunk with the pressure inside a mated DSRV so the hatch could be opened for egress. Scott removed a small plastic bottle filled with milk. He opened it and held the stream next to the E-valve stem and watched. Like a slow-moving jellyfish, the milk floated away with the currents. Had it been sucked toward the valve, it would have indicated that the E-valve was open and the hatch was not flooded. This combination would cause a pressure imbalance, resulting in a stream of milk being sucked into the trunk.

Scott grabbed the E-valve handle with his gloved hand and tried to crank it counterclockwise, as instructed by Verich. It did not budge. He tried again. Still no movement. He confirmed the order to turn counterclockwise. Legg glanced at Verich, who was adamant about the direction to open the valve. Legg relayed the information to Scott, who asked his supervisor to have a welder aboard the *Eagle* create a makeshift key and fit it to the end of a rod. He thought it might help provide leverage if he could insert it into the finger guides on the valve handle. While waiting for the part, he and Dinessen continued to examine the area and record video. They saw no apparent reasons the DSRVs could not mate, unless the *Kursk* had been at a steep angle as originally reported.

Long minutes passed before a crane operator aboard the *Eagle* lowered a cable holding a basket. A key welded atop a rod lay nestled inside. Scott retrieved the rod, slipped it into the finger guides, and tried again but to no avail. The handle did not budge. Scott poured out some more milk. No suction. It floated away as before.

Aboard the *Eagle*, Mann and Legg considered whether the valve had previously been opened by one of the divers on the AS-34 DSRV when it tried to mate. They asked Verich, who looked incredulous and swore no DSRVs had mated and the valve had not been opened. Mann considered whether the crew aboard the *Kursk* had flooded and equalized the trunk while trying to escape and reach the surface. He shuddered as he wondered if the divers might find the body of a submariner on the other side of the hatch. If so, the buoyant corpse might shoot toward the surface while news cameras broadcast the gruesome scene.

To ensure the divers didn't need to grab a buoyant body, while the media filmed the event, Mann ordered a temporary halt to the operation so they could discuss their options. They decided to fashion a mesh net to trap any ascending bodies once the hatch was opened. During the wait, the Russians stepped away from the control room and Scott took the opportunity to examine the area more closely. He wiped away some slime near the valve. He squinted and read something printed next to the handle. There appeared to be the letter O at the end of one arrow pointing counterclockwise and the number three at the end of another arrow pointing clockwise.

Scott asked his supervisor what the two markings meant. Legg asked the translator, who said the O probably stood for "открываться," which meant "open," and the three was Cyrillic for E, which stood for "shut" or "close." Scott then asked if anyone would mind if he turned the handle clockwise instead. Though in violation of the strict instructions given by Verich, Legg approved the request. Scott turned clockwise, and the valve handle moved. Verich must have given them incorrect instructions, but why? He stopped for a moment and sucked in a breath of helox as the truth congealed. *Verich had not given them incorrect instructions.* The Russians obviously followed international standards, so "open" was counterclockwise. This meant the E-valve had been open all along.

Scott tried the milk again but did not see any flow. He reported his findings, and a representative at Stolt, stationed in Bodo, Norway, made a note in the daily log.

There was now little doubt that the escape trunk was flooded. Although the lower hatch could still be closed, any rescue attempt would now be difficult, if not impossible. The *Kursk* had no power, and by this point, no air or hydraulic systems were working. Without help from the LR5 team, which had been rejected by the Russians, there was virtually no way the Russian teams could equalize and drain the trunk for a DSRV rescue.

The Russians returned to the control room to discover that their instructions had been overruled, the valve was open, and the trunk was most likely flooded. Verich's face turned red when Legg said the E-valve had apparently been in the fully opened position all along. The vice admiral made no comment about this fact and immediately ordered the divers to open the upper hatch. Working together, Scott and Dinessen pulled as hard as they could, but the hatch did not budge. They tied a bag filled with air to the hatch to provide a constant upward pull, but it made no difference. Verich grew impatient. He demanded that Mann use the *Eagle's* crane to yank the hatch open.

Mann refused. A vehement stalemate ensued for several minutes until Admiral Popov arrived by way of a small boat at around four thirty p.m. Mann and Ball went topside to greet him. Popov came aboard along with a few of his men. One of them, a stocky sailor with a chiseled jawline, was introduced as a DSRV diver. Taut muscles bulged under his uniform shirt. As the man stepped inside, an interior light illuminated his face. Ball's adrenaline surged. The man's eyes were the brightest green he'd ever seen, but they were also extremely bloodshot and dilated. His eye sockets were bruised black and blue, as if he had been pummeled in a street fight. Ball had seen this condition before. In fact, he'd once had it himself.

If a diver's face is exposed to a sudden pressure differential, a condition known as barotrauma can occur. This typically happens when the diver is wearing a mask filled with air and an unexpected pressure change, usually due to an accident, creates tension that causes tissue ruptures. Tiny blood vessels in the eyes erupt. The diver's eye sockets become bruised and swollen. The diver looks like the Russian who had just come aboard the *Eagle*. Ball knew this man had been squeezed in a recent...and severe...diving accident, probably on one of the DSRVs while diving on the *Kursk*. Based on the man's condition, Ball estimated the accident had occurred less than a week earlier.

Mann guided Popov and his team into the control room. Popov's back straightened as he expressed concerns that the *Eagle*'s divers "were not mentally prepared for the task at hand." Respectfully but firmly, Mann reminded Popov that the Stolt dive team had many years of experience and were not only mentally prepared but had been involved in several far more dangerous operations in the past. Popov conceded, but when he was asked why the LR5 was not also involved in the rescue, the admiral said he'd been informed it could not mate with the *Kursk* as the area around the hatch was damaged.

Mann politely corrected Popov and told him the dive team had done a thorough inspection and saw no reason why a DSRV could not mate with the submarine. Popov's face wrinkled in surprise as he took a step backward. He furrowed his brow, raised his voice, and pointed a finger at Verich. An argument erupted between the two naval officers related to the obviously inaccurate information Popov had received, as well as concerns about opening the upper hatch. Verich did not directly report to Popov, however; he was a vice admiral in charge of rescue operations, whereas Popov was a more senior admiral in command of the flotilla. As with all navies, there was a definite pecking order.

Popov asked Mann his opinion about forcing the hatch open. Mann said his team needed more details and specifications before attempting to pry it open. Popov agreed and then suggested the unthinkable. Verich flung his eyes open when Popov recommended that two foreign dive supervisors from the *Eagle* fly to a Russian naval base and examine the hatch on an *Oscar*-class sister sub.

While listening to the conversation in the control room, Garry Ball at first thought the translator had misinterpreted the admiral's words. She had not. Less than an hour later, Popov sped away on his small boat while Ball and Nankivell, along with a female translator, boarded a Norwegian helicopter. They lifted off from the *Eagle*'s pad and took a five-minute flight to the *Peter the Great* flagship. As he stepped onto the deck of the Russian warship, Ball was awestruck by the armament, missile launchers, and array of electronic surveillance systems. While walking away from the aft heli-copter pad, he glanced upward. On an upper deck, several Russian sailors clad in blue uniforms stared at him. One of the men nodded and tapped a hand over his heart, indicating his gratitude for helping in the rescue effort. Ball's eyes misted as he nodded back.

On the deck of the Russian cruiser, Ball and Nankivell met with Admiral Popov and the ship's captain. They asked permission to enter the sister sub and take internal and external hatch and space measurements. Without hesitation, Popov agreed.

Moments later, Ball, Nankivell, and the translator strapped into an uncomfortable Russian helicopter. The pilot wore a tattered leather flying jacket and ruffled hat, popular decades earlier during the Cold War. Dishev-eled and unshorn, he looked hungover and half asleep as he fired up the motor. Engine fumes filled the small cabin. The helicopter lifted off and sped toward Severomorsk, and Ball wondered if they'd make it there alive.

They flew low across the Russian countryside, and by way of the poorly fitting doors on the helicopter's rusted metal sides, Ball felt occasional gusts of wind on his face. They sped past military bases and flew directly toward the side of a mountain. To Ball's surprise, something akin to a large door had been carved in the mountain's side. Less than an hour later, the helicopter banked and descended toward the naval base at Severomorsk.

On the *Eagle*, while waiting for Ball and Nankivell to complete their mission, Mann again strongly advised Verich to allow the U.K.'s LR5 team to attempt a rescue. With the hatch flooded, the LR5 was now the only hope for any survivors. Verich firmly said *nyet*. He was interested only in getting the hatch open to verify that the entire sub was flooded. Mann insisted that if they opened the lower hatch to verify flooding, they'd be sentencing to death any crew still alive. Verich dismissed the plea and said he was certain there was no one still alive. When Mann started to question how he could be so sure, Verich cut him short and demanded he follow orders, as if Mann were a subordinate Russian sailor.

A few minutes later, Admiral Popov radioed Mann. On a speaker in the control room, he again put Verich in his place and agreed to allow Commo-dore Russell and the LR5 team to attempt a rescue at noon the following day. By then, nine days would have passed since the accident, and the odds of anyone's being alive were almost nil, but the LR5 crew would be allowed to verify such. His face crimson with anger and embarrassment, Verich stormed out of the control room. Mann ordered divers Scott and Dinessen back into the diving bell, and the team went into standby mode.

Ball and Nankivell Tour the *Orel*

Near midnight, Ball, Nankivell, and the translator landed at the military base in Severomorsk. They were met by three Russian personnel. One of them was the *Orel's* captain, and another introduced himself as the chief engineer. The third person was a Russian translator. They climbed aboard a minibus and rumbled toward the naval base. Near the gate, Ball spied a wooden shack manned by women selling booze. Off-duty sailors stood in line and licked their lips. As they approached the gate, another woman in sneakers and a dirty uniform checked credentials and let them in. They parked and walked across a set of pontoons on the water toward a floating drydock. Much of the gray paint on the side of the dock had peeled off, and patches of orange rust covered the metal. Ball's mouth fell open as they entered the dock.

Inside, a whale of a vessel rested on concrete blocks. Dull black skin covered the beast and reflected no light. Sleek and ominous, the *Oscar*-class submarine sat silent, guarded by a half-dozen soldiers with machine guns. To the left and right, two large warships flanked the sub. Ball marveled at how the Russian Navy, in its current state of disrepair, could have built such a massive enclosure. The *Orel's* captain, through the interpreter, said the drydock had been built in Finland and was the largest in the world. Ball glanced around and noticed that unlike with a typical NATO drydock, there were almost no machines, compressors, paint containers, or workers. He wondered what repairs could be done on these vessels, but surprisingly, they appeared to be in good condition.

Ball followed the Russians across a gangway and stepped onto the acoustic tiles of the *Orel*. Several of the Granit tube doors were open. Inside, Ball saw live missiles pointing upward. He had to remind himself that his mission was not to aid a foreign country in potentially starting a conflict, but to rescue fellow human beings from a gruesome death.

Ball took a deep breath. The gritty smell of the drydock filled his nostrils as he walked toward the aft hatch above compartment nine. There, he and Nankivell studied the design and took measurements. They were trying to determine why the hatch on the *Kursk* was not opening. They asked permission to take photos, which was granted, but only if they did not photograph the propeller blades or other ships in the drydock. They agreed and entered the escape trunk through the hatch. The space was small and claustrophobic. Ball's breathing escalated. His palms moistened as he looked at the bottom hatch and imagined the survivors on the *Kursk* staring up at a similar hatch, praying for a miracle. He and Nankivell ran fingers across the inner workings of the trunk and asked questions about the pressurization procedure. They opened the bottom hatch and climbed down the ladder.

Inside the compartment, they stood on the upper-deck platform, about nine feet below the top of the hull. They saw an assortment of valves, systems, boxes, and equipment. The small space tapered downward toward the aft. Facing the bow, a round white hatch led into compartment eight. Two placards were mounted on the hatch with information and instructions printed in Cyrillic. Large red block letters specified the volume and pressure as 550 cubic meters and ten kilograms per square centimeter, respectively.

Unlike Western hatches, which use O-rings to make tight seals, the Russians use unidirectional lip seals. Ball marveled at this, as well as the lower-hatch designs. On U.S. subs, sailors shut the hatch, spin a wheel, and "dog" it shut. On the *Orel*, there appeared to be a hatch within a hatch, wherein the outer one could be dogged but the inner one could be opened by negative pressure, or by other means from inside by the crew.

Ball asked dozens of questions about the operation of the hatch and the typical escape procedure. The *Orel*'s CO answered these without hesitation and wanted to ensure Ball and Nankivell understood that while the sub was at rest, water leaked past the shaft seals. Eventually, compartment nine would fill up, but not before the CO_2 buildup and pressure became lethal.

Ball and Nankivell verified the E-valve open direction on the hatches, and once the tour was concluded, they left the drydock. Unable to get a flight back until six a.m., due to nighttime flight restrictions, they boarded the bus and drove to Murmansk, thirty minutes away. There was no available radio or phone, so Ball and Nankivell walked from the hotel to the Norwegian consulate and radioed Mann on the *Eagle*. They described what they'd seen, including the potential flooding past the shaft seals, and then strolled back to the hotel. As Ball shut the door to his room, he noticed a gas mask hanging on the back side with instructions in Russian. The following morning, the translator said the masks were there in case of a nuclear accident...or a war.

Early that morning, nine days after the incident and hours before Ball and Nankivell returned, something unexpected happened on the *Kursk*.

Three hundred and fifty feet down, as if caused by an unseen supernatural force, the top hatch swung open. In the control room on the *Eagle*, no one had been watching. Mann deployed divers Alistair Clark and Stewart Bain of team two, led by Norwegian diver John Hvalbye. At seven a.m., Clark and Hvalbye swam over to the hull and noticed that the hatch had opened by about twenty-five degrees. They assumed the previously deployed air bag had done its job. The dive team fully opened the upper hatch and secured it with a cargo strap.

Ball and Nankivell landed on the *Eagle* and sprinted down to the control room. After having examined the hatch on the *Orel*, Ball did not believe the air bag alone could have pulled it open. He thought for a moment while Mann looked for the local tide tables. Ball and Mann studied the tables, took out a calculator and punched in some numbers, and concluded it was likely a combination of the air bag and reverse pressure caused by the receding tide.

Verich was elated and demanded the divers immediately open the lower hatch. Mann was hesitant. He was still hopeful they could find a way to verify whether there were any survivors, flooded trunk or not. Once the lower hatch was opened, the entire sub would fill with water, killing anyone still alive. He excused himself from the control room and asked Ball and Nankivell to follow him to the conference room, where they shut the door and sat at a table.

Mann discussed his concerns about opening the lower hatch with his two dive supervisors and asked if anything they had learned aboard the *Orel* could shed light on the situation. The two men relayed details and measurements and confirmed the E-valve opening direction as being counterclockwise from outside the sub. Also, Russian sub designers had elected to use a lip seal on their hatches instead of an O-ring like NATO subs. If the AS-34 had mated and opened the E-valve, the pressure buildup inside the sub could have burped gas past the O-rings and potentially caused the DSRV to blow off.

Ball then described the Russian DSRV diver he'd seen with the squeezed eyes. If the AS-34 had blown off, the sudden pressure change could have caused a squeeze to any divers wearing a mask. Mann nodded and mentioned the bent ball pin on the *Kursk*'s hatch, as reported by divers Scott and Dinessen. If there had been a blow-off, the DSRV might have careened sideways and smacked the pin flat. Also, dive team one had speculated that the E-valve had already been in an open position. Silence filled the room. No one spoke for a long moment until Mann stood from his chair and motioned toward the door.

Though unspoken and unprovable, evidence pointed to the strong probability that Verich and his rescue teams were hiding the truth from Popov and other Russian officials. The AS-34 had likely mated with the *Kursk*, opened the equalization valve, and was blown off by pressurized gas escaping past the hatch lip seals. During this incident, they might have also inadvertently flooded the escape trunk, making it nearly impossible for the DSRVs to affect a rescue.

Entering the Tomb

Video streaming from the ROV projected spectral images of the escape trunk's lower hatch onto monitors in the *Eagle*'s control room. The final bastion. Mann lowered his eyes as a wave of dysphoria hit him in the gut. He forced himself to look up again in time to see Ball point at a screen. He noted that a small amount of gas was bubbling out from around the lower hatch seal. He and Ball had seen this before on other missions and knew that this type of pulsation could result from small pressure changes caused by ocean currents. Having examined the hatch design while visiting the *Orel*, Ball knew the inner hatch could be burped open briefly by occasional pressure imbalances. This allowed a small amount of gas to escape and float upward, and it appeared to be the final proof. There could be little doubt now that compartment nine was completely flooded.

Mann concurred with Ball and no longer argued with Verich. He did not discuss the details of the conversation he'd had with his team in the conference room, but he did finally agree to open the bottom hatch and enter the tomb. At ten thirty that morning, dive team two used a mechanical device attached to the larger WOROV to push open the hatch. A flurry of bubbles escaped and shot upward. Mann's stomach knotted at the thought of what they'd find inside.

On the video screens in the control room, dark interiors were seen in the glistening bubbles, which had likely been caused by a fire. Though no one spoke the obvious, they all knew of the danger posed by the air-regeneration canisters. If exposed to oily saltwater, they could have exploded and ignited a fire. If that tragic event had occurred, it would have consumed the remaining oxygen, and no one could have survived.

All eyes inside the control room aboard the *Eagle* filled with tears as they stared at the video monitors. They were acutely aware that hundreds of relatives from across Russia had boarded railways and travelled to Murmansk to huddle together and pray for their loved ones. Their last breath of hope was now streaming toward the surface along with the silver bubbles escaping from the *Kursk*.

Mann forced himself to remain calm and focused while he conversed with Scott, Hvalbye, and the other divers, who were now back inside the chambers aboard the *Eagle*. They debated whether the sat divers should try to slip down inside the escape trunk and recover some of the bodies. Scott and his fellow divers unanimously agreed to go. They not only wanted to help bring closure to the mourning families, but they also wanted their own closure. They wanted to know if it might have made a difference had they been allowed to attempt a rescue days earlier.

The team agreed to take discreet and small steps toward a recovery, as they had not yet cleared the operation with Stolt management. Scott said he didn't see any way the divers could squeeze through the narrow trunk safely given the bulk of their suits and bailout bottles. They could, however, improvise a special air hose to allow the removal of the bottles. Mann discussed this idea with a management representative monitoring the operation from Bodo, who said that "under no circumstances are Stolt Off-shore divers to enter into the hull of the submarine *Kursk* through the rear escape hatch." Mann was reminded that his team was "onsite to support a rescue mission to save life and limb; consequently, the divers were not to be exposed to unnecessary risk."

Still, the team wanted to see inside, and so did the Russians. An hour later, dive team one relieved team two and mounted a CCTV videocamera onto a long metal pole. Scott remained in the bell while Dinessen and Mallen swam over and carefully lowered it through the open hatch. The grainy images were broadcast to the control room as well as to other monitors throughout the ship. In the control room, Mann held his breath as the camera panned about the dark and cramped compartment. The images were dense and misty, as if broadcast through a dirty windshield.

The pole plunged deeper into the compartment. Almost sixty fathoms down in the Barents Sea, the *Kursk*'s ninth compartment offered no warmth or light. Blanketed by small pockets of CO_2-filled air, swirls of freezing-cold and pitch-black ocean tossed about empty air-regeneration cartridges, while several unopened packages floated past.

The camera came within a few inches of the port bulkhead. Ball pointed. The bulkhead had been scorched black, and the gray paint was blistered and cracked. Mann nodded. They had seen this phenomenon before while conducting various operations. The discoloration had definitely been caused by a severe fire. So had the dim visibility. Millions of carbon particles had been mixed up in the water like granules of sugar in a glass of liquid. The team in the control room gasped as a body shot past the camera lens. The sailor was clad in blue coveralls and his lifeless eyes stared at nothing. The room fell silent. No one moved or said a word until Mann ordered the team to prepare to retrieve a gas sample.

From a pocket of air trapped above the waterline, they extracted a gas sample and brought it back to the *Eagle*. They measured the carbon monoxide level at 2.3 percent, lethal to humans. The oxygen had been diminished to 6.1 percent and was not breathable. It was obvious the compartment had not been completely flooded when the fire had been ignited, and the incendiary reaction had consumed the remaining oxygen and removed any hope of survival.

Having seen enough, the Russians shuffled out of the control room. The team on the *Eagle* extracted the camera and started securing equipment for an imminent departure. They could not help but imagine the final terrifying hours endured by the submariners. The disquieting images they had seen haunted them and would continue to do so for many years to come.

CHAPTER 11

THE COVER UP

*"In the best case, the real truth about what happened
on the Kursk may pop up in some 25 years."*

—SVETLANA BAIGARIN,
widow of *Kursk* Torpedo Chief Murat Baigarin

On Tuesday, August 22, ten days after the *Kursk* went down, the rusted metal gates leading to the Vidyayevo naval base swung open. A line of black limousines roared past while dwarf birch trees swayed in the breeze. The vehicles bounced and squeaked as worn tires thudded across potholes. The cars pulled to a halt near a run-down building. A door swung open and President Vladimir Putin, sharply dressed in a dark suit and black shirt with no tie, stepped from a limo. A swarm of bodyguards, with faces grim and curled wires dangling from ears, ushered Putin toward the Officer's Club in the center of the small city.

Along the way, Putin stopped briefly to pay respects to Irina Lyachin, the widow of Captain Lyachin. Putin rested undisturbed for the remainder of the evening. The following day, he officially declared a national day of mourning. In the late afternoon, the crew's relatives gathered inside a large meeting hall and awaited the president's arrival. They had been told he would speak to them at four p.m. He finally arrived four hours later. The media had been told to leave the meeting hall, but Andrei Kolesnikov, a reporter from the newspaper *Kommersant*, hid among the relatives. He had slipped a recorder inside his coat and clicked it on when the president arrived.

Putin marched to the front of the hall. He was silent for a long moment as he surveyed the crowd. The sobbing and crying diminished as he started to speak.

"We planned to hold a meeting at the Navy headquarters in Severomorsk," Putin said, "but I decided first to meet you here...."

A man yelled from the back of the room, "We can't hear you!"

"Well, I will speak louder," Putin said. "I would like to talk to you about the situation. It is a terrible tragedy. Words of condolences and apologies have been offered to you, and I add my voice to that."

A woman shouted, "Tell us why the rescue operations were stopped when the hatch was opened to the ninth compartment. What about the seventh and eighth sections—maybe there is no water there?"

"I put the same question to the experts," Putin said. "I called them every three or four hours, and I wanted to phone them every few minutes, but I was worried about distracting them from their work...."

"Why didn't you ask for foreign help immediately?" a mother asked.

"The Northern Fleet had all the rescue facilities we needed," Putin said. "I was called by the defense minister, Marshal Sergeyev, on the thirteenth of August at seven in the morning—"

A man interrupted, shouting, "The submarine is lost on Saturday, and you were called on Sunday?"

Putin waved a hand in the air. "The submarine was lost at eleven p.m. on Saturday, and the search was started then. It was found at four thirty a.m. The minister of defense called me at seven in the morning and reported, 'Something has gone wrong in training—contact with the submarine has been lost, and we have found it on the seabed. Rescue operations are underway.' My first questions were, 'How about the reactors? What can we do to save people? Do you need extra resources?' The answers were clear. The military officials considered that they had all the facilities they needed—"

Several relatives grumbled and shook their heads.

"Wait," Putin said, "I must finish my answer. Foreign assistance was suggested on the fifteenth, and Admiral Kuroyedov agreed to it."

The grumbling escalated, as if a volcano were about to erupt.

Putin's brow furrowed as he leaned into the microphone. "The television tells lies. It lies. It lies. It lies. There are people on the television who like to speak about all this, but they've been trying to destroy the Army and Navy for ten years. Their purpose is to discredit and ruin the armed forces. They have stolen money for years—"

A mother at the front of the crowd wrung her hands and sobbed. "Where is my son? Where is my son?"

Another woman joined in. "How long must I wait for my son?"

A third woman wiped away a tear and said, "I have no more money...."

Putin spent the next several minutes promising the relatives monthly payments for ten years in an amount equal to the average pay of an officer on the *Kursk*.

Near the end of the meeting, an old man in a tattered coat stepped forward. "I am sorry to interrupt you, but what are these hundred men for Russia? You must raise the submarine and rescue those poor boys who died."

Putin lowered his head and cleared his throat. "I give my word of honor that we will do our best to raise the submarine."

ON WEDNESDAY, AUGUST 23, ADMIRAL POPOV informed the rescue ships *Normand Pioneer* and *Seaway Eagle* they could head home. Commodore Russell pointed the bow of the *Pioneer* toward Norway's North Cape, but not before sending a radio message to the crew aboard the *Peter the Great*: "On behalf of the first sea lord, all members of the Royal Navy, and all those onboard the *Normand Pioneer* and myself, please pass on our deepest sympathies to all those associated with the submarine *Kursk* and in particular on this day, their families. We have all worked well together during these last few days in tragic circumstances. With Admiral Popov's permission I will depart now and leave the area. We go with a heavy heart and hope we will meet soon under happier circumstances."

Admiral Popov replied with: "Thank you for your sincerity at this moment, which is tragic for us all. In your honor and as a mark of our thanks, the warship *Admiral Chabanenko* will accompany you from the area."

White curls of foam swept across the bow as Commodore Russell leaned over a railing on the port side of the ship. The *Admiral Chabanenko* pulled near and escorted them out of the area. Along the railings of the ship, a line of blue-clad Russian sailors waved their caps in the air and cheered in gratitude. Russell's throat tightened as he waved back. During his entire naval career, he had never seen a more touching tribute.

The *Eagle* turned toward the Norwegian port of Kirkenes while the supervisors monitored the sat divers inside the two heated chambers below decks. A week would pass before Tony Scott and the other divers could "decom out" and fully decompress back to surface pressure. Normally chatty and in good spirits after a successful dive, the teams were now quiet and somber. Garry Ball suspected it would be far longer than a week before the divers would begin to decompress from their brush with death on the bottom of the Barents Sea.

Shkval or Fat Girl?

On Sunday, August 27, 2000, Rustam Usmanov, head of the Dagdizel military plant on the Caspian Sea, revealed that his chief weapons design engineer, Mamed Gadzhiyev, and his assistant, Arnold Borisov, had been aboard the *Kursk* when it went down. Although he denied that the two men had been supervising the test-firing of a new secret weapon, a British weapons expert said the Russians would not send two top experts from this factory to test older-model torpedoes. He and other Western experts believed the *Kursk* had been test-firing a new Shkval torpedo.

On Monday, August 28, the ONI in Maryland updated its maritime intelligence report. It began with the statement: "...a new type of torpedo, fitted to the OSCAR II class submarine KURSK in 1998, contributed to the disaster that sank the submarine on 12 August 2000. This torpedo [redacted]... reportedly was abandoned in the late 1980s amid safety concerns associated with the torpedo's thermal propulsion system, but recently was reportedly reintroduced to the Russian fleet."

The Russians claimed that an older-model Type 65 Fat Girl torpedo had exploded and caused the demise of the *Kursk*; however, Fat Girls use a propeller and not a thermal propulsion system. The Shkval rocket torpedo *does* use thermal propulsion.

The ONI report verified that Aleksander Rutskoy, the governor of the Kursk region, said the submarine was carrying "a new torpedo and two civilian engineers.... It is possible that the 'civilian engineers/employees were onboard the *KURSK* to monitor testing/implementation of a new torpedo.'"

The Chinese had previously bought forty of the first-generation Shkvals from Kazakhstan, and they had indicated a desire to buy hundreds of the newer, more capable units. The U.S. Navy had received reports that a high-ranking Chinese official had also been onboard the *Kursk* to observe the test-firing.

While withering away in a Russian prison, Edmond Pope watched the Russian news broadcasts about the Norwegian dive team's examination of the downed *Kursk*. He heard Russian government and military officials claim that a U.S. submarine had collided with their beloved *Kursk* and caused its demise. He also heard other experts point to a potential explosion of a Fat Girl torpedo as the culprit. No one mentioned the Shkval rocket torpedo.

Pope knew the *Kursk* had planned to test-fire a Shkval during the August exercise. The sub had been refitted with a new and potentially dangerous torpedo-launching technology in 1998—over the objections of several Russian Navy experts—that could better accommodate the firing of a rocket torpedo. The trigger mechanism, when pulled, ignited the liquid fuel and produced a gas stream that propelled the torpedo out of the tube. The liquid fuel had also been replaced by a different type with a lower flash point, and it could become unstable unless extra safeguards were used. NATO navies had once considered the use of this type of fuel for torpedo expulsion but rejected it for safety reasons.

At the time of the test-firing, the *Peter the Great* flagship had been over thirty miles away. The maximum range for a Type 65 "Kit" Fat Girl, which the Russians said had exploded just prior to firing, was less than thirty miles. The top speed was fifty knots. A gathering of high-ranking Russian Navy admirals and officials had crowded onto the bridge of the warship to watch the *Kursk* fire its torpedo. Why would these officials stand on the bridge for over thirty minutes to watch a Fat Girl torpedo run out of gas before it reached the flagship? The short answer is, they would not.

Obviously, the *Kursk* had been test-firing a Shkval, which would have taken less than ten minutes to reach the *Peter the Great.* The sub's crew was most certainly using the trigger mechanism to propel the torpedo out of its tube, whereupon the rocket engine would ignite. If the trigger mechanism had been pulled and the Shkval was not able to eject from the tube, perhaps due to a collision or scrape across the bow, that could very well have caused the initial explosion. The potential scenario is terrifying.

What if the *Kursk*'s torpedomen pulled the launch trigger mechanism right before the USS *Memphis* or *Toledo,* while trying to record the event, came too close and either scraped a bow plane across the hull or caused the *Kursk* to evade a potential collision? A scrape or sudden evasive jolt could have caused the Shkval torpedo to become lodged in the narrow tube. When the time-delay mechanism kicked in, the onboard rocket fired. A hot stream of ignited jet fuel blasted from the rocket nozzle and blew the aft torpedo tube door off its hinges. Two minutes later, the raging fire overheated the fuel in a half-dozen nearby torpedoes and caused a cataclysmic explosion that disintegrated compartment one.

Could this be what happened to the *Kursk*? If so, the Russian Navy may never divulge the truth, and neither may the U.S. Navy.

THE ONI REPORT REMAINED SECRET for many years after the incident. A heavily redacted copy released later validated Pope's speculation. The last two pages of the report ended with these sentences: "If the propulsion system had been initiated, the system possibly could have quickly overheated within the confines of the launch tube which may have led to an explosion.

"Detonation of the warhead due to the reported arming modifications and/or propulsion hazards could have caused the catastrophic event leading to the sinking of the KURSK."

The *Toledo* Arrives in Faslane

When the Russian Navy started leaving the Barents Sea, the USS *Toledo* was ordered to depart its station and head toward Scotland. It had not originally been scheduled to dock in Faslane, and the crew wondered if the *Kursk* incident had prompted the destination change. Control room watch-standers also knew something was up. The boat was not operating or responding normally, but they had not been briefed as to why. The sub cruised at slow speed while leaving the Barents and made a long trek away from Ivan's playground. They surfaced and cruised toward Her Majesty's Naval Base (HMNB), Clyde, near the end of August.

One worker at HMNB Clyde watched with curiosity as the *Toledo* cruised toward the docks during daylight hours. In his experience, U.S. subs usually came in under cover of night to avoid detection by Russian satellites. As the sub neared the pier, the worker noticed submariners on the deck pointing toward one of the bow planes, apparently to warn tugboat and dockside personnel that the bow plane was still extended. Normally, the planes were retracted into the hull to prevent damage when docking. The worker wondered why the *Toledo* was docking with one of its planes still extended.

"We pulled into Faslane during daylight so the Russian spy satellites could see that our topside wasn't damaged," says a *Toledo* petty officer. "We were debriefed by our command and then by a Vice Admiral from COMSUBLANT. They told us not to say a word to anyone about anything and if we did, we'd be in deep shit. One night I was on a sat phone call with a relative, and he was asking me questions about what had happened. I didn't divulge any details, but I mentioned the *Kursk* a few times. Someone overheard the call and told the Chief of the Boat, who called me on the carpet and told me that if I did it again, I'd be arrested and sent stateside. I kept my mouth shut tight after that."

A former employee described the base departments at Clyde in August 2000. They included logistics, which oversaw accommodations, stores, catering, and so forth. Also, engineering, which took care of waterfront services such as berths, tugboats, pilotage, and the like. The executive admin team oversaw base security and police duties, which included a large Ministry of Defence Police force ashore and afloat, supported by the Royal Marines.

The base had a robust Sea Training group that manned shore-based simulators and a Trident submarine training facility. If an American boat needed support for repairs, Clyde base workers offered assistance, but they were usually confined to cranage, internal slinging assistance, and other common functions. Lacking the proper security clearance, base personnel were not normally allowed near sensitive systems or equipment. For certain, no U.K. personnel were allowed admittance to the aft reactor area on a U.S. submarine.

There were a few exceptions to the "no clearance" rule. The base had a strategic weapons system facility with personnel familiar with systems used on U.S. SSBN submarines, as these are similar to those on U.K. "boomers." Also, the Navy Technical Department (NTD) was manned by a mixture of Royal Navy and civilian personnel. This group was assigned to several workshop facilities that conducted a variety of jobs, such as repairing a damaged sonar dome or replacing a bow plane part, should that be required. Any decision to use U.K. personnel to conduct such repairs was predicated upon a formal request from the U.S. Navy, coupled with an assessment by the U.K. regarding their competence to conduct the work.

The Clyde base worker on the pier had received such a request and was standing by, along with his team, to complete a repair in the bow of the *Toledo*.

U.S. boats typically use the "northern area" next to the ship lift. This section is also used by U.K. SSBNs. Access to the jetty where American submarines moor is controlled by U.K. security forces, but as with all submarines, only the topside watch can allow passage across the brow that connects the sub to the pier.

On that day in late August, U.K. personnel were allowed aboard the USS *Toledo* to conduct a hull inspection for damage and recommend appropriate repairs. The *Toledo* remained at Faslane for three weeks—far longer than U.S. boats typically remain in port during a northern run. Most visits, unless repairs are required, last less than a week.

Says one petty officer, "We were told that something had broken forward in the bow; I think it was a cylinder assembly. We waited four or five days for the part to show up before we could leave port. In fact, we started up the reactor a few times in anticipation of leaving only to shut down and wait another day."

Part AGAV for a *Los Angeles*-class submarine is described as a "retractable bow plane lock-in/lock-out cylinder assembly." The part might need to be replaced if the bow plane is damaged, perhaps in an accident. Without this part, it can't be retracted into the hull.

ONCE ALLOWED TO FINALLY LEAVE THE SUB and venture out into town, Petty Officer Pat Moore and his shipmates found a dingy pub in downtown Helensburgh. While they were sitting at the bar and downing a few pints, a few Scots wandered in, grinned, and walked over. They bought Moore and his mates another round and bantered about their doing a "good job" by taking down a Russian submarine.

Moore's fingernails dug into his palms. While the Russians were technically "the enemy," he was dismayed by the tragedy that had befallen the crew of the *Kursk* and did not appreciate a joke about their demise. He and his fellow sailors politely excused themselves and proceeded toward the door. On the way out, Moore stepped into the men's room and froze. Someone had used a black marker to etch a message on one of the stall doors.

It read: "Toledo Northern Run 2000: Into the Kursk."

Evidence or Coincidence?

The *Toledo* left Faslane in late September and mysteriously returned a few weeks later. All American submarine captains keep detailed logbooks. Included are dates and times of almost every important event and port visit. While most of the contents of these logbooks are classified, the dates and times subs enter or leave port is not only considered public knowledge but is often readily available on the internet or via unclassified sources. For example, the deployment history for the *Memphis* can easily be found and includes details about the sub's departure from Groton, Connecticut, on June 14, 2000. Also, entries validate that the sub moored at berth six in Haakonsvern Naval Base in Bergen, Norway, on August 18—eight days after the *Kursk* went down.

Conversely, a similar log for the USS *Toledo* from the same source offers deployment details beginning with the sub's launch and commissioning in 1995. However, there are *no* entries between 1995 and the *Toledo*'s deployment on February 16, 2002. Even inside sources with access to this information cannot find a single log entry for the years 2000 and 2001. Verification that the *Toledo* docked in Faslane in August 2000 and remained there for three weeks can be verified only by interviewing HMNB Clyde employees and submariners who were there. During that time, the crew described a repair to replace a cylinder assembly in the bow, a *Kursk* incident debriefing from a Vice Admiral, and a hull inspection to check for damage.

Years later, in July 2009, when the sub was undergoing an overhaul, two serious cracks were found in the hull of the USS *Toledo*. Experts said they possibly had been caused by a collision years earlier.

CHAPTER 12

THE EXHUMATION

"If you can't get back to the bell, you're dead."

—DON DEGENER, Saturation Diver

On September 4, 2000, Russian defense ministry officials made a shocking announcement via the Itar-Tass news service. They claimed to have recovered a piece of metal railing from the *Kursk* site, which Defense Minister Igor Sergeyev swore was a fragment from a NATO submarine conning tower.

U.S. naval submarine experts briefed President Clinton's national security advisor, Sandy Berger, prior to his meeting in New York on September 6 with Russian Security Council secretary Sergei Ivanov. They informed Berger that both submarines in the area were *Los Angeles*-class boats, which did not have metal conning tower railings. If indeed the Russians had recovered a railing, it was not from the *Memphis* or *Toledo*.

In the session, Berger cautiously offered Ivanov details about the *Kursk* incident that had been obtained via U.S. intelligence platforms. This included an array of ACINT (acoustic intelligence) and other recorded data. He had hoped this might unwind any arguments about a U.S. sub colliding with the *Kursk*, but it did not.

That same day, President Bill Clinton met with Vladimir Putin at the Waldorf Astoria hotel in New York. Strobe Talbott, deputy secretary of defense, told reporters the two world leaders met for ninety minutes to discuss several topics, including the loss of the *Kursk*. Clinton expressed condolences on behalf of the U.S. for Russian lives lost when the submarine sank in the Barents.

Other sensitive topics were discussed, including the sale of military technology by Russia to Iran and the release of Edmond Pope, still imprisoned on espionage charges for trying to obtain secret plans about the Shkval torpedo. Despite pleas made by Mark Medish, Pope's wife and doctor had been denied access to check on the retired officer's deteriorating condition. Putin was noncommittal about any actions involving Pope.

Some experts, privy to inside information, speculated about a secret deal made between Clinton and Putin involving the loss of the *Kursk*. They intimated that perhaps there was indeed a collision or near scrape between a U.S. sub and the *Kursk*, and the two presidents conspired to cover up the incident to avoid a potential conflict.

As if on cue, nine days after the New York meeting, two members of the lower-chamber Russian Duma sent a demand to inspect the USS *Memphis* for collision damage. Naturally, Berger refused. U.S. Navy officials were paranoid about allowing potential spies near one of their secret subs. The Russians were not surprised that the U.S. denied the request and used this as further proof of a collision the Americans were trying to cover up.

Having made their case, the Russians turned their attention toward the next obvious move: they needed to exhume the *Kursk* and recover its secrets before anyone else could. They had been badly burned during the Cold War by Project Azorian—the clandestine mission led by the famous Howard Hughes, mentioned earlier, wherein he'd designed a massive ship to snatch the remains of the Russian submarine K-129 from the bottom of the sea. The Russians decided on a double mission for the *Kursk* but lacked the resources to tackle either one. They did not have trained saturation divers, proper cutting tools, specialized equipment, or capable teams to pull off a salvage of one of the world's largest submarines.

One side of the mission involved the very public recovery of the bodies on the *Kursk*. The other needed to remain top-secret. Like consummate magicians, they wanted to keep the world focused on their left hand, which sought to recover the bodies from their underwater grave, while their right hand completed a secret four-part mission.

The first part of that mission entailed an examination of the twin reactors. They had to ensure no leakage or damage. If there was a leak, the last thing they wanted was a contamination PR nightmare. The second part required finding and recovering any intact secret encoding devices or code books, systems or weapons manuals, and of course, the ship's log and audio recordings. The latter included any conversation recordings in the GKP prior to the incident. If the crew had made any serious mistakes, they did not want this leaked to the press.

While the Russian Navy had changed communication codes, they knew NATO had archived thousands of hours of taped transmissions and could use old codes to decipher them, so this took precedence. However, it was not as important as the third part of the secret mission: locating evidence to support a collision with a NATO spy sub. Russian officials had been publicly adamant about this claim, and subsequently announcing to the world that they were looking for evidence would be paramount to admitting they had none. The truth was, they did have something, but it was not definitive. They wanted absolute proof.

Part four could be equally damaging to Russia's reputation. The Russians desperately needed to find out what had caused the explosion. Even if they found definitive proof of a collision, a collision alone could not have caused the second, massive detonation. Video evidence pointed to overheated torpedoes exploding, but what had caused the initial, smaller blast? Had a collision or near collision unsettled a Fat Girl? Had a Shkval triggering mechanism malfunctioned? No one could say for sure, and from Putin on down, questions demanded answers.

Entering the downed sub would be no easy task. Each meter of entry required a reel out of that much diver umbilical cord, which contained HeO2, heated water, power, and video and audio communication lines. Any snag or damage could end a mission, if not a life. Two Russian divers had been killed during a similar operation in 1986 while trying to enter the *Admiral Nakhimov*, a Soviet passenger liner, to rescue survivors after a collision sent that ship to the bottom.

Proper entry points and safe maneuvering inside the *Kursk* had to be planned for, down to the smallest detail. To do this, the Russian Navy recruited experts from Rubin Design, including marine architects and design engineers who now had to think backward. Instead of figuring out how to build a sub, they had to determine how best to dismantle one. They started by deciding how to cut through the thick hardened steel of the outer hull, and then into the inner hull. They had to find the best locations to slice into areas that were free from obstructions such as line lockers, missile tubes, and pipes. They also needed to avoid cutting into bulkheads or support beams. They decided to create full-size metal templates the divers could use to help them find cutting locations, like a paper sheet with drill marks used to mount a television on a wall.

While the Russians were confident in their ability to plan for a slice and dice, they were not so buoyant about their sat-diving or metal-cutting abilities. For saturation divers, they had two choices: find foreign divers and teach them the basics of submarine design, or find knowledgeable Russian scuba divers and train them on sat diving. They chose the latter, as it was more expedient and reduced the concerns about foreign spying or leakage of mission secrets. Also, the Russian divers could be supported by experts via video links without the need to translate or hide secret details.

The Russians recruited mission divers from the 328th Emergency Search and Rescue detachment, including Captain Vladimir Salutin. He had served with Russian naval special forces and had once been given the difficult assignment of removing unstable World War II mines from the Baltic Sea. Salutin joined divers Sergey Shmygin and Andrey Sviagintsev, and together they completed courses on forensic body recovery, which entailed working in a morgue and taking classes at the Saint Petersburg City Hospital Number 40. Meanwhile, dive masters devised an entry plan to have one diver enter a hole and drag in lights, videocameras, and other items while his dive buddy reeled out the umbilical cord and monitored for obstructions and other dangers.

Once inside the sub, the divers planned to use ropes to pull out any remains found and place them in a container for transport. The bodies would be placed in a cold room on the support ship manned by examination and autopsy doctors. Despite desires to conduct all four parts of the mission using Russian personnel, some outside help was needed. The Russians decided to let foreign divers assist, but only Russian divers would be allowed inside the sub. As Stolt Offshore of Norway had proven reliable and trustworthy during the *Kursk* rescue operation, Russian government officials turned to that company once more for the body recovery.

In early September 2000, Ramsey Martin was a marine and subsea engineer working for Stolt Offshore. Although employed by a Norwegian firm, he was decidedly British. In fact, he'd received the Member of the British Empire medal awarded by the queen for "public service outside the military service." His "public service" had been to help design and manage the successful lifting of the Piper Alpha *Accommodation* after a tragic explosion had occurred on the North Sea oil and gas platform in July 1988. Even though sixty-one workers survived, 167 had perished. Because Martin had been a project engineer working on the recovery and handling of the bodies, and due to his unrivaled experience with submarine escape systems, he was seen as the ideal candidate to manage a similar project with the *Kursk*.

Since Garry Ball had previously examined the *Orel* submarine, he had started the run toward a Stolt proposal during a Saint Petersburg meeting with Rubin Design in August. Martin had now taken the baton, and while Salutin and the team of Russian divers prepared to complete saturation dive training with Stolt, Martin travelled to Severomorsk to tour the *Orel* in harbor. The Russians had agreed to allow him to examine the sub to see the areas that would need to be cut away so the divers could gain access, and to help Stolt complete a bid on the salvage job. Martin arrived in Severomorsk and climbed through the hatch of the *Oscar II*-class submarine. He studied every detail and walked through each compartment. He was amazed when he stepped through the compartment-six hatch and spied a lounge area that looked like a European café, complete with an espresso machine and small swimming pool.

Martin returned to Norway in time to learn that the project was on hold. Stolt had bid twelve million dollars for the job, and the Russians did not want to pay north of nine million. Negotiations stalled on Wednesday, September 20, as it was the fortieth day after the sinking of the *Kursk*. Russian Orthodox followers believe the soul leaves the body and ascends to heaven on day forty after someone perishes. All work stopped for most of that week while citizens swarmed into cathedrals or countryside chapels to mourn. In Severodvinsk, where the keel of the *Kursk* had been fashioned, city officials unveiled a large monument to the crew. The inscription read: "This sorrowful stone is set in memory of the crew of the nuclear submarine *Kursk*, who tragically died on August 12, 2000, while on military duty."

In Moscow, however, angry crowds held up signs and shouted protests at Putin and the government for refusing help from the West until it was too late. They also demanded an official inquiry into the collision they had been told caused the submarine's demise. Some questioned why the government was risking even more lives—those of the divers—to exhume the bodies during the winter. The son of a *Kursk* sailor scowled on the RTR television network and asked, "Why risk additional tragedies? Why deprive those divers' families of fathers, as happened in this case?"

An article in the *Komsomolskaya Pravda* suggested the bodies should remain on the *Kursk* in keeping with Russian naval traditions, wherein a downed vessel should become the crew's tombstone. Seventy-eight relatives of the deceased crew members banded together and wrote a letter to Putin, requesting the recovery mission be postponed or cancelled altogether. Like so many others, they did not want to see anyone else die while trying to exhume the bodies of their loved ones.

During this upheaval, negotiations between Stolt Offshore and Rubin Design screeched to a halt. Russian Navy and government officials had no intention of cancelling the mission, but they could not divulge the four secret mission parts planned in concert with the body recovery.

Concerned that negotiation delays might set back or even derail the *Kursk* salvage operation, Deputy Prime Minister Klebanov called a meeting of senior government officials. He ordered Rubin to finalize a deal with Stolt, or another firm, as soon as possible. Rubin created a list of eight companies capable of undertaking the project and delivering the required dive training. Meanwhile, at the *Kursk* site, the Russian Academy of Sciences Institute of Oceanology vessel *Akademik Mstislav Keldysh* undertook the first step on September 26. Over the previous twenty years, the aging but capable *Keldysh* had completed forty-five scientific expeditions in seventeen ocean locales. Originally designed for marine studies, the *Keldysh* had been used for several military missions as well. It can transport two *Mir* deep-diving minisubs on its back, like a marsupial carries its young. Shaped like footballs, the orange-and-white subs are driven by a single propeller spun by a battery bank. They can't stay submerged longer than fifteen hours due to limited battery life, but they can dive to almost twenty thousand feet deep.

The *Mir* subs came equipped with active sonar systems, manipulator arms for grabbing objects, high-resolution cameras, and enough room for a few passengers. They had been recalled from the North Atlantic, where they had been used to take tourists on excursions to view the *Titanic*. Now, they were poised to take close-up shots of the *Kursk* and gather debris for inspection. Their primary mission was to help the Russians complete objectives three and four—find evidence of a collision and collect samples to determine what had really happened.

Trained sonar technicians aboard the *Keldysh* were ordered to work in tandem with the *Mir* craft while they scoured the ocean floor in a grid pattern, inch by inch, to find anything that might convict in a court of law or at least provide more clues for analysis. While the original plan called for complete stealth, officials changed their minds and authorized Admiral Vladimir Valuyev, first deputy commander of the Baltic Fleet, to speak with reporters. He did not offer many details but did say that "apart from moral liability, there will also be financial sanctions" against those responsible, should evidence be found of a collision.

Operators aboard the *Mir-1* and *Mir-2* had gained extensive experience working with various Russian submarines. The two minisubs had descended upon the downed *Komsomolets* nuclear sub in the late nineties, and to prevent plutonium from leaking out of the nuclear warheads, they had used the manipulator arms to shove plugs into the torpedo tube doors. Now, during the mission at the *Kursk* site, the *Mir* craft started showing their age. One or both vessels experienced failures and were out of commission for hours. In all, the difficult combing of the seabed took four full days while the subs crisscrossed imaginary grid lines in the search area. They covered a three-square-mile sector around the site while collecting scattered bits of metal and debris.

Days later, the samples collected confirmed what everyone already knew: a massive explosion in the torpedo room had sent the *Kursk* to the bottom. Strangely, Klebanov went public to say they had found no indication of a collision with a foreign submarine. The announcement angered Russian naval officers involved in the search, who grumbled that just the opposite was true. They apparently leaked their opinions to the press, which led to a story about how the *Mir* subs had hauled in definitive proof that a U.S. sub had smacked the *Kursk*. Also, they speculated that during the New York meeting, Putin and Clinton had agreed to suppress any evidence found, to prevent a potential war. U.S. officials dismissed the story as rubbish and hearsay, and it was never picked up by Western media.

On October 2, while the *Mir* subs continued to peck at the ocean floor, Rubin Design finalized its decision and signed a contract in Saint Petersburg with a firm to complete the salvage and dive training. The total cost was only seven million dollars—two million less than the initial desired fee. When Ramsey Martin heard the news from executives at Stolt, he was shocked.

Not only was the bid almost half that quoted by Stolt, and most certainly unprofitable to the firm that had won the job, but the selected company, Halliburton AS, made no sense. Although a Norwegian company, it was a subsidiary of a giant U.S. firm. Why would the Russians allow operators with direct ties to the Americans access to their top-secret submarine? The idea seemed incredible. Even more unbelievable, the former president of Halliburton U.S. was none other than Dick Cheney, the U.S. secretary of defense from 1989 through 1993. Cheney had resigned from Halliburton in August 2000 to run for vice president of the United States alongside George W. Bush.

Although Cheney no longer ran the multibillion-dollar firm, he had been granted thirty-nine million dollars in stock options. He obviously had a large vested interest in Halliburton's success, but if elected—which seemed likely—he would also be directly involved in U.S. national security.

Through Halliburton AS, he'd naturally have access to any confidential information found at the *Kursk* site.

Even more concerning, U.S. saturation divers had conducted top-secret Ivy Bells missions during the Cold War by descending to one thousand feet to wiretap Soviet communication lines. The Russians never knew about these missions, as they had no such capability and never surmised it could be done. After the Cold War, what few sat divers Russia did have fled for greener pastures, so Russia never had the ability to conduct these types of missions.

Now, an American firm once run by the former U.S. secretary of defense and likely the next vice president of the United States had just won a bid to teach Russian divers how to sat-dive—a skill they most certainly would use in later years to wiretap or even cut U.S. and U.K. communication lines.

Sea Hunt

In late September 2000, cold winds whipped across the chilled waters of the Barents Sea as the Norwegian Radiation Protection Authority tested the area for radioactivity, coming from either the submarine's reactors or nuclear warheads. They found no discernible traces of contamination. Six Russian divers had completed the saturation-dive training in Saint Petersburg for Halliburton AS; they would be supported by a Halliburton dive team consisting of nine Brits, a South African, a Norwegian, and one American, Don Degener. Degener had grown up near Kansas City, Missouri, and had always been captivated by what might be found under the surface of large bodies of water.

"One of my favorite TV shows when I was a kid was *Sea Hunt*," said Degener, referring to the classic television drama starring Lloyd Bridges. "Then those Jacques Cousteau documentaries came along. I thought I was going to be an oceanographer."

Fearless at the age of eleven, Degener attached an air hose to an old bucket, dropped down to the bottom of his swimming pool, and walked on the bottom for almost thirty minutes. Hooked on diving, he worked in Wyoming oil fields until 1975 and then signed up for a civilian dive school.

"I haven't worked a day in the United States since," Degener said.

After graduating from dive school, Degener worked for more than thirty years on oil platforms and completed several dangerous construction projects in overseas locales such as Nigeria, Malaysia, the Persian Gulf, the Red Sea, the Mediterranean, and the Caribbean. On one dive, Degener helped recover the body of a British fighter pilot after his plane crashed into the sea, and on another, he performed one of the deepest salvage dives in history by descending to 810 feet to look for gold on the HMS *Edinburgh*, a British ship that sank in 1942. He and his fellow divers had to move large pallets of still live forty-year-old bombs to find the gold and haul it out of the wreck. "That was much more dangerous than the *Kursk*," Degener said, "because of the depth, cold water temperatures, bad weather conditions, and an old ship with bombs."

In early October 2000, Degener landed in Norway and stepped aboard the *Regalia*. In many ways this dive platform resembled the *Seaway Eagle*. Looking more like a large rectangular building than a ship, the vessel had been built in Sweden in 1985. The rugged decks held a helipad, tall cranes, derricks, and a variety of construction equipment. Pontoon hulls extended down into the ocean, turning the ship into a semisubmersible platform that was quite stable, even in high seas.

On Monday, October 9, 2000, the *Regalia* headed toward Honningsvåg, Norway, where it stopped briefly to load more helium and sat-diving equipment. The Halliburton engineers had spent weeks working with Russian experts to determine the best locations and methods to cut through the *Kursk*'s outer and inner hulls. The procedure would be challenging even in calm seas. Unfortunately, during that time of year in the Arctic, weather forecasts called for large storms and rough seas.

Concerned about not being able to properly cut through the metal hulls, Halliburton's engineers contacted Oil States MCS, Ltd. in England for help. The reputable firm was well known for its expertise in custom abrasive waterjet cutting equipment. It had designed systems and processes used to make complex cuts through underwater pipes and pilings in oil fields and elsewhere. The process used abrasive copper slag and high-pressure water pumped through a hose to a cutting head. Like a water jet used to clean teeth, the system creates a high-powered stream that strikes the metal with almost fifteen thousand pounds of force per square inch.

The Halliburton team tested the system for six hours before approving it for use on the *Kursk*. They packed the system parts into portable cargo containers and sent them by truck to Honningsvåg, where they were hefted aboard the *Regalia*. Once loaded, the ship cruised at a slow six knots toward the Barents site.

While the *Regalia* voyage was underway, on Friday October 13, Deputy Prime Minister Klebanov reported publicly that the *Mir-1* and *Mir-2* minisubs had failed to gather any evidence of a collision. This again angered naval officers involved in the operation, who claimed privately that the report was wrong. The *Regalia* reached the site on October 20. As the ship approached, the crew spied the warship *Peter the Great* dropping warning depth charges to ward off snooping NATO submarines. Geysers of ocean water shot upward with each explosion off the stern of the large ship.

Degener and the rest of the dive team were grateful that, at least for the time being, the sea was calm. It was unusual for that time of year, and they knew it would not last long. The forecast still called for bad weather, and they feared it might soon be impossible to hold the platform steady above the dive site, which might force them to delay or abort the mission. The ship used advanced satellite navigation systems and thruster propellers to hover over the site, but they might not be adequate in a high-sea state.

While the team was preparing equipment for the dive, a large group came aboard. Included were family members of the *Kursk*'s crew, along with naval and civilian officials. They performed a memorial service to honor the lost crew and then departed. The dive team lowered radiation monitors and video equipment and prepped an ROV for a site survey. In the control room, as the ROV beamed back images, the supervisors were awestruck. During all their underwater projects, they had never seen such a site. A giant mutilated beast lay quietly on the ocean floor. A gaping wound had replaced the bow, where shiny fish now darted in and out of the tangled wreckage.

On the eleven-thousand-square-yard deck of the *Regalia* support ship, oil field and marine construction equipment and systems filled every open space. Windowless superstructures rose from the deck like high-rise buildings in a small city. One prefabricated portable building had been strapped down on the deck like a large trunk atop a pickup truck. Technicians in this makeshift additional control room monitored the progress of the ROV as it circled the *Kursk* and broadcast unnerving images from the depths. Meanwhile, Degener and his two fellow divers on team one, along with three more divers on team two, entered the sat-dive chambers and started the hours-long process to "press down." Engineers and experts on the *Regalia* studied the wire templates provided by Rubin Designs and decided on the best locations to attach the manipulator arm and cutting nozzle on the sub's hull. They completed a final inspection and were given a green light to proceed.

On October 21, Degener and the team one divers opened their chamber hatch and squeezed into the diving bell. The system lowered the bell to the ocean floor. One diver remained in the bell as Degener and another diver clamped on SuperLite Kirby Morgan masks and stepped out into the black ocean. Swaths of bright yellow light shot out from the tops of their helmets and created dim circles on the smooth deck of the *Kursk*. They descended toward the sand and silt. Degener glanced up. His eyes opened wide as he took in the five-story expanse of the giant monolith before him. He turned to his right and left, but in the gloomy darkness, he could not see the bow or stern in either direction.

Degener and his fellow diver ascended again and found the escape-trunk hatch in the conning tower. If the survivors in the aft section had been able to move forward of compartment five, they might have reached the escape module in the sail. Four tall cylinders jutted upward toward the surface. Degener recognized these as the periscope, radar, and radio masts, indicating that the *Kursk* had been near the surface before the initial explosion.

Degener searched for and found a thick high-pressure line that shot compressed air from a storage tank into a ballast tank to allow the sub to surface. He was told by his supervisor to cut the pipe and allow any remaining air to vent to sea. This was a dangerous operation. If the line still contained high-pressure air and a diver happened to get in the way, he could be injured or killed. Also, as Degener put it, the cutting jet could easily "cut your leg off like a light saber out of *Star Wars*." With great care, the two sat divers attached the cutter's robotic control unit, high-resolution video-camera, and pressurized cutting head to the air line. They triple-checked everything and informed their supervisor that the site was ready.

Degener and the other diver kicked fins and swam away from the area, with their long umbilicals trailing. Silence filled the void for several long minutes. Degener heard only the whisper of his own breathing as his lungs filled with helox. The cutting torch lit off with a loud whine. Bubbles spewed upward, followed by a burst of air escaping from the pipe. Degener instinctively shot backward in the water. The technician in the *Regalia* shut off the torch until the air dissipated. He then resumed cutting and completely severed the line.

The process was repeated several more times to ensure that no high-pressure air lines could rupture and injure a Russian diver. Between cuts, from 350 feet above, Degener heard the churn of the *Regalia's* propellers as advanced GPS systems automatically adjusted the ship's position in the water. Long hours passed as the divers worked while occasionally checking each other for signs of High-Pressure Nervous Syndrome. Once their shift was complete, Degener and his dive buddy, shivering from exhaustion and cold, reentered the bell. Team two suited up and swam over to the *Kursk*. The second shift ended with all the compressed-air lines cut and vented. The next shift could now begin the grueling process of cutting entry holes through the three inches of sound-dampening elastomer before slicing through the outer and inner hulls. Cutting through the honeycomb rubberized coating on the outer hull took far longer than planned. The glue holding it in place was so strong that the divers were forced to use underwater jackhammers to peel it away. The extra work placed the team behind schedule. They were hoping to get as much done as possible before the storms hit.

The divers had made good progress but were not yet done when at 5:15 p.m. on October 23 their Kirby Morgan speakers lit up with an urgent plea. They were told to reenter the bell for immediate ascent. The storm had arrived and kicked up waves to over thirty-five feet high. Even with its high-tech thrusters working overtime, the *Regalia* started to rock back and forth. The divers clambered back into the bell, and the techs cranked them upward toward the ship.

Unfortunately for the divers, now crammed back into the tight dive chambers on the *Regalia*, the storm lasted for a day and a half. "Rough weather," Degener wrote in his diary. "Can't cut or burn through the pressure hull. I watched the report on BBC World News about our job." He passed the time in the six-bunk compartment by reading books or watching television through a porthole while watch-standers delivered food and fresh laundry through the pressure lock.

The dive team was not allowed to return to the *Kursk* until 1:45 a.m. on October 24. Bottom conditions were still rough. The storm had stirred up silt that turned the water murky and dropped visibility down to a few feet. Shifting sea currents swatted them about like thin trees in a high wind. They did not last an hour before struggling to climb back into the bell in time.

"If you can't get back to the bell," Degener said, "you're dead."

The next day, the clouds finally cleared and the sea calmed. The divers went back to work and finished cutting a six-foot-wide hole into the three-inch-thick steel covering the compartment-eight inner hull. They lined the ragged edges of the cut with a rubber collar and then sent in a team to clear away pipes, support beams, equipment, and other obstacles that might make it difficult for the Russian divers to enter. Degener and another diver on his shift completed cutting the first access hole at midnight on October 24.

Underwater Graveyard

Degener returned to his pressurized chamber and watched the video feed from helmet-mounted cameras as the Russian dive team left the bell. "Everybody watching was rather sad about it, grim," he said.

Russian divers Sergey Shmygin and Andrey Sviagintsev swam over to the *Kursk*. Captain Vladimir Salutin, on Russian dive team two, stood by in a chamber aboard the *Regalia*. Shmygin had a smaller frame, so he had received the honors of first entry, while Sviagintsev provided assistance. Experts at Rubin Design had decided that due to the blast location, and given the rising CO_2 and pressure in compartment nine, many of the well-preserved bodies might be found in compartment eight.

Shmygin's pulse sped up as he was poised above the compartment-eight hole. A large cod shot past his mask and made his heart race even more. He flipped upside down and entered the hole. His helmet light illuminated the gravesite as it danced across bulkheads, pipes, and equipment. Restricted by his umbilical, he swam slow and steadily and examined the upper-deck area. Seeing no bodies, he turned aft and approached the round hatch that led into compartment nine. There, a large fish, which had apparently entered the hole before the divers arrived, stood guard and refused to let Shmygin near. Having seen the fish in the video feed, a dive supervisor on the *Regalia* warned Shmygin to stay back until the creature decided to leave. Precious minutes passed while Shmygin repeatedly checked his watch. Finally, the large fish tired of the game and moved away. Shmygin swam to the hatch, undogged it, and tried to pull it open. It did not budge. He tried again. Still no movement. He then worked on the latch ring with his diving knife until the hatch budged. He kicked it open with the ball of his foot and swam into compartment nine.

Shmygin held his breath as a soaked mattress drifted past his mask. The light on his helmet lit up the gray rectangle, which resembled a floating gravestone suspended in murky water. He used his knife to push it to one side and then froze as the outstretched fingers of a dead sailor brushed his arm. The man's eyes were wide open, and his face was wrinkled with pain. After regaining his composure, Shmygin fastened a rope to the sailor's legs and pulled the cadaver back through the compartment-eight hatch. He approached the hole and handed the rope end to Sviagintsev, who pulled the body up through the compartment-eight entry point. The sailor's upper body was charred black, but his lower body was not.

Shmygin returned to compartment nine to recover more bodies while Sviagintsev placed the dead sailor into a yellow steel-mesh box resting on the deck. Shmygin found another man in compartment nine who had been badly burned. He felt nauseous and almost threw up in his mask. The sailor's head flopped to one side, like a rag doll's, as Shmygin maneuvered the body out of the compartment. After three bodies were recovered, the two divers returned to the bell to rest. Hours later, near midnight, Shmygin retrieved a fourth corpse and the *Regalia*'s crane operator lifted the body box to the surface.

The operator lowered the box into a white shipping container in which medical examiners were standing by to do makeshift autopsies. Russian medical personnel shivered inside the chilled container. When the bodies were placed on tables, the small area filled with the rancid odor of saltwater and burned flesh. Russian Navy pathologist Colonel-Lieutenant Sergey Chernisov, clad in white coveralls, stretched latex gloves onto his hands before bending over a body. When the dive team on the *Seaway Eagle* had previously recorded evidence of a fire in compartment nine, Chernisov had been expecting to see burned bodies, but the other details he was now witnessing not only were unexpected; they were shocking.

Chernisov had been told by Russian naval officers that the crew had died within hours after the accident. The evidence before him now belied that fact. Some of the sailors had changed clothes. One wore a waterproof emergency escape suit from the waist down. Others appeared to have lasted much longer than a few hours, perhaps even a few days.

Chernisov stepped aside to allow backup Russian diver Renat Gizatullin to video the morbid scene. He then supervised while pathologist Shamil Shamshudtinov completed an exam. Shamshudtinov carefully peeled away dark, oil-soaked layers of damp clothing to expose the skin of one corpse. The examiner stopped and reached his gloved fingers into the breast pocket to retrieve a handwritten note.

Chernisov stepped closer as Shamshudtinov grabbed a magnifying glass, squinted, and read the scribbled words on the paper: "Aryapov and Kuznetsov," he said. The dead man had apparently recorded the names of the survivors of the initial blast. Shamshudtinov continued reading. "Olga! I love you! Do not suffer too much! Regards to G.V. Regards to mine. No need for despair. Mitya." The letter had been written by Captain Mitya Kolesnikov, and the initials "G.V." obviously referred to his wife's mother. The writing at the top of the note was clear and legible, and all the letters fit neatly within each line on the page, indicating that flashlights had still been working.

The note also provided a situational update: "It's 13:15," Kolesnikov had written. "All personnel from section six, seven, and eight have moved to section nine, there are 23 people here. We feel bad, weakened by carbon dioxide.... Pressure is increasing in the compartment. If we head for the surface, we won't survive the compression. We won't last more than a day."

In the second part of the note, written at 15:15, Kolesnikov's handwriting was barely legible. The letters were no longer contained within the lines. "It's dark here to write, but I'll try by feel. It seems like there are no chances, 10–20 percent. Let's hope that at least someone will read this. Here's the list of personnel from the other sections, who are now in the ninth and will attempt to get out. Regards to everybody, no need to despair. Kolesnikov."

Chernisov could not believe what he had just read. The *Kursk* submariners had obviously lived much longer than reported by Russian officials. They had likely survived for at least a day if not several, and had had time to change clothes, tap out SOS signals, and write notes. Although the second note had been written at 3:15 p.m., Chernisov wondered if it had been written on Saturday the twelfth or possibly the following day. The sub had gone down at eleven thirty a.m., so the initial letter had been scribbled less than two hours later, while light was still available, likely from a flashlight. The second note had been written in the dark, and it seemed unlikely that the batteries in the flashlight would have died in less than four hours.

Fearing that he might become the messenger who gets shot, Chernisov placed the notes into a clear plastic bag and sent it to Vice Admiral Verich, who had come aboard the *Regalia* to observe the operation. Given no choice, Verich forwarded the note to Admiral Popov, who in turn sent it up the chain of command to Kuroyedov, who then had it forwarded to Klebanov in Moscow. Klebanov was then forced to inform Putin, who made a fateful decision that changed history.

While still inside his dive chamber, Degener recorded his own note in a diary: "Operations on section 9 halted due to a note found on a body. A grim reminder of life's frailties."

Kolesnikov's note travelled up the proverbial monkey chain while Vice Admiral Mikhail Motsak arrived at the Northern Fleet headquarters in Severomorsk in the early morning hours. Using a secure line, he contacted Verich on the *Regalia* at eight thirty. Verich told him about the note and the two discussed how to handle the explosive information. Both men concurred that the tapping heard between Saturday, August 12 and Monday, August 14 had come from the submariners. Popov probed Verich for more details about what had happened when the AS-34 did a fast recharge and tried again to mate with the *Kursk* on the fourteenth, but Verich was not forthcoming. Popov asked whether there were any additional details about the AS-34 dives that Verich might now want to reveal. Verich revealed nothing.

By nine thirty that morning, Kuroyedov was already on the phone with Moscow when Motsak entered his office at headquarters. Kuroyedov turned to Motsak and said, "It is agreed that this note must be made public, to make clear to all that nobody is concealing anything."

Kuroyedov said Deputy Prime Minister Klebanov had ordered the public announcement, but Motsak knew the decision had come down from Putin himself. The two officials concurred with the instructions, given that the possibility of a leak was too great and concealing the truth at this point could backfire. However, they agreed to keep the personal parts of the note private for the time being. "Read only the service part of the note," Kuroyedov told Motsak.

Disclosure

Vice Admiral Motsak made a formal announcement on Russian television that afternoon at two o'clock. He informed the world about the recovery of the bodies and the note written by Kolesnikov. "The note is of a very private nature and will be passed on to his relatives," said Motsak with a somber face, "but it also gave us a lot of operational information."

The disclosure by Motsak put into motion a fervent campaign to release a copy of the full note to the families of the crew. The media seized the opportunity to rail against Putin and other officials and demand the full text be read on television. More leaks surfaced, and the press discovered that additional notes had been found but suppressed from public view.

In the wake of the furor over the note, or notes, Russian officials placed a clamp on salvage mission communications. Henceforth, all discoveries had to be cleared through official channels before any release to the public. Still, the contents of another note leaked to the media. Penned by Captain-Lieutenant Rashid Aryapov, the note discussed a shortage of oxygen-regeneration canisters and belts used for the escape suits. "Our condition is bad," Aryapov had written. "We have been weakened by the effects of carbon monoxide. Pressure is increasing. We can't make it more than 24 hours."

Aboard the *Regalia*, the weather turned from bad to worse while the divers huddled inside the dive chambers. Decisions were made to reenter compartment nine. Based on Kolesnikov's note, they expected to find several more bodies there. The divers went back in at four a.m. on October 28. Over several grisly days, they recovered eight more bodies. On October 31, Degener assisted the Russians on the final dive by staying inside the bell as the designated "bellman."

"They showed courage," Degener said of the Russian divers. "Here were some of their comrades inside. All of us agreed they did their job very well."

Having recovered as many bodies as could be found, the divers shifted focus on November 1 and entered the third compartment. The Russians wanted to complete one of their mission objectives: recover the code books and encryption equipment and any other secrets they might find. With mission time running thin, winter storms churning the ocean, and public opinion roiling, the divers extended their shifts and worked overtime. On several dives, Degener helped cut access holes into the compartments. Two dozen of the crew had been stationed in the GKP during the explosion, but when the Russian divers entered compartment three, they found no bodies. There was not much left to recover, so they turned their attention toward compartment four. The crew's section of the sub held staterooms, bunks, a gym, a galley, a sauna, and other facilities. At the time of the accident, a dozen men had occupied this space.

Before they could enter compartment four on November 3, storm conditions worsened and blew harsh sheets of icy rain onto the decks of the *Regalia*. Work was stopped until Sunday, November 5, when the dive team went back down and entered the compartment. Although visibility was dismal, cameras revealed that the second blast had caused an unbelievable amount of damage. Miraculously, the bulkhead separating compartments four and five had held. The Russians were relieved to discover that the reactor had shut down as designed and there was no apparent radiation leakage. Although Rubin Design and members of the Russian team were eager to continue with the operation and enter compartment five, the decision was made to conclude the operation and return to port. After a difficult and dangerous eighteen days on station, the team had recovered a dozen bodies and accomplished all their secret mission objectives. The Russian divers closed the internal hatches and exited the *Kursk* for the last time.

Having made a total of sixteen dives on the *Kursk*, Degener helped the Russian divers plug the access holes and then stood on the deck and faced the submarine's massive conning tower. Guided by directions from the dive supervisor, he tilted his head to line up his videocamera while two Russian divers posed in front of the red-and-white eagle emblem painted on the tower. Degener then returned to his chamber and started his five-day decompression.

"I've been on a Russian submarine," Degener said, "and I've had the honor of being the only American to have been there."

THE *REGALIA* RETURNED TO PORT, and the twelve bodies were delivered to forensic scientists and medical doctors to identify the remains and confirm the causes of death. All the sailors had high concentrations of CO_2 in their blood. Also, there had definitely been a fire. One seaman had an emergency breathing mask welded to his face. Others were badly burned, but only from the waist up. They had obviously been standing in water when the fire started. Examiners determined that the fire had likely been caused by an exploding air-regeneration canister.

On November 2, after the examinations had concluded and the remains were released to families, a funeral with full military honors was held for Captain-Lieutenant Dmitry Kolesnikov at Admiralty Hall of Dzherzhinsky Naval College. More than three thousand officials, dignitaries, colleagues, and friends were present. The families had wrapped the tall marble columns in the hall with ribbons and lined the walls with flags.

In keeping with Russian Orthodox traditions, the family members sat near the zinc-and-wood coffin. Kolesnikov's father struggled to hold back tears, while Kolesnikov's mother and widow sobbed into trembling hands. Standing nearby, guards in dress uniforms occasionally dabbed at an eye. Thousands of mourners, many in uniform, marched or shuffled past the flag-draped casket. A framed copy of Kolesnikov's final note had been placed in front of the coffin, just below a picture of his smiling face. No one uttered a word or gave a speech, other than a priest, who muttered a prayer for Kolesnikov's "warrior soul."

As the saga of the *Kursk* unfolded, more details about the survivors came to light. Rashid Aryapov's body had been found lying in his bunk, below the waterline. He wore an oxygen mask, and his brown eyes were wide with shock and fear. He had stuffed a short letter into one of his pockets. It had been written by another sailor, Sergei Sadilenko, who had been unable to don an oxygen mask. Aryapov apparently had snatched the note from Sadilenko after he died, perhaps hoping he could deliver it to the man's loved ones.

Warrant Officer Andrey Borisov had also written a final note to his wife and son and shoved it into a water bottle. It read: "My dear Natasha and Sasha, if you are reading this letter, it means I am no longer with you. Natasha, Sasha—I love you so very much."

Another line in the note had been written to the Russian Navy officials. It said, "We did everything according to the instructions."

The Implausible Lies

Official reports later released by Russian naval and government officials made the following claims:

1. There had been no collision between the *Kursk* and a NATO submarine.
2. The unstable fuel in a Type 65 Fat Girl torpedo had overheated and caused the initial explosion.
3. Two minutes later, other torpedoes had "cooked off" in the fire and caused the second, massive explosion.
4. Twenty-three crew members had survived in the aft compartments but died on the first day in an accidental fire when an air-regeneration canister exploded.
5. None of the DSRVs had been able to mate during repeated attempts, but as the crew had died on Saturday, August 12, it made no difference.
6. The Russians had not accepted help from the West as it was assumed the crew had perished long before help could arrive.
7. Notes found on the survivors tended to support these claims and assumptions.

Two decades after the most terrifying submarine tragedy in naval history, new insights, evidence, and testimony shatter the lies told by the Russians and cast a new light on the truth. What really caused the *Kursk*'s demise? Was a U.S. submarine involved? How long did the crew survive? Could they have been rescued? Was there a cover-up, and if so, why? What lessons can we learn from this sad event?

Like any jury in a court of law, we do not possess the ability to peer back in history and witness events unfolding in real time. We can only examine the evidence presented to us in the present and do our best to determine the most likely truth.

The Shocking Truth

Shkval?

The Russians claimed unstable propellant in an outdated Fat Girl torpedo caused the initial explosion. They suggested the torpedo was loaded into an unclean tube moments before the scheduled firing, and the irritants ignited the unstable fuel. Any torpedoman, whether NATO or Russian, knows better. Torpedoes are loaded and ready in tubes, hours before a test-firing. Tubes are meticulously inspected prior to loading. Two civilian experts from the Dagdizel military plant were in the torpedo room monitoring the exercise, yet allowed an unstable weapon to be loaded into a dirty tube?

The question asked earlier remains unanswered. Why would high-ranking officials aboard the *Kursk* and the *Peter the Great* warship have an interest in observing the test-firing of an outdated torpedo that did not have enough fuel to reach its target? Numerous sources verify that the *Kursk* was test-firing a Shkval torpedo and not a Fat Girl. Ramsey Martin long suspected this, and to assist with the publication of a book about the *Kursk* a few years after the incident, he journeyed to Moscow to meet with naval officers and others involved in the recovery operation. While downing shots of vodka at one in the morning, the officers revealed several interesting details.

They said video taken by the AS-15 spy sub had documented deep scratches in what remained of the bow section of the sub near a torpedo tube door. They also knew the *Kursk* was test-firing a Shkval rocket torpedo. They were told that a faulty inner tube-door mechanism had malfunctioned or the sub had experienced a collision or near collision, which caused the rocket torpedo to be lodged in the tube. After the firing mechanism was triggered, the Shkval was programmed to light off. Unable to leave the tube, the torpedo blew off the aft torpedo tube door, and two minutes later, the fire ignited the fuel in several Fat Girls and other torpedoes and caused the second, catastrophic explosion.

Edmond Pope knew the Russians were test-firing a Shkval, and in his book, speculated that the above was the most likely scenario. If the *Toledo* did not brush the *Kursk*, then the culprit may well have been a defective tube-door mechanism. If the U.S. attack submarine did cause a sudden jolt, it may have triggered a domino effect that led to the initial explosion. Either way, this part of the truth will probably never come to light.

Collision?

When Edmond Pope failed to obtain technical documents on the Shkval torpedo, the NSA and NSG were highly motivated to gain intel on this new weapon. They tasked the USS *Memphis* and *Toledo* with Holy Stone espionage operations to gain that intel. Operating in Arctic waters increases the danger of mistakes, incorrect system information, and potential collisions. By August 2000, submarine crews were not as experienced at close quarter tracking and surveillance as they were during the Cold War. This elevated the risk of a smack. Did this "perfect storm" lead to a collision or near collision?

Not a single submariner interviewed confirmed such in any manner, and therefore violated no secret oaths, but circumstantial evidence points to a potential incident. Coffee cups crashed to the deck during the second explosion, so the *Toledo* was obviously at a very close range to the *Kursk*. Russian officers divulged to Ramsey Martin that a scrape or near scrape may have caused the Shkval to be lodged in its tube. The *Toledo* did a last-minute port of call change to dock at Faslane. This facility is one of the most suited in the area to complete repairs. The *Toledo* was delayed from leaving due to a repair, possibly related to a bow plane part. The *Toledo* logs for the year 2000 are mysteriously missing. The Russians claimed to have photographed scrape marks on the *Kursk* that led them to believe there was a collision. Even so, there is no smoking gun and if neither the *Memphis* nor *Toledo* caused that gash, they are owed an apology from an over-zealous media. However, if they did scrape or almost scrape the *Kursk*, how might that have affected the outcome?

Rescue Cover-Up?

Logs from the *Peter the Great* warship verify SOS and code-signal-tapping, heard at various intervals from the *Kursk* between 2:28 a.m. Saturday, August 12 and 6:07 a.m. Monday, August 14. Sonarmen aboard the *Toledo* also heard and recorded the tapping during those time frames. The AS-34 DSRV made its first rescue attempt dive on Sunday, August 13 but was not able to mate. However, the crew most certainly would have tried to communicate with the survivors by using the minisub's manipulator arms to tap out code signals. They would have told the crew to huddle near the compartment-nine hatch and await an imminent rescue. Kolesnikov's note appears to confirm this. Otherwise, with CO_2 levels rising, it made no sense to cram twenty-three men into one compartment until the rising water level forced them to do so.

Autopsies and other evidence belie claims by the Russians that the crew did not survive more than a few hours. Captain-Lieutenant Sergei Sadilenko's note logged increasing pressure in compartment nine. Given the compartment's volume and the likely rate of water leakage past the shaft seals, experts agree that the pressure recorded by Sadilenko would likely not have been reached until Monday, August 14. This conclusion is supported by the analyses completed on water samples and autopsies on the recovered bodies.

The AS-34 made an unsuccessful docking attempt at three a.m. on Monday, August 14, and after its batteries were depleted, it was rushed back into service at five a.m. The accelerated recharge risked damaging the battery and placing the DSRV out of commission. Why did the Russians take this risk? Did they know from the crew's signal-tapping that the water and CO_2 levels were not far from lethal? On that fateful last dive, the AS-34 remained down for three hours, and final taps from the *Kursk* were heard at 5:35 a.m. through 6:07 a.m. According to reports from Vice Admiral Verich, the DSRV again failed to mate with the *Kursk*.

Verich also claimed that since the AS-34 did not mate, its crew never opened the equalization valve. However, Tony Scott and Paal Dinessen— the first sat divers to examine the *Kursk*'s hatch—were told by Verich to turn the valve counterclockwise. Ball and Nankivell examined the lower escape-trunk hatch on the sister sub *Orel* and verified the open direction. Photos of the hatch confirm this. Logs kept by a Stolt representative record the divers stating that the valve "had been in the open position all along."

If so, who opened it?

There were no bodies found inside the escape trunk, and no one tried to escape, so none of the survivors could have opened the E-valve. That leaves only one possibility: the DSRV crew. During the *Orel* inspection, Ball and Nankivell also noted that the Russians use a lip seal around the edge of their hatches instead of an O-ring as used by NATO subs. If the AS-34 did mate with the *Kursk* on its five-a.m. dive on Monday, the divers would have opened the E-valve to equalize pressure with the escape trunk. By that time, the pressure in compartment nine was most likely around eight BAR. (eight times sea level atmospheric pressure), if not fully equalized at more than ten BAR. During equalization, pressurized gas from the nearly flooded ninth compartment would have burped past the lower-hatch lip seal and rushed into the trunk. Then it would have burped past the upper-hatch lip seal and rocketed up through the open hatch on the DSRV. The sudden pressure differential would have caused the AS-34 to lose suction and fall off the back of the *Kursk*. When this happened, the gas bubble would have prevented the DSRV from flooding until the divers could close the hatch. Since the divers were wearing full-face masks plugged into air manifolds, the pressure change would also have caused serious barotrauma. Ball saw one of these divers and noted the black-and-blue indications of a recent squeeze.

When the AS-34 blew off, perhaps it smacked into the ball pin and flattened it against the hatch. Dive-video examination by experts indicates that this may be the most likely cause of the bent pin. The AS-15 made a subsequent dive after the AS-34's final descent. Did they also close the upper hatch to conceal what had happened?

Stolt logs record Admiral Popov as being "visibly taken aback" by revelations that the hatch was not damaged, and the divers saw no reason why a DSRV could not mate. He and Vice Admiral Verich argued over this and other details. Obviously, Verich did not divulge accurate or complete details to Popov or other Russian officials. Pleas from Commodore Russell and Graham Mann to allow the LR5 to attempt a rescue were dismissed by Verich, who expressed certainty that the crew had already perished. Why was he so sure? Did he know that the AS-34 DSRV had been blown off, and in the process the escape trunk filled with water, which made it nearly impossible to rescue any survivors?

Accidental or Consequential Deaths?

Forensic evidence confirms that the survivors were standing waist-deep in water when an explosion occurred. This also indicates they were alive at least until Monday morning, as compartment nine should not have been flooded to that level only twelve hours after the explosions. Video shows burn marks on the inside of the compartment nine hatch, and scorch marks on the compartment-nine bulkheads that verify a waterline about waist deep. Several recovered bodies were burned, but only above the waist. What caused the fire? The obvious explanation is an accident wherein an air-regeneration canister hit the oily water and exploded. When considering the CO_2 levels present by early Monday morning, the survivors would have been suffering from nitrogen narcosis. In a delirious state, one of them could have accidentally dropped a cartridge. It's also possible that the unthinkable happened.

Many of the survivors were standing just below the lip seal on the bottom hatch. Experts agree that if the AS-34 caused a sudden gas burp by opening the E-valve, the event would have been startling. Perhaps enough so to cause a sailor to knock a canister into the rising water?

Verich had said the SOS tapping stopped on Monday morning, August 14. *Peter the Great* logs and *Toledo* sailors confirm this. No further DSRV rescue attempts were made after that date. The vice admiral was not interested in a rescue, as he was certain the survivors were no longer alive. Perhaps he knew the truth about what had happened during the AS-34's final rescue attempt, and to save face, chose not to divulge it to Popov, Burtsev, or anyone else.

Regardless, the sad truth is that it's evident the E-valve was opened by the AS-34 crew. Experts agree this would have caused them to blow off the *Kursk*, which may have sealed the fate of the submariners aboard the *Kursk*. Any subsequent rescue attempt made by the Russians would have been impossible, as there was no longer a way to properly equalize and drain the trunk.

Epitaph

If by Monday, August 14 the survivors aboard the *Kursk* had indeed been on the verge of death, neither the *Seaway Eagle* nor LR5 could have gotten to the site in time to save them. Despite the evidence pointing to an accidental blow-off that might have sealed the fate of the crew, the DSRV teams had apparently done the best they could with the inadequate and aging equipment they'd been given. The fault lies not with them but with the Russian government for investing in prideful warships and planes while shuffling rescue vehicles and crews to the bottom of the deck. Perhaps one day Putin and his military advisors will learn from this tragic incident and place a higher priority on the safety of their dedicated sailors and officers. For without them, sophisticated new ships and subs are just useless hulks of metal.

Pope's Pardon

On December 6, 2000, after eight months in prison, Edmond Pope was convicted of espionage by a Russian court for attempting to steal plans for the secret Shkval rocket torpedo. During the six-week trial, Pope conceded he'd purchased documents related to the Shkval but said the information was not confidential as it was already in the public domain. The plea fell on deaf ears, and Pope was sentenced to twenty years in prison.

Congressman Greg Walden from Pope's home state of Oregon publicly stated, "If Russia forces Ed Pope to serve prison time, that country's relationship with the United States will be forever scarred."

One week later, on December 15, President Vladimir Putin pardoned Pope and set him free. Putin said he had granted the pardon because he wanted to preserve good relations with the United States. Was his real reason to prevent a war with the U.S.?

CHAPTER 13

THE SECRET DEAL

"The U.S....sunk the ship; there will be a war!"

—GENERAL VALENTIN KORABELNIKOV, Russia's GRU chief

Few understand how close the U.S. and Russia came to a conflict or an all-out war due to the *Kursk* incident. Prior to the salvage operation, while the official inquiry was still in process, Admiral Popov and Vice Admiral Motsak were interviewed on October 2 by the Spanish newspaper *El Mundo*. They repeated their belief that a NATO submarine observing the exercise had collided with the *Kursk* and caused its demise. That same day, Admiral Kuroyedov bolstered this theory by saying he was 80 percent certain the accident had been caused by a collision with a foreign submarine. He and the other admirals reminded the world that since 1967, eleven collisions had occurred between submarines operating in the Barents Sea. They also said the Russian Navy had video footage of the wreck to prove the validity of their claims.

On November 5, near the end of the salvage mission, a Northern Fleet general staff representative told the Russian NTV station that the incident had been caused by a collision. Motsak repeated this statement twelve days later in an interview with the Russian newspaper *Izvestia*. He insisted that an American submarine had negligently gotten too close while spying on the *Kursk* and caused a collision. He pointed to satellite photos of the *Memphis* pulling into Norway and the original radio communications claiming the sub needed to "conduct repairs."

A Russian commission, headed by Deputy Prime Minister Klebanov, met on November 8, 2000. Based on the evidence available, members pointed toward a collision with a U.S. or British submarine. The belief that the *Kursk* had collided with an "underwater object" remained "first among equals" with the Russians. In a press conference after the meeting, Klebanov said the collision theory "received very serious confirmation" from expert testimony and images showing a "very serious dent."

By November 19, after divers had recovered bodies and forensic evidence from the *Kursk*, the Russian commission publicized its official stance, wherein Klebanov said Russia had obtained "a great deal of indirect evidence proving that the Russian submarine sank as a result of a collision with a foreign one."

On December 7, 2000, the CIA published a secret report titled *Russia's Kursk Disaster: Reactions and Implications*. The heavily redacted report, obtained via the Freedom of Information Act, states: "Government officials, in response to U.S. officials, have refused to put a 'national origin' to the 'object,' but this is a small fig leaf given pointed reminders by Klebanov and others that two U.S. submarines were reported to be in the area."

Also, "Russian officials almost certainly do not yet know what sank the *Kursk*. Continued claims that the triggering event was a collision with a U.S. or British submarine probably result from a combination of genuine suspicion, bureaucratic blame-shifting, and the lack of irrefutable disconfirming evidence. Consequently, these views will be hard to dislodge.

"We assess that the Russians have enough seismic and acoustic data to conclude that the *Kursk* was lost due to two explosions, but they lack the quantity and quality of data to point to a triggering event or to rule out the presence of another submarine in the vicinity of the *Kursk*. Consequently, they are unable to completely rule out a collision as the initiating event."

The CIA report mentions a press conference during which Klebanov said video and photos taken by Russian divers and DSRV crews showed a "deep hollow, which must have been caused by an impact and nothing else." Klebanov also mentioned streaks that proved something scraped across the submarine's bow after an impact, "tearing the rubber of its outer hull."

Based on these claims, and the clamoring within Russian military ranks, tensions between the U.S. and Russia escalated. Many on Putin's staff and in the military were calling for retaliation, up to and including a nuclear response. Russia's GRU chief, Army general Valentin Korabelnikov, commented angrily: "The U.S....sunk the ship; there will be a war!"

The Deal

A Russian financial crisis, also known as the Russian Flu, had descended upon the population in August 1998. The Russian government and central bank devalued the ruble and defaulted on debt, which negatively impacted the economies of nearby countries. Declining productivity and a high fixed exchange rate between the ruble and foreign currencies were blamed as the "patient zero" causes of the crisis, along with the high cost of the first war in Chechnya, estimated at $5.5 billion. A 1997 financial crisis in Asia had also triggered declines in demand for Russian crude oil and metals.

In March 1998, President Boris Yeltsin fired Prime Minister Viktor Chernomyrdin and his entire cabinet and named thirty-five-year-old energy minister Sergei Kiriyenko acting prime minister. Three months later, to bolster the declining currency, Kiriyenko increased interest rates to a shocking 150 percent.

One month later, the International Monetary Fund (IMF) and World Bank stepped in and approved a $22.6 billion financial package to help support reforms and stabilize the Russian market. Still, by August 1998, Russia owed its workers almost thirteen billion dollars. Confidence fell even further and stoked investor fears. This ignited a ruble sell-off and dumping of Russian assets, which pushed the burning economic wagon even faster down the hill. Left with no alternatives, the central bank spent twenty-seven million dollars in U.S. reserves to stabilize the Russian currency, which further eroded investor confidence and undermined the ruble.

Inflation reached an unbelievable 84 percent, while welfare costs skyrocketed. Unable to keep their doors open, several prominent Russian banks shut down. Many experts believe the financial crisis was the beginning of the end for Yeltsin and paved the way for Putin. Russia did eventually pull out of its downward spiral as oil prices rose in 1999, but by July, the country had inherited more than one hundred billion dollars' worth of debt from the former Soviet Union and owed more than one hundred and fifty billion dollars to Western governments, the World Bank, and the IMF. Russia had been hinting at asking its debtors for relief, and on July 18, 2000, four U.S. senators, led by Senate Foreign Relations Committee chairman Jesse Helms (Republican of North Carolina), sent a letter to President Bill Clinton advising him that they "strongly oppose any further debt rescheduling, reduction or relief for the government of Russia absent significant changes in Russian spending priorities."

On July 25, Putin begged for mercy at the G8 summit in Okinawa. He asked the G8 leaders to write off almost a third of the debt. He claimed Russia would have to spend up to 40 percent of its revenue on servicing the debt unless it was granted this relief. The G8 turned him down. On the eve of the summit, German chancellor Gerhard Schröder said that since Russia was a world power and not a developing or emerging country, it didn't need the write-off. Other Paris Club members agreed and instead offered Russia more time to repay the debts.

As noted earlier, during the Millennium Summit in early September 2000, Bill Clinton met with Putin and discussed the *Kursk* crisis along with other important topics. On October 25, two days after the first Russian saturation diver entered the *Kursk* and took detailed photos of the wreckage, the U.S. House approved a fifteen-billion-dollar foreign aid bill. The bill earmarked three hundred million dollars to help fight AIDS in Africa and one hundred million dollars for Serbia but was strangely vague on where almost fourteen billion dollars went. One of the bill's primary negotiators, Senator Joe Biden (Democrat of Delaware)—a close friend of Bill Clinton's—insisted on fairly mild reporting requirements for recipient countries. Several of these countries had strong economic ties to Russia.

While little proof exists that Russia indirectly received debt-relief payments from the U.S. to squelch the claim that a U.S. submarine clipped the *Kursk* and potentially caused its demise, we do know that Putin was having trouble muzzling his dogs. They insisted that evidence obtained at the site all but proved the involvement of a U.S. submarine, and they were demanding retribution. Putin needed a bargaining chip. Money speaks volumes and often has a way of softening stances. Given how difficult it is to uncover secrets buried under two decades' worth of dirt, we may never know the truth, but the facts do increase the suspicions that some kind of deal was struck between the two superpowers to silence the barks and prevent a potential conflict.

If indeed a deal was cut between Clinton and Putin, the U.S. certainly would have insisted upon the cessation of any Russian claims that a U.S. sub had smacked the *Kursk*. The two most vociferous supporters of this theory, and the two most in a position to have access to evidence to support such a claim, were Northern Fleet Commander Admiral Vyacheslav Popov and his chief of staff, Vice Admiral Mikhail Motsak.

In early 2001, not long after the October 25 bill went into effect, Prosecutor General Vladimir Ustinov began an internal investigation into the *Kursk* incident. On December 1, Ustinov presented a preliminary report to Putin, wherein he wrote that the August 2000 naval exercise had been "poorly organized" and the investigation had revealed "serious violations" by Popov and Motsak. Putin quickly demoted and transferred both admirals. During their public dismissal, Putin vehemently repudiated any *Kursk* collision claims made by the pair.

Others who may have harbored or supported collision beliefs were also sacked that year, including Minister of Defense Igor Sergeyev, Deputy Prime Minister Ilya Klebanov, and Northern Fleet submarine commander, Vice Admiral Oleg Burtsev. In total, a dozen high-ranking Northern Fleet officers were dismissed, but the official public line was that it had nothing to do with the *Kursk* disaster, even though all of them had been directly involved in the exercise or rescue operations, or in some other way with the *Kursk*.

Kursk Raised

Putin had made a commitment to the crew's families to eventually raise the *Kursk* from the bottom and recover the rest of the crew's remains. The operation was estimated to cost sixty-five million dollars. The Russians contracted with Halliburton and the Dutch marine salvage firms Mammoet and Smit International. Aside from the raising of the K-129 by Howard Hughes, the complex *Kursk* project would be the largest salvage operation of its kind in history.

The operation carried extreme risk due to potential radiation leakage from the reactor, as well as from several hazardous obstacles. Sat divers and ROV cameras found only seven of the *Kursk*'s twenty-four torpedoes; the rest were presumed destroyed in the second blast. Deemed necessary to raise the rest of the submarine, and given that the sub might still contain unexploded warheads, Halliburton divers cut away the bow from the rest of the *Kursk*. To accomplish this, they used two massive hydraulic suction anchors and a tungsten carbide abrasive saw pulled back and forth across the hull. The operation took ten days.

When the bow was finally free, several divers proceeded to bring up smaller parts of the wreckage, including a torpedo tube section weighing over a ton. They also grabbed a high-pressure compressed-air cylinder weighing half a ton and a piece of the sonar system dome. These were analyzed to help determine the cause of the explosions.

The Mammoet team converted a Giant 4 semisubmersible deck barge into a platform that could support the weight of the raised submarine.

Although the barge could carry large loads on its deck, they decided to raise the *Kursk* up to a point just beneath the hull, where it could then be transported back to port. Accomplishing this required the teams to design an array of new technologies and build a cadre of unique lifting equipment. Programmers had to write custom software to automatically compensate for the wave motion caused by unstable ocean currents that could snap the cables holding up the *Kursk*.

The sat divers also had to cut a huge hole in the ship's hull to allow the sail to come through. The saturation-diving teams worked in six-hour shifts from a diving bell and remained pressed down in chambers for a total of twenty-eight days. As they had done the year before to cut entry holes in the sub, they used hydraulic abrasive water jets to create twenty-six holes in the inner and outer hulls. Then they mounted custom guidance rings around the cuts and lowered guide cables to eventually raise the wreck.

On October 8, 2001, fourteen months after the *Kursk* went down, the joint salvage teams took fifteen hours to slowly raise the remains of the *Oscar II*-class submarine from the ocean floor. They carried the hulk back to the Roslyakovo Shipyard in Murmansk while the Russian Navy destroyed what remained of the severed bow section.

Once in drydock, observers pointed to a curious round hole in the starboard side of the *Kursk*, about the same diameter as a torpedo. Uninformed politicians and media reporters sensationalized this evidence to catapult the collision theory back to the forefront, but with an added twist. They claimed that the USS *Memphis* or *Toledo* had collided with the *Kursk* and then two minutes later fired a torpedo that sliced through the outer and inner hulls in the bow and caused the second explosion.

Submariners and torpedo experts disputed this claim. A MK-48 ADCAP is not designed to penetrate anything. It's designed to go underneath the hull of a ship or get near a sub and then detonate, breaking the back of the ship or shattering the hull of the sub. Also, even the best-trained crews can't possibly execute a snapshot torpedo firing in less than a minute, such that the torpedo could have reached the *Kursk* within two minutes.

Few believed the stories, and the truth about what really happened never came to light.

CHAPTER 14

UNDER THE ICE

*"There is a potential for conflict in the Arctic
due to natural resources."*

—REAR ADMIRAL ROBERT KAMENSKY,
Former head of NATO Submarine Operations

Was there a collision between a U.S. submarine and the *Kursk* in August 2000? The *Kursk* was lost with all hands in the Barents Sea, which is inside the Arctic Circle. The Arctic Ocean is the world's smallest ocean, but it can stop your heart in a matter of seconds. The ancient Greeks named the region after the northern constellation Arktos when Pytheas discovered the frigid sea in 300 B.C. Sheer walls of ice, some hundreds of feet high, loom above the ocean's surface during winter, when temperatures plunge to minus thirty degrees centigrade. Only the native Inuit, polar bears, seals, and other wildlife have dared call this desolate place home.

As noted earlier, every few years, the U.S. Navy sends two or three nuclear-attack submarines to the Beaufort Sea, two hundred miles north of Alaska, to hone tactics and test the latest weapons, communications, navigation, sonar, and fire control systems in icy conditions. The program is called ICEX, which stands for "ice exercise." It is now the Navy's primary method of maintaining submarine dominance and proficiency in the Arctic region. Also as mentioned earlier, the USS *Memphis* had participated in ICEX fewer than eighteen months before the *Kursk* incident.

To better understand what happened in August 2000, and what factors might have contributed to a possible scrape or near miss between an American submarine and the *Kursk*, I petitioned the Navy's chief information office for almost a year. I asked the staff to allow me to join four dozen officers, sailors, scientists, and engineers at the ICEX camp and spend several days aboard a nuclear fast attack submarine under the Arctic ice. With the help of ICEX Camp Director Jeff Gossett, I finally gained approval and packed my bags.

The English language holds few metaphors that can match nature's palette, and describing in these pages what I saw and felt during my journey was quite a challenge. I hope the following account does justice to the sailors, officers, and civilians who made this experience of a lifetime possible.

Arctic Dangers

I boarded a plane to Prudhoe Bay, where I met a team from the Navy's Arctic Submarine Lab. These guys help run the ICEX camp in concert with the University of Washington's Applied Physics Laboratory (APL). Flat, treeless, and white, Prudhoe resembles a snow-covered oil field in Texas. Alaska Airlines ferries in daily a slew of oil workers, sporting red flannel shirts, who maintain the Trans-Alaska Pipeline. The Navy commandeered a hangar near the terminal, where Charlie Johnson from ASL told us how to keep from freezing our family jewels off at minus twenty degrees below zero. I learned that wool makes for the best defense against the ultracold. Cotton can cause you to sweat, and sweat tends to refreeze, which can turn your skin into a Brillo pad. I trudged out to the single-engine Cessna on the runway, the engine sputtered to life, and we roared down the runway.

The ICEX camp appeared from nowhere, as if conjured by Houdini. More than a dozen wooden boxes dotted the ground, resembling large rectangular coffins hammered together from plywood. The camp had been built weeks earlier by a hired construction crew, who ferried parts from Prudhoe Bay and would burn the remains after the April shutdown (rather than haul them back to Alaska). Camp Director Jeff Gossett met me at the plane and ushered me to my quarters—a hooch ironically called Truk, as in the Pacific island near Guam.

Gossett eloquently informed me that the difference between operating in Arctic waters versus other areas, such as the Pacific Ocean, is like the difference between driving a car on a four-lane freeway in Nevada versus a one-lane road on the edge of a cliff in Colorado. In the Pacific, you can run at flank speed for days with little worry of hitting anything. Water conditions make it easier to hide from the enemy, and positioning your sub to fire a torpedo doesn't require an engineering degree. In the Arctic, all that changes, and the nation with the best training, tactics, and technologies to operate in these waters will win the day.

"Arctic waters are not very friendly," Gossett says. "Over time, salt leeches out of the ice and freshwater rivers flow into the ocean here. There's little to no evaporation, or any wave action to mix the fresh with the saltwater, and the result is lower density and less salinity."

I asked how that affects submarine operations.

"Things are a lot more treacherous up here," Gossett says. "As subs move toward the surface, due to water conditions, they can feel thousands of pounds heavier. That makes sub driving much tougher. There are also stalactites—or long icicles—that form keels beneath sea ice when a flow of saline cold water mingles with ocean water. In shallow water, some of these spikes can extend all the way to the bottom. Maneuvering around them can be quite dangerous."

Having served as a submariner, I asked about surfacing through the thick ice, as most subs were not designed to do this.

"We only have three submarines of the *Seawolf* class that can safely crack through thick ice," Gossett says, "and only two of them have participated in ICEX training. Some older *Los Angeles*- and newer *Virginia*-class boats can crack through thinner ice, but don't have sails that can handle thicker ice without causing some damage. So if they had a casualty, like a fire, toxic gas leak, flooding, reactor scram, or were damaged by an enemy attack, they'd have to search for a thin ice area to surface. If they couldn't find one quickly, they'd be in serious trouble."

Gossett says that for ice exercises, which last about six weeks, ASL and APL teams install a special set of equipment and systems, and then provide sub crews with guidance and training on their usage. The extra gear includes a low-light, upward-looking camera mounted in the sail. The camera stares at the ice above to help the crew determine ice conditions for surfacing and better assess relative position in relation to a constantly moving ice floe.

A monitor in the control room, mounted in a one-foot-square metal housing, displays the video captured by the camera. The image looks like a dull white blanket dotted with mud spots, which are caused by ice imperfections and small holes bored into the ice by melting water.

A marine conductivity, temperature, and depth (CTD) sensor on the hull broadcasts data to a customized display to inform the CO and crew about environmental conditions and changes and the like. This can be critical for surfacing, as it monitors things such as density changes, which could affect the sub's weight and thus cause issues with the rate of ascent. As Gossett says, "It's like being able to see an upcoming hill ahead when you're driving a car so you can speed up before climbing."

All submarines have "factory installed" high-frequency top-sounder and ahead-looking sonar systems, but crews are not trained on how to use these in northern waters unless they attend ICEX. The USS *Toledo* crew did not receive this training, and this equipment is more often used to search for enemy mines or ASW ships. ICEX personnel also conduct training and supervise exercises to teach crews how to repurpose their high-frequency sonar to determine ice thickness and look for ice keels to avoid smacking one. The sonar has limited range, only about five hundred yards on either side, so crews need to go slowly to avoid ramming something or missing an open area for surfacing.

ASL teams set up shop in a wooden command hut at ICEX, which is chock-full of monitors and systems. During the program, over more than a month, they assist subs with exercises to improve under-ice operations; learn how to use the special ASL gear; test communications, sonar, navigation, and weapons capabilities; and practice Arctic operational skills.

Under the Ice

The USS *Connecticut* is one of three submarines that comprise the *Seawolf* class, which were built in the late nineties. The original design was completed toward the end of the Cold War, when large Soviet warships and submarines were a major threat. In my book *Red November*, I discuss the primary missions of fast attack submarines during that time period. Submarines today still undertake such missions, and this class of boat is well suited to the task.

Submariners love code names, and that year the ICEX team used the movie *Top Gun* and the game Monopoly as inspirational sources. The USS *New Hampshire* became "Goose," and the *Connecticut*, "Iceman," with their respective surfacing locations named "Waterworks" and "Marvin Gardens." Once the *Connecticut* had received final instructions to surface at Marvin Gardens, a helicopter descended and whisked us away to the rendezvous location. The chopper blades whipped the snow off the ice at our landing spot a few miles away and turned the sky white. A wooden warming hut, no larger than a walk-in closet, sat on the frozen ground next to a couple of bundled figures.

One of the ICEX guys approached and waved us away from the chopper. A fat cigar dangling from his lips, icicles coating his beard, a bright red glow on his Rudolph nose, he said his name was Hector Castillo. He cupped a pair of headphones and called the *Connecticut* via Gertrude—a short-range underwater communications system that uses hydrophones to send open voice messages. "Iceman, this is Marvin Gardens. Media is ready for your surfacing."

Camera in hand, fingers numb, and heart thumping, I stood on the polar ice cap and waited. No French horns blew when the *Connecticut* punched through the ice, as they had in the movie *Ice Station Zebra*, but I heard them all the same. I also heard the ice crumble as eight thousand tons of steel cracked through the hard cover and pushed skyward. The ground rumbled like the prescient warnings of an avalanche. Where only nature had once painted the landscape, a dark intruder emerged. Foreboding and mysterious, the monolith inched higher until a black rectangle loomed large. Orange-suited sailors popped up from the front of the mound and attacked large chunks of ice, pushing them over the side. Boulders of white flew from the submarine's sail and crashed to the ground below.

More orange-covered suits appeared; one man had a chainsaw dangling from his hand. He resembled a cross between Jason from the horror movie and a pumpkin patch worker. Another sailor came down from the sail and used a line to measure the distance from the back of the sail, to mark the approximate location of the after-entry hatch. Pumpkin Jason walked over to the marked spot and brought the chainsaw to life with a roar. As if spewed from a refrigerator gone mad, crunched ice flew into the air while he cut into the snowpack covering the boat. Thirty minutes passed before a glint of sunlight reflected from the black steel of the submarine hatch. The orange clad sailor completed his sculpture by notching a large square step into the ice just in front of the hatch.

The spring-loaded hatch opened, and a distinct "boat smell" wafted up from below. Stored diesel fuel, amine, something electronic, and something deep-fried combined to create the odor. Those of us who have served aboard nuclear submarines recall this scent well. Still bulk-bundled, I climbed down the ladder and landed near the galley. The XO welcomed us aboard and motioned us into the crew's mess. We stripped from our Arctic gear and followed a petty officer to the sixteen-man berthing section, one deck up. We stowed our gear and made our way to the officers' wardroom.

Meals in the wardroom are formal affairs, and our lunch followed submarine officers' protocol. We stood when the commanding officer,

Commander Michael Varney, entered the room, and then sat in our assigned seats. A steward entered from the galley, dressed formally in serving attire, and placed a bowl of soup in front of the captain. Soup bowls clicked atop plates in a counterclockwise direction until everyone had been served. No one ate until the CO consumed his first spoonful. The rich French onion soup rivaled recipes found in top New York restaurants.

During our meal, Commander Varney assured me that should a troublemaking enemy vessel threaten the USS *Connecticut*, it could handle the challenge. This boat and the other two subs of its class are uniquely outfitted with eight torpedo tubes and a fully automated system to load MK-48 ADCAP torpedoes and Tomahawk cruise missiles.

Later that day, the crew demonstrated the loading of a weapon in a tube, sounding off warnings and completing procedures with polished precision. We were told that the *Connecticut* could sink eight warships and be prepared to do it again in less than fifteen minutes. As a former fire control technician, I couldn't help but marvel at this capability.

That evening I was allowed into the control room to watch the boat submerge. While the crew prepared to dive, Varney pointed to various control stations and explained their functions. Most of this I already knew, and I was overcome by nostalgic memories of my ninety-day jaunts into enemy waters during the Cold War. I also had a twinge of jealousy and wished the two classes of boats I had served on had been this modern. Digital displays blinked and flickered near the diving stations, which fronted two operators who gripped airplane-like steering wheels. One sailor operated the rudder to go right and left, and the other, the bow planes to go up and down. Nearby, sat the chief of the watch, who is responsible for various operations, including flooding the ballast tanks to make the boat heavy enough to dive.

The diving alarm sounded, orders were issued and repeated, and the boat slowly dropped from her icy perch to mingle with the fish below. We leveled off at four hundred feet and were promptly escorted from the control room, but not before I caught a glimpse of the BYG-1 (pronounced "big one") fire control panels.

The digital BYG-1 panels resemble large videogame consoles and can keep tabs on dozens of contacts without breaking a sweat. My eyes wandered from them to the sonar shack, just forward of the fire control area, where headphone-wearing operators stared at BQQ-10 sonar stacks. With this advanced system, they can practically hear a pin drop from dozens of miles away.

Drill or Die

The following morning, after a brisk run on one of the boat's treadmills, I had the privilege of interviewing Commander Varney in his stateroom. What he told me opened my eyes to what's really happening in the Arctic, and why it's imperative that U.S. research labs continue to develop new technologies and systems to fight under-ice battles. Also, for fast attack submariners to learn how to use these systems and practice tactics and maneuvers in Arctic waters.

Varney grew up in Kittery Point, Maine, next to a shipyard that built submarines. Several of his classmates' fathers were submarine captains, and his own dad, a harbor master and a firefighter, had served as a sonar technician on a destroyer involved in the Cuban Missile Crisis. It was natural that Varney grew up intrigued by submarines, their technology, and their missions. When *Top Gun* hit theaters, all his friends wanted to be Maverick, except Varney. "I wanted to be the guy who gets to hunt for *Red October*," he says.

"My father was a firefighter," Varney says. "He used to say that fighting fires was ninety-five percent boredom and five percent sheer terror. I learned something from that I live by today. I believe that it's not how you train that prepares you for the unexpected, but how you live. I think that how an individual or a team performs in combat comes down to what they know instinctively, and not just what they've been taught. Even the best-trained crews can crumble under intense pressure and stress. You can avoid that by introducing instinctive behavior into their everyday life."

Varney drew a straight line from this to the importance of ICEX training. Even just one month in the Arctic can make a difference. Running drills every day creates muscle memory, or instinctive behavior, that can save lives. All too often the unexpected happens and instincts need to kick in to quell the situation immediately.

Varney's words made me reflect again on what happened on August 12, 2000, in the Barents Sea. Even though sheets of ice do not cover the surface of the ocean at that time of year, the sea currents make submarine operations difficult and tricky. As Gossett explained, during the summer, freshwater ice melts and mingles with colder seawater. This creates shifting layers that can reflect underwater sounds before they reach a sonarman's ears. Especially in shallow waters, like the Barents, sound can refract off the surface layer. On its way back down, the refraction might be exacerbated as the sound hits a cold or warm layer. When it finally hits a submarine's sonar array, an untrained crew that does not properly adjust for this might report inaccurate sonar bearing and range estimates.

Eighteen months prior to the *Kursk* incident, the *Memphis* had completed ICEX training to help deal with those anomalies, and most of the crew still had muscle memory. They still had Arctic instincts. They knew how to consider warm and cold layers and sonar refraction. Conversely, the *Toledo* had not been to ICEX. Its crew had not had this advantage. Did this handicap contribute to an unfortunate set of circumstances?

Varney conducted a few simulated drills to show us how his crew might respond in situations in which they were trailing a Russian sub in Arctic waters. As he ran drill after drill, I watched the crew hone their skills and improve their abilities with each run. A few seconds faster here, a bit more efficient there. Hours later, the instincts were ingrained and muscle memory set.

If the *Toledo* had completed such rigorous training during ICEX along with the *Memphis*, would 118 submariners aboard the *Kursk* still be alive? We may never know, but Varney's final words during our interview were profound. When asked why he felt ICEX was important to the submarine Navy, Varney said this was the *Connecticut*'s fourth training exercise in the Arctic. He felt that without the knowledge and experience gained in these operations, his crew would be at a severe disadvantage if they were tasked with a surveillance mission in northern waters. He intimated that without ICEX training, serious collisions might occur, placing hundreds of lives at risk.

As noted earlier, Rear Admiral Robert Kamensky and I served together aboard the USS *Drum* during the Cold War. Kamensky later did a stint as the flag officer heading up all submarine operations for NATO—an organization that is undergoing one of the most profound command structure reforms in its long history, due primarily to recent developments in the Arctic. When I asked him about this topic, he said, "There is a potential for conflict in the Arctic due to natural resources. Conventions are in place, but how are we going to enforce them? That's going to be our biggest challenge. NATO has a very strong concern with this. Up until now we've been focused on Europe, because that's where all the sparks were. Meanwhile, things are continuing to fester up in the Arctic region without a lot of national attention."

That statement raised the hairs on the back of my neck and made me wonder what might happen if the world continued to watch Putin's left hand and completely miss the deadly moves made by his right hand.

CHAPTER 15

THE FIRST DOMINO

"[T]he [Kursk] accident also has strengthened trends in military reform—pointing toward increased defense resources...aimed at building a more capable military."

—CIA REPORT, December 7, 2000

Many historians believe the *Kursk* incident became the first toppled domino that propelled the superpowers toward another cold war that could be far more frightening than the first. The *Kursk* tragedy provided Putin with the political clout to muzzle several energy oligarchs, put them behind bars, and steal their riches. He then gained control of key gas and oil firms and used the profits to inject enough wealth into the Russian economy to drive up the gross domestic product (GDP).

Putin knew that any resurgence in Russia's prosperity would not be possible without exploiting the country's vast reserves of natural resources, and the oligarchs were in control of most of these.

Wresting that control away from several of these wealthy rulers, and placing it under his thumb, was the first step in Putin's plan. His initial target was Mikhail Khodorkovsky, the most prominent and wealthiest of the lot. The outspoken businessman had amassed more than eighteen billion dollars from oil profits and had made it no secret that he hated Putin. Through a series of questionable and essentially illegal tactics, Putin seized all of Khodorkovsky's bank accounts and holdings and tossed the man in jail at the culmination of kangaroo court proceedings.

By August 2003, Putin was well on the way to bringing Khodorkovsky's Yukos oil company under the complete control of the Russian government. Less than a year later, he forced the firm's largest enterprise, which accounted for most of its oil production, onto the auctioning block. The Russian government's oil firm, Rosneft, eventually gained complete control of Yukos, thereby tripling Rosneft's oil production. Within the week, Rosneft became Russia's third-largest oil producer and Putin became one of the wealthiest men in the world, with an estimated net worth of more than seventy billion dollars.

Now rich, Putin was elected to his second term in March 2004 by an overwhelming margin. A year later, he backed reforms in education, health care, agriculture, and housing. During the initial years of his reign, Putin led Russia through an unprecedented economic transformation. Wages tripled, and real incomes went up by 250 percent. Poverty and unemployment were cut in half, and the self-assessed life satisfaction of the average Russian shot upward. Putin understood well that energy revenues had contributed greatly to his country's gross national product (GNP). He also knew that the oil and gas fields under Russian control would eventually run dry, and without new energy resources, his country could once again be propelled toward third-world status. Avoiding this outcome became Putin's primary motivation.

During the decade after the *Kursk* incident, Putin invested heavily in a formidable new Navy and military infrastructure. His unyielding ambitions to rebuild Russia's military caused world leaders to question whether NATO was headed toward a new cold war.

This concern was voiced by the CIA in the December 7, 2000, document referred to earlier, wherein experts stated that "the [*Kursk*] accident also has strengthened trends in military reform—pointing toward increased defense resources...aimed at building a more capable military as an instrument of Russian national security policy."

Two decades later, this prophecy has come true, and Putin has rebuilt and repositioned Russia's naval forces to dominate key Arctic routes and resources. Disputes stemming from international maritime law definitions could soon lead to regional conflicts or full-scale wars.

UNCLOS

In the seventeenth century, a Dutch jurist named Hugo Grotius became the founder of international maritime law. Grotius postulated that a sea could belong to no man or nation, which prompted the term "freedom of the seas" in the eighteenth century. During that time, Cornelius van Bynkershoek, also a Dutch jurist, contended that a bordering state could lay claim to an area extending beyond the coastline equal in distance to the average range of a fired cannonball—or about three nautical miles. This tenet remained until 1958 when, during a Geneva conference, efforts were made to better define the Law of the Sea and create legal guidelines related to internal waters, territorial waters, contiguous zones, exclusive economic zones, continental shelves, and international waters.

The conference did little good, as most nations disputed the definitions. Arguments continued for another two dozen years, until the United Nations Convention on the Law of the Sea (UNCLOS), which defines the term "sea" as any watery area containing salt (such as an ocean, a gulf, or a strait), was adopted at Montego Bay, Jamaica. Another dozen years passed before the agreement was signed by all 158 of the industrialized nations involved, except for the United States.

As defined by UNCLOS, territorial waters are found between baselines and exclusive economic zones. This is where a two-hundred-nautical-mile rule comes into play, granting countries the right to resources found within that range. This does not supersede the traditional territorial definition of twelve nautical miles, which governs geopolitical disputes involving foreign vessels or aircraft that might "cross the line." Most nations guard their territories with fervor. Conflicts and even wars have almost started when a ship or plane crossed over or skirted these invisible but highly protected lines.

That said, some ships, including commercial and military vessels, are often granted the right of "innocent passage" through a nation's territorial waters, so long as they are quick about it and do nothing that might be considered "prejudicial to the peace, good order, or the security" of the coastal nation. Territorial waters are subdivided by coastal inner bands, known as archipelagic waters, which extend twelve miles beyond the farthest island.

The term "international waters," also known as "the high seas," is defined as sea areas extending beyond the economical two-hundred- or maximum 350-nautical-mile limit. No nation owns these waters, and no "keep out" signs can be posted here, so anyone can motor or sail through these areas unfettered by angry landlords. Still, one must obey traditional laws that govern crime and environmental protection. Drug runners and litterbugs beware.

UNCLOS defines how oceans can be used or governed. Unfortunately, the guidelines in this treaty are often incomplete and difficult to interpret, which opens the door to arguments and conflicts. When drawing lines around Arctic or South China Sea assets, for example, verifying which areas belong to which government could escalate disagreements beyond international courts, with winners decided by muscle and might rather than by lawyers and judges.

The Arctic Eight

Since fingers of the Arctic Ocean touch upon the shores of the United States (Alaska), Russia, Norway, Canada, and Denmark (Greenland), these nations comprise the "Arctic Five" bordering nations. The wider Arctic region is roughly the same size as the African continent and covers around 8 percent of the earth's surface. This area cuts across Iceland, Finland, and Sweden. Those three countries plus the Arctic Five comprise the Arctic Eight voting council members. There are also twelve permanent observer states on the Arctic Council: France, Germany, the Netherlands, Poland, Spain, Great Britain, China, Italy, Japan, South Korea, India, and Singapore. Ad hoc observer states, which do not have permanent seats or voting rights, include Turkey and the European Union.

The council formed in 1991 when the Arctic Eight signed the Arctic Environmental Protection Strategy (AEPS). The Ottawa Declaration of 1996 certified the Arctic Council as a forum to promote coordination, cooperation, and interactive discussions between the Arctic nations, along with indigenous populations, regarding issues such as trade routes, the environment, natural resources, and development. The Arctic Council is also commissioned to conduct various studies on oil and gas, climate change, and Arctic shipping. Council chairmanship rotates every two years. The U.S. chaired from May 2015 through May 2017, whereupon Finland took over in May 2017 and served until May 2019, and then Iceland grabbed the baton. While the council discusses Arctic issues, members do not govern or enforce any laws, but instead defer such matters to the United Nations.

A UN Commission on the Limits of the Continental Shelf (CLCS) has been appointed as the adjudicator in this northern court, but its gavel has largely been silent. CLCS members have done little to carve out territorial guidelines or resolve disputes, instead choosing to "just say no" to virtually every claim filed.

The Arctic region comprises around 6 percent of the world's surface area, but the U.S. Geological Survey believes the frozen north could yield some 1.7 trillion cubic feet of natural gas, or about 30 percent of the undiscovered reserves, and over ninety billion barrels of oil, or 13 percent of the reserves. Like a sought-after bride, the Arctic also promises a dowry of rich veins of precious metals such as uranium, iron ore, gold, and platinum. Engagement ring manufacturers are salivating.

Until recent years, extracting Arctic riches had been almost impossible. Much of it lies hidden beneath thousands of feet of ocean shrouded by miles of ice pack. But with the ice now receding, that changes the game. Many nations have already invested millions over the past decade to collect geological and bathymetric data to verify their economic rights to drill, dig, or sell. Although most of the parties launched these quests with visible smiles and concealed daggers, smiles are now fading and knives are being stabbed into the wood atop negotiating tables. One of the hottest arguments stems from ownership claims to trillions of tons of oil and gas reserves across the Lomonosov Ridge.

Putin Stakes a Claim: August 2, 2007

Anatoly Sagalevich's heart thudded as he seated himself inside the tiny submersible. Although the sixty-nine-year-old undersea veteran had trained for this momentous occasion, no amount of preparation could quell the excitement of a journey such as this. A harsh wind whipped across the Arctic Ocean and sent it splashing against the Plexiglas canopy of his *Mir-1* minisub. Years earlier, Sagalevich had led similar dangerous missions to the bottom of the Atlantic and other seas to explore the murky remains of the *Titanic* and the *Bismarck*. As the department head of the Shirshov Institute of Oceanology, he had an often-perilous job that had brought him to the far north. Russia had invested in Sagalevich's vast geological and environmental knowledge, and was counting on him to discover the evidence needed to claim a prize of great wealth.

Russia was also counting on Sagalevich's colleague, the sixty-eight-year-old Artur Chilingarov, who was commanding this mission from the cockpit of the *Mir-2* minisub. The calm, easygoing polar scientist had been the recipient of Russia's most prestigious Hero of the Soviet Union award after completing several harrowing treks to the South Pole and other treacherous locales. Well known throughout his country, Chilingarov had served as a deputy chairman for the Russian Federal Assembly.

Chilingarov looked up from his instrument panel, winked at Sagalevich, and flashed the okay sign with an O-shaped finger and thumb. Sagalevich winked back. The minisubs housing the two explorers had been lowered into the water from the *Rossiya*, a nuclear-powered Russian icebreaker. While roiling about in the choppy waters, Sagalevich focused on his panel and completed a mental checklist. Satisfied that all systems were green, he gave Chilingarov the sign to dive. From his cockpit, Sagalevich glanced up at the gray clouds above and watched them disappear, gradually replaced by an ink-black sea. He switched on the forward running lights, but they did little to illuminate the dark. He and Chilingarov would need to rely on instruments and instincts to find their way to the bottom, almost fourteen thousand feet below.

Reaching their destination would not be easy. Water temperatures average just below zero degrees centigrade in this region, which can freeze equipment and systems needed to navigate, maneuver, and survive. Even if they reached their destination and found the evidence they sought, returning with the proof could prove impossible. Pushed by ocean currents, ice floes in this region move often. If the two scientists did not break the surface in their exact original location, they could wind up stuck under a thick pack of ice. Teams from the *Rossiya* would not be able to break through the hard cover in time. Trapped in their vessels, both explorers would soon ache for air as supplies grew thin. Their bodies would eventually be found with faces wrinkled in agony, having succumbed to a slow death by asphyxiation.

Sagalevich had little time to ponder this thought as he guided his craft into the abyss, careful to keep an accurate track of his path. An hour passed, then another. Finally, four hours into the journey, Sagalevich smiled. He had reached the bottom. He settled onto the rocky floor and received a report from Chilingarov that *Mir-2* had also touched down nearby. Sagalevich did a systems check and then extended the minisub's retractable robotic arm. The metal hand scooped up soil and rock samples and deposited them into a container. Satisfied that he'd collected enough, Sagalevich swelled with pride and excitement. Although gathering samples had been his government's primary goal, he had risked his life for more than just geological evidence. He radioed his colleague and told him to stand by. Chilingarov acknowledged in an excited voice.

Sagalevich retracted the arm and carefully cinched the metallic fingers around a cylindrical piece of titanium. The metal pole was attached to one edge of a small rectangle. He extended the arm and drove the pole into the silt and sand. Beaming broadly, staring at the Russian flag planted on the seabed at a depth of 13,980 feet, he radioed Chilingarov and told him their mission had been accomplished. The two minisubs ascended and managed to find their way back to the awaiting icebreaker. Later that day, Sagalevich made an entry in his log: "Today we set the flag of the Russian Federation on the floor of the Arctic Ocean."

Back in Moscow, the two explorers were greeted by cheering crowds, red carpets, and brass bands. Both congratulated their teams and all of Russia for "reaching the North Pole of the earth." Sergei Balyasnikov, a Moscow-based Arctic Institute spokesman, told the press, "This is like placing a flag on the moon; this is really a massive scientific achievement."

Sagalevich and Chilingarov had a right to be proud. This expedition marked the first plunge beneath the polar ice cap made by manned minisubs down to that depth. But their pride had little to do with being first, as if this were another space race. This mission was part of a strategic plan to outmaneuver other players on the international chessboard. Knight to queen's pawn two. Artur Chilingarov was a close friend of President Vladimir Putin's. Together, the two had plotted their moves carefully, aware that to the victors go the spoils.

"The Arctic Is Ours"

Putin had more than once previously announced Russia's dire need to lock up "strategic, economic, scientific, and defense interests" in the Arctic. Chilingarov had seconded the motion by stating that "the Arctic is ours, and we should manifest our presence." He and his colleague Sagalevich had done just that. First, they had brought back geological evidence they hoped would secure their claim to a chunk of the Arctic seabed under international law as governed by UNCLOS. Although the law grants countries exclusive economic rights to natural resources discovered in areas extending up to two hundred miles offshore, Russia wanted more. If the Russians could prove that the "natural prolongation" of their underwater continental shelf stretched beyond that two-hundred-mile limit, they could lay claim to all the riches buried there. All the oil, gas, minerals, and food worth trillions of dollars would belong to Russia. They could either extract these resources or sell the rights to the highest bidders, profiting like pirates who had found the proverbial X on the map. But first, they'd have to win their case.

Six years before the 2007 minisub mission, referring to UNCLOS, the Russians had petitioned the UN CLCS for exclusive economic rights to the Lomonosov Ridge, a three-thousand-mile-long shelf that runs from the New Siberian Islands, past the North Pole, to Ellesmere Island of the Canadian Arctic Archipelago near Greenland. No spot in this icy ocean is shallower than three thousand feet deep. Before recent increases in global temperatures, most of the area lay beneath large chunks of ice. Any resources found there were inaccessible. With the ice melting, and with new extraction technologies entering the scene, Russia's interest had escalated.

Unfortunately for Putin, the CLCS voted against the initial petition, stating that Russia did not have enough evidence to verify ownership of the ridge. An infuriated Putin then met with an eager Chilingarov to mastermind the plan to find irrefutable evidence that Russia owned the Lomonosov Ridge. When the two Russian explorers planted their country's flag on that ridge, to them it was more than just symbolic. They intended to make a statement to the world that effectively said, "First come, first served."

"If a hundred or a thousand years from now someone goes down to where we were," said Chilingarov, operator of the *Mir-2* minisub, "they will see the Russian flag." While Chilingarov was certainly aware that stabbing a flag into the sand does not necessarily constitute ownership, he believed that it set a precedent that could sway CLCS voters to rule in Russia's favor. Also, it would send a clear signal to other nations that Russia was dead serious about claiming large portions of the Arctic.

When asked about this incident, Rear Admiral Robert Kamensky had this to say: "What bothers us is when the Russians send out deep-submergence vehicles and plant a Russian flag in an area that used to be covered by ice, but is now mostly ice free, and state that it's part of their territorial shelf. Then they claim that all the mineral resources, including sizable petroleum deposits, are all theirs."

Tom Casey of the U.S. State Department commented publicly on the incident, stating that, "I'm not sure whether they put a metal flag, a rubber flag, or a bedsheet on the ocean floor. Either way, it doesn't have any legal standing." Canadian foreign minister Peter Mackay vehemently commented: "This isn't the fifteenth century. You can't go around the world and plant flags."

In Russia, Chilingarov shot back by saying, "We are happy that we placed a Russian flag on the ocean bed, where not a single person has ever been, and I don't give a damn what some foreign individuals think about that." Chilingarov then referred to Soviet Arctic researcher Ivan Papanin, who had led an expedition in the winter of 1937 to a remote ice floe: "Russia [has] always expanded its territory by northern lands.... [S]eventy years ago, they would say, 'Bolsheviks have conquered the Arctic.' Now our crew is United Russia. The Russian flag is the point of the North Pole of the earth. Full stop. If someone doesn't like it, let them dive as deep as fourteen thousand feet and try [to] leave something down there."

Putin served in his second premiership between 2008 and 2012. During that time, the pink cloud turned gray when the Great Recession delivered low blows to the Russian economy. Under his leadership, Russia waged war with and defeated the state of Georgia, then a NATO ally. Putin helped maneuver Russia through its economic crisis by leaning on the reserve Stabilization Fund of the Russian Federation, which had been accumulated in large measure through lucrative oil and gas exports.

Having come from meager beginnings may have provided Putin with the will and the wits to survive rough seas. One need only visit the Russian continent once to witness the toughness and resolve of its people. Most have endured lives of hardship that few in the U.S. or many European countries have seen or understand. As their leader, Putin has repeatedly demonstrated his resolve to ensure that his people are fed, clothed, and warm.

To accomplish this goal, Putin has repeatedly demonstrated his ability to step onto the stage as a calm, controlled, rational ruler with an engaging smile. On the flip side of his coin, he is ruthlessly wresting control of vast swaths of natural gas and oil. He also invaded Ukraine to protect the half-dozen gas pipes that run through that country and feed Europe with a third of its natural gas. Putin obviously shared the opinion of his friend Chilingarov when he said, "The Arctic is ours!"

At the time, world leaders shrugged off Chilingarov's claim as arrogant and baseless. Years later, they all changed their tunes.

Russia's *Arktika* Expedition

In the wake of the *Mir-1* and *Mir-2* expedition of 2007, the Russian Federation expressed bitter disappointment over the CLCS's unexpected denial of their territorial claims. Five years later, on November 7, 2012, to prove once and for all that Russia had sole economic rights to the Mendeleev and Lomonosov Ridges, the Russians sent a new class of submarine to the bottom of the Arctic Ocean to gather soil samples. These samples, they surmised, would ultimately verify to the CLCS that the underwater ridges had the same geological "DNA" as their parent continent, Russia. As part of the special *Arktika* (Arctic) 2012 expedition, the deep-diving *Kalitka* spent twenty days on station to explore the entire ridge area.

This unique submarine contains a series of linked spherical pressure chambers inside its outer hull, which allows it to dive as deep as fourteen thousand feet. Submariners aboard the *Kalitka* renamed their oddly shaped vessel the *Losharik*, in reference to a character in a poem written by

Genrikh Sapgir, a popular Russian poet. The character, who also appears in an animated film, is a toy horse consisting of small spheres joined together. The name is a portmanteau of "*loshad*," which means "horse" or "donkey," and "*sharik*," meaning "small sphere." Designated AS-31, the *Losharik* is a next-generation vessel after the AS-15 spy sub used to survey the *Kursk*. The submarine's special design allows it to deploy on repetitive dives to the bottom of the ocean to collect geological samples or, like the AS-15, conduct ultra-secret espionage operations.

Commissioned in 2004, the *Losharik* is similar in design to the NR-1—a U.S. deep-diving submersible launched in the 1960s. Powered by a nuclear reactor and hardened by a titanium hull, the *Losharik* minisub is carried on the back of an adapted Project 667 *Kalmar* submarine—a former *Delta III* ballistic-missile boat with its launching tubes removed. Since its introduction in 1973, the *Delta* class once formed the backbone of the Soviet strategic deterrent fleet during the Cold War. The boats carried sixteen R-29R (SS-N-18 Stingray) nuclear ballistic missiles equipped with multiple warheads. Fortified with Arctic-hardened capabilities, as well as improved electronics and noise reduction, *Delta III*s gave U.S. attack submariners heartburn by hiding under the polar ice cap, which made them hard to detect.

For the 2012 mission, the *Losharik* assisted the on-station *Kapitan Dranitsyn* and *Dikson* diesel-electric icebreakers in their efforts to pinpoint exact locations to drill for the desired samples. During the expedition, crews onboard the icebreakers drilled three wells at two sites and collected soil samples at a depth of almost two miles. The Russian Ministry of Natural Resources and Environment intended to use the samples to convince the UN CLCS of Russia's ownership of the two ridges in question.

"The joint effort resulted in a substantial amount of geological material," a Ministry of Defense source said. "More than five hundred kilograms of classifiable rocks were selected. The results of the survey will underlie Russia's application to the UN Commission on the Limits of the Continental Shelf, to allow extension of Russia's continental shelf—the initial [2007] application having been rejected because of a lack of geological evidence—and grant Russia the priority right to develop the deposits located on the shelf."

The *Mir* minisubs used in 2000 to survey the *Kursk*, and again during the 2007 flag-planting expedition, operate on batteries that die after fewer than seventy-two hours underwater. In contrast, the *Losharik* is a nuclear-powered craft capable of operating without surfacing for several months. Crews can work and live in a self-contained environment that includes a recreation room, workrooms, and a mess hall. The air- and water-regeneration systems are as good as those installed in the international space station.

The Russian Ministry of Defense source stated, "We are in need of such machines. Besides *Losharik*, only *Mir* deep-sea stations are capable of working at depths of two to three kilometers [up to two miles]. We used both *Mir* stations during the previous expedition led by Artur Chilingarov, but the operations we performed recently were even more complicated and took more time. *Mir* stations can't support themselves that long, so we decided to use *Losharik*." He went on to say, "The *Mir* stations are pleasure bathyscaphes rather than research machines—they have weak manipulators with limited mobility, and you can't install deep-sea sounding equipment on them."

Putin undoubtedly watched this operation with a great deal of anticipation. Geological experts had estimated that the reserves extractable from the 1.2 million square kilometers of territory could add almost six billion tons of oil equivalent, as well as 426 billion cubic meters of natural gas, to Russia's kitty. The expedition did indeed bring back a bevy of sediment and other samples that were subsequently submitted to the CLCS as "proof" that Russia owns the ridges, but as of the writing of this book, the outcome is still pending. If the CLCS casts final votes in Russia's favor, Russia will be granted exclusive economic rights to 463,000 square miles and at least five billion tons of oil and gas, making it the world's leading nation for these reserves.

On July 1, 2019, the *Losharik*'s lithium batteries overheated and, similar to the *Kursk* incident, caused a fire that led to an explosion. The crew was unable to quell the flames, which spread to other compartments. They fought the fire for ninety minutes but lost the battle. Fourteen of the nineteen men aboard perished in the accident. Two of the men had received the Hero of Russia award, equivalent to the U.S. Medal of Honor. Four surviving crew members, along with one civilian specialist, managed to initiate an emergency blow, and the *Losharik* surfaced off the coast of the Kola Peninsula. Nearby fisherman watched in amazement as the 230-foot-long sub broke the surface and bobbed in the roiling sea. The crew shut down the nuclear reactor and flooded all the spherical compartments before clambering onto the *Kalmar Delta III*.

The five survivors were rescued, but the *Losharik* was no longer seaworthy. NATO military officials had long speculated that mission parameters for the super-secret spy sub included using saturation divers to wiretap or slice through Western communication cables. Many of these officials commented that the U.S.-owned Halliburton had helped push Russia back down the underwater espionage path by training and equipping six sat divers in October 2000 in preparation for the *Kursk* salvage operation.

Broadway

More than 95 percent of Russia's natural gas and 60 percent of its oil reserves are in the Arctic, but they will eventually run dry. The Prirazlomnoye oil field in the Pechora Sea will pump out more than 120,000 barrels of oil per day in 2020. Gazprom, Russia's gas giant, sent its first oil-laden tanker from the area on May 1, 2014. Putin hailed the news as "the beginning of great and large-scale extraction of minerals and oil by our country in the Arctic." He also said that Russia's Arctic assertiveness would "positively influence Russia's future presence on the global energy markets and will strengthen both the whole economy and the energy sector."

Putin needs the resources buried along the Lomonosov Ridge to ensure economic longevity, but that sector of the Arctic is only Park Place on the Monopoly® board. Unfortunately for the rest of the world, Russia has already won Broadway. It's an area that's thirty-five miles wide and three hundred miles long in the Sea of Okhotsk known as the Peanut Hole. The Russians refer to it as "Ali Baba's cave" because it contains more than one billion tons of oil and two trillion cubic meters of gas.

Putin's maneuvering to control resources in the Peanut Hole was nothing short of brilliant, not to mention ruthless. He had the world focused on his left hand during the Ukraine crisis while four thousand miles away, with his right hand, he grabbed an Arctic area the size of Switzerland and secured the rights to all its oil and gas. This invasion required no guns, rebels, tanks, or planes, yet had a far greater impact on world power than the cessation of Crimea.

Using sleight of hand, in similar fashion to the card tricks he employed against President Obama in Syria, Putin created panic over the mundane issue of pollock fishing in the Sea of Okhotsk to influence the seven-member CLCS subcommission to expedite its decision. Of course, Russia's track record flies in the face of any real environmental concerns.

Putin arrested more than two dozen Greenpeace activists who were peacefully protesting near one of Russia's offshore oil rigs in 2013. The activists said the rig lacked a contingency plan in the event of a spill. Russia threatened the activists and their U.S. ship captain with seven years in prison, even though the rig had suffered no damage or operational setbacks.

More than half of Russia's fresh water is no longer potable, and around three-fourths of its surface water has become seriously polluted. The country's air is barely breathable, with over 85 percent of the population subjected to intense smog, and two major cities are consistently on the world's top-ten most-polluted list. Clouds of poison are so bad in Dzerzhinsk that Guinness World Records rates it as the planet's worst, and no one who resides there is expected to live beyond the age of fifty. In 1993, Russia callously dumped nuclear waste in the Sea of Japan—not far from the Peanut Hole. Yet Putin expected the world to believe Russia was concerned for the environmental safety of fish in the Sea of Okhotsk.

Putin intimated that if the UN did not do his bidding by voting positively for his territorial submissions, he would be "forced" to use Russia's naval fleet to prevent foreign vessels from transiting the Sea of Okhotsk, but of course, only to protect the precious pollock. Perhaps swayed by this threat, the UN subcommittee gave Putin what he wanted. In late 2013, they agreed with the arguments presented and granted Russia exclusive rights.

"Thanks to recognition of this enclave as a part of the Russian continental shelf, our country will gain more reserves of valuable minerals and other natural resources," Natural Resources and Environment minister Sergey Donskoy said in a press release. "It took Russia many years to achieve this success."

Putin invested vast amounts of resources, time, and effort to further his Arctic plans, at a time when the entire world was hammering him about his "illegal" European conquests. This speaks volumes about his ambitions and priorities. Putin had placed several submissions before the members of the UN CLCS, but none more important than the two concerning the Peanut Hole and the Lomonosov Ridge.

Referring to the CLCS positive vote for the Peanut Hole, Donskoy said: "This water area of the Sea of Okhotsk has many biological and natural resources, which have not [been] considered as the main income source of the country's economy and now we can consider and include it in our long-term plans." Donskoy said it would eventually drive "enormous opportunities and prospects for the Russian economy."

Just two weeks prior to the CLCS vote, Putin announced the construction of a "united system of naval bases for ships and next-generation submarines in the Arctic" to defend Russia's interests in the region. One week later, U.S. defense secretary Chuck Hagel warned of a "dangerous potential for conflict there." He further said that "the melting of gigantic ice caps presents possibilities for the opening of new sea-lanes and the exploration for natural resources, energy and commerce, also with the dangerous potential for conflict in the Arctic."

Putin Wants the Entire Monopoly Board

The Lomonosov Ridge and Peanut Hole are only the tip of the proverbial iceberg. In recent years, Arctic sea ice has reached its lowest level in recorded satellite history, which dates to 1979. Non-satellite observations made by sea and land travelers prior to the seventies indicate that the record-breaking low has not been seen since the Little Ice Age. The melt is self-perpetuating. As more ice melts, less heat is reflected, causing more ice to melt, and so on. Scientists call this the albedo effect and note that dry snow reflects around 80 percent of the sun's radiation, bare ice 65 percent, and open water only 5 percent. Each summer, more and more open water areas lead to faster ocean heating, resulting in less ice—and that ice is thinner and easier to melt the following year. "Less and thinner" has rolled downhill, and the current Arctic sea ice volume is now less than 20 percent of its 1980 level.

Alarmed by this fact, four scientists hailing from Russia, Norway, and the U.S. wrote a paper wherein they said, "The long-term outlook is disturbing. Our view is that a seasonally ice-free Arctic Ocean might be realized as early as 2030."

If these scientists are correct, the results may be catastrophic for global weather patterns but compelling for global transport companies. Formerly treacherous sea-lanes have become more traversable, offering the promise of far shorter routes and less expensive ocean transport. What's important here is not whether skeptics believe these changes are only temporary or believers think global demise is just around the corner. What may be of more immediate concern is what world leaders believe and what they are doing about those beliefs.

Shipping is critical to our world economy. Seaborne trade represents 90 percent of the world's total trade; transported items are mostly fossil fuels, natural gas, dry goods, raw materials, equipment, parts, and various other container-housed cargo. Trade between Europe and Asia is escalating in importance and frequency, creating high-seas bottlenecks through the Strait of Malacca and Suez Canal, increasing the risk of collisions and slower transport times. More time at sea translates to more cost, which translates to higher prices for goods.

Melting Arctic ice now allows shippers to shorten sea time by shipping goods through the Northern Sea Route (NSR), past Russia, or through the Northwest Passage, which winds around Canada. Icebergs and harsh weather prevented Captain Richard Chancellor from sailing all the way through the NSR in 1553, but more modern commercial ships have no such limitations.

Less than a decade ago, few ships traversed the NSR. By early 2013, twenty massive merchant ships were traversing the Arctic's "great circle route" each day, humping goods between Asia and North America along the 1,200-mile Aleutian chain. Hundreds of tankers were starting to haul goods between Asia and Europe while cutting their journey times and costs by 40 percent as compared to traveling through the Suez Canal. The Chinese did somersaults. They estimated that up to 15 percent of their trade could eventually go through the NSR and save them more than five hundred billion dollars per year.

In the summer of 2014, Mitsui O.S.K. Lines, Ltd. and China Shipping Development Co. Ltd., in Japan and China, respectively, announced the start of a regular service to carry Siberian natural gas across the Arctic Ocean to East Asia. The two companies now ship natural gas, by way of the Arctic NSR, from Russia's twenty-seven-billion-dollar Yamal LNG facility in Siberia, to harbors in Japan and China. In 2017, shipping through the NSR grew by an unprecedented 40 percent to more than ten million tons. According to NSR administration logs, on many days, more than a hundred vessels were navigating through those Arctic waters, conducting a total of 1,800 voyages from ninety-four countries. It's important to note that a vast majority of the ships were Russian.

By 2018, Russian gas company Novatek was shipping large quantities of LNG through the NSR, as it took only nineteen days instead of the usual thirty-five days through the Suez Canal. Buoyed by profits from these energy sales, Russia's investment possibilities have expanded, and Putin seems eager to own more Monopoly® properties and place more hotels on the game board. Russia owns a vast majority of the NSR's coastline and is uniquely positioned in the region, so anyone who wants to "roll logs down the river" must pay tariffs to Russia. Such fees reportedly pay for icebreaker assistance, safety patrols to thwart piracy, rescue efforts when needed, and resources to clean up any ecological spills that may occur.

Putin is continuing to build a series of military bases along the NSR and has beefed up Russia's warship presence and slated several new *Borei*-class ballistic missile and other attack submarines to patrol the area. A more open NSR could upend the naval balance in the Pacific. Russia's Atlantic and Pacific fleets may soon be able to reinforce each other with greater ease and speed, resolving the two-front problem that has plagued Moscow since 1905, when Japan destroyed two-thirds of the Russian fleet in the Tsushima Strait.

If the U.S. and Europe allow Putin to gain complete control of this route, Russia could start acting like a Chicago gangster, demanding higher fees for icebreaker escorts, whether needed or not. It could become a dirty cop, deciding who gets to save 40 percent on transport costs and who does not, perhaps depending upon who bids the highest. It could also try to block the U.S. from shipping oil and gas to Europe, to thwart competition and to maintain Russia's energy stronghold on EU countries.

Should any of these scenarios occur, how might the U.S. and its allies respond? Would they send submarines or ships to the Arctic to pry loose Putin's grip on the region? If so, how might Russia respond? Are we headed toward conflicts in the icy north, and if so, could they lead to war?

Two days before the nineteenth anniversary of the sinking of the *Kursk* in the Arctic, the Northern Fleet's warships once again conducted a show of strength in the Barents Sea. An area of focus included mock searches for snooping NATO submarines, including *Los Angeles*-class subs—like the *Memphis* and *Toledo*—and the newer *Virginia*-class attack submarines.

With the Arctic warming even more during the summer of 2019, the Russian military constructed new bases and upgraded older ones. Russian forces also tested a new surface-to-air Bastion missile system designed to take out large warships, including aircraft carriers. U.S. officials, of course, dispute Russia's claims over a vast majority of the NSR and have threatened to send warships and subs to the area to conduct a Freedom of Navigation Operation (FONOP). Secretary of the Navy, Richard Spencer, publicly stated that freedom of navigation must be applied to the region. General Curtis Scaparrotti, former supreme allied commander in Europe, testified before Congress and suggested that an Arctic FONOP should be directed toward Russia as a warning. In May 2019, Secretary of State Mike Pompeo echoed this sentiment by saying, "We are concerned about Russia's claim on the international waters of the North Sea Route."

Many geopolitical experts, however, believe that an Arctic FONOP is a bad idea. Such an action could spark a naval battle not seen since World War II. Putin has staunchly expressed his desire to dominate the NSR, and as evidenced by his actions in Ukraine, he will not be easily outmaneuvered. Directly challenging Russia with military action could lead to even more aggressive Russian moves and may also risk relations between the U.S. and Canada by setting a dangerous precedent about that nation's claim over the Northwest Passage.

Putin knows that one fifth of his nation's gross domestic product (GDP), and almost a third of his government's income, are derived directly from Arctic resources. Much of this comes from natural gas and oil fields along the Yamal Peninsula. By controlling the NSR, Russia now gains additional revenue by slapping NSR ships with exorbitant tariffs and tolls. NSR travelers must request permits, use Russian ice pilots, and make advanced payments before passing through. If transport ships violate any of these requirements, they can be fined, boarded and inspected, and have their cargo confiscated or destroyed. Even so, most travelers do not object to the charges given their 40 percent time and cost savings as compared to using other routes.

Should the U.S. conduct a FONOP to loosen Russia's grip, it could easily lead to a skirmish, and submarines might shoulder the brunt of any conflicts. Again, only a handful of U.S. subs can break through thicker ice, and given ICEX cutbacks, most crews are not well trained to operate in this icy region. Conversely, Russia's naval forces are highly prepared for a polar fight.

The Russians have dozens of subs and surface ships, along with numerous NSR shore facilities, to support their naval assets. The U.S. has almost no ice-hardened warships or Arctic infrastructure to sustain a war in this region. They have one bullet in a six-shooter compared to a fully-loaded AK-47. In fact, Russia is armed to the teeth along five NSR strangulation points. All these flow between Russian land masses or are within twelve-mile territorial claims. The Russians could easily deter or stop traffic in any of these chokepoints and cause economic upheaval.

To date, the U.S. has been powerless to stop Putin from militarizing and controlling much of the NSR, and a potential FONOP appears to be the only way to put up a geopolitical roadblock. However, to conduct such an operation, the U.S. Navy would need to turn to its allies, such as Norway, Finland, or Sweden, to borrow enough Arctic ships to make a show. These nations would need to risk losing the economic benefits derived from NSR shipping to join the U.S. in defying Russia, which they be will reluctant to do, especially considering UNCLOS Articles 21 and 234.

The Russians have pointed to UNCLOS to justify its actions. Article 21 says they can regulate territorial waters within the twelve-mile limit. Article 234 gives them the right to govern adjacent ice-covered waters, if in doing so, they seek to protect the environment. This is the case the Russians made to lock up resources in the Sea of Okhotsk. The problem with 234 is that it's vague and leaves much to interpretation. Russian Foreign Minister Sergei Lavrov stated publicly that Russian naval assets could threaten or sink any

U.S. ships, borrowed or not, that attempt a FONOP. When threatened in Ukraine, Putin did not back down from defending what he believed to be his backyard. The NSR is not only his front yard, it's a highly coveted and valuable part of his territory that he will protect with tooth and nail.

In late 2019, Putin validated his determination to control the Arctic by launching Russia's most extensive underwater naval exercise since the one that caused the demise of the *Kursk* in August 2000. At least ten submarines participated in the North Atlantic show of might, and according to Norwegian intelligence, eight were nuclear powered. The Russians tested several new weapons, including what may be the next generation of rocket torpedoes with capabilities that surpass the Shkval.

A key Russian objective in conducting these war games included the protection of strategic naval ports along the Barents Sea and maintaining dominance over the NSR. Unfortunately, after decades of atrophy, U.S. and NATO ASW forces are far behind the proverbial eight ball and have only recently started bolstering P-8 Poseidon patrol aircraft that operate out of Iceland. A year earlier, in response to increased Russian threats, the U.S. Navy reactivated the famous 2nd Fleet with a primary mission to keep a watchful eye, and possibly a thumb, on the new cold war brewing with Russia.

Clearly Russia is poised for a fight, especially in the Arctic, and Putin is setting the stage to use his large arsenal of weapons to protect his claims. NATO officials are likewise poised for imminent battles, with most officials expressing concerns that Russia is even more unpredictable now than during the Cold War. Unfortunately, as of yet, NATO has no means to defend against Russia's terrifying new doomsday weapon.

Status-6 Doomsday Weapon

Russia is launching several new classes of submarines to patrol the Arctic and other regions, the scariest of which is called the Project 09581 *Khabarovsk*— named after a Russian city. This new class of attack submarine is infused with a host of advanced technology that makes it formidable and nearly undetectable. The *Khabarovsk*, or "*Khabbie*," as some call it, is reported to be faster and quieter and to carry more firepower than almost any attack-class sub in the world. It has also been optimized for Arctic operations. Most experts are deeply concerned that once the *Khabbie* slips beneath the ice, NATO's attack submarines will be hard-pressed to find it, let alone stop it. But that's not what worries them the most.

The *Khabbie* has been built to do one thing: carry a new type of torpedo that is ten times larger than anything ever built. This Status-6 torpedo, codenamed *Kanyon* by NATO and dubbed *Poseidon* by the Russians, can hit speeds of more than eighty knots and devastate targets more than six thousand nautical miles away. The weapon achieves this speed by using a miniature nuclear propulsion system and an updated version of the super-cavitating technology used in the Shkval torpedo that destroyed the *Kursk*. NATO torpedoes, including the MK-48 ADCAP, can only hit about fifty-five knots on a good day. The *Khabbie* can fire a Status-6, quietly and unde-tected, from across the Pacific and take out San Diego. In fact, it can take out most of Southern California, because the Status-6 carries a one-hun-dred-megaton nuclear payload. For comparison, this terrifying weapon of mass destruction has 2,300 times more destructive power than the bombs dropped on Nagasaki and Hiroshima *combined*.

The *Khabbie* can carry up to six Status-6 torpedoes and shower a half-dozen seaports or ocean transit points with enough "dirty bomb" radioactive fallout to render them useless for centuries. Given that almost 90 percent of the world's oil trade goes through only six maritime chokepoints, such as the Strait of Hormuz or Malacca, one *Khabbie* on a mission from hell could cripple the global economy.

The ten-thousand-ton *Khabarovsk* looks a lot like a *Borei*class SSBN and is powered by an ultraquiet pump-jet propulsion system, making it hard to find or track. Submariners shiver at the thought of trying to chase one of these subs, especially if it's about to fire a Status-6 torpedo.

In my latest novel, *Status-6*, I depict this scenario in detail as the pro-tagonist, a former SEAL team-two operator turned NCIS agent, teams with a British female scientist to stop a rogue *Khabbie* controlled by infected artificial intelligence. The captain of a *Seawolf*-class sub faces his greatest challenge—and fear—as he tries to corner the Russian submarine. Spoiler alert! In my thriller, the good guys win the day. In the next chapter, we'll learn why that might not be the case in real life.

CHAPTER 16

PRELUDE TO WAR

*"We've seen a dramatic escalation in hostile actions
and confrontations by Russian and Chinese naval vessels and
aircraft over the past few years. All it takes is one accident
or incident to incite a costly skirmish or war."*

—PETER DALY, CEO,
U.S. Naval Institute, and vice admiral of the U.S. Navy (retired)

China Claims Near-Arctic Status

No part of the Arctic touches China, but that hasn't deterred the Chinese from referring to their country as a "near-Arctic" state. In March 2010, retired Chinese Navy Rear Admiral Yin Zhuo declared, "The Arctic belongs to all the people around the world as no nation has sovereignty over it." He went on to say that China "must also have a share of the region's resources." Strong words given that China now has submarine-launched nuclear missiles, has started sending attack subs to the Arctic, and owns the world's largest icebreaker.

Expressing concerns about potential Chinese aggression, NATO submarine flag officer Rear Admiral Robert Kamensky says, "Who has a very large appetite for new fisheries opening up in the Arctic? China. So what do they have up there in force right now? A lot of fishing vessels harvesting and taking their catches down to China. So there's a potential for conflict in that area over natural resources."

China is not one of the Arctic Eight nations, so it is not compelled to send minisubs to the North Pole to plant flags. The Chinese are, however, masterful negotiators, and China was granted a permanent observation seat on the Arctic Council. China can observe what goes on but has no voting rights. They petitioned the council for years to obtain that seat and have been an active player in the High North over the past decade.

China is now the world's largest economy, and although the country is responsible for more than 13 percent of the world's oil consumption, it has limited production capabilities. The Chinese see the Arctic as a potential way to level the playing field and become less dependent upon Russia, especially considering energy deals they recently inked with Putin.

Shorter sea routes are almost as important to China as Arctic oil, gas, and minerals. As mentioned earlier, the NSR shaves nearly 5,200 kilometers and nine days off the traditional European excursion, which typically requires going through the Suez Canal and Malacca Strait.

Chinese ambitions have encouraged the development of an NSR route guide, published in July 2014; it is a "comprehensive, practical, and authoritative" informational document to help Chinese cargo ships navigate the NSR to Europe. The guide comes complete with nautical charts, icebreaker hotlines, sailing suggestions, geographic data, climate information, and even the laws and regulations of foreign lands that crews will pass along the way, including Russia.

China's strategic report says the country's growing involvement in Arctic affairs is motivated in part by the desire to prevent a handful of Arctic Council nations from gobbling up all the riches. Also, the Chinese have long harbored supply-chain fears, given that a bulk of their supplies must travel through the narrow Malacca Strait, which connects the Indian Ocean to the Pacific. Recent posturing by China's Navy to exert control over various sea-lanes, coupled with massive increases in defense spending, have U.S. military leaders worried.

China has dramatically increased its weaponry, technology, and capabilities to do serious harm to its enemies. Most troubling are recent improvements in nuclear submarine warfare. U.S. Defense Department's annual reports on Chinese military developments have depicted a worrisome trend: the Chinese Navy is sailing ahead at a rapid pace, and the U.S. Navy will have difficulty keeping up.

According to one recent report, the People's Liberation Army Navy is "the region's largest Navy, with more than 300 surface combatants, submarines, amphibious ships, patrol craft and specialized types. It is also an increasingly modern and flexible force."

Beijing has been deploying its vast submarine fleet to "achieve maritime superiority within the first island chain (running from Japan to The Philippines), as well as to deter and counter any potential third-party intervention in a Taiwan conflict." By mid-2019, China had acquired six nuclear-attack submarines and fifty conventional subs. "The speed of growth of the submarine force has slowed and will likely grow to between 65 and 70 submarines by 2020," the report said.

In March 2019 congressional testimony, U.S. Navy admiral Philip Davidson said, "Potential adversary submarine activity has tripled from 2008 levels, which requires at least a corresponding increase on the part of the United States to maintain superiority. There are four hundred foreign submarines in the world, of which roughly seventy-five percent reside in the Indo-Pacific region. One-hundred and sixty of these submarines belong to China, Russia, and North Korea. While these three countries increase their capacity, the United States retires attack submarines faster than they are replaced."

In December 2016, the U.S. Navy needed sixty-six attack subs to maintain equity in the region. By early 2019, it had only fifty-one, and many of these were aging *Los Angeles*-class boats, like the *Memphis* and *Toledo*. Building a new *Virginia*-class SSN costs more than two billion dollars, and given tight budgets and the decommissioning of older subs, the U.S. Navy undersea fleet will likely shrink to just forty-two vessels by 2028.

With the NSR opening to more seagoing traffic, China has its eye set on using the route to transport more natural resources and goods to bolster its trade economy while lowering transport time and costs. It isn't yet aggressively trying to dominate the area, like Russia, but it's obviously placing a foot in the water—or perhaps an entire leg. That's why U.S. Pentagon officials issued a warning report in May 2019 suggesting an increase in attack-submarine patrols to act as nuclear-attack deterrents.

Meanwhile, U.S. Navy admirals are asking for more subs in the South China Sea to retaliate against increased Chinese aggression that could cause serious sea route disruptions.

Assassin's Mace

While the U.S. was embroiled in a war with Iraq, the Chinese acquired a newer version of the Shkval rocket torpedo from the Russians and reverse-engineered the supercavitating technology to design a new type of supersonic submarine. Fifteen years later, reports surfaced that this new rocket sub could jet from Shanghai to San Francisco—about six thousand miles—in less time than it takes to watch a movie. If true, this could be a serious game-changer should conflicts erupt over sea-lanes and sand islands. The Chinese have also created the Assassin's Mace Mach 10 missile, which can take out an entire U.S. aircraft carrier strike group in a matter of minutes.

It's no secret that Beijing has its heart set on owning large swaths of the South China Sea, and for good reason. The U.S. Energy Information Agency estimates that this area holds around 190 trillion cubic feet of natural gas and twenty-three billion barrels of oil worth almost ten trillion dollars. Given China's insatiable demand, it needs more resources. That's why the Chinese have built sand islands in remote locales like the Spratly Islands near Malaysia and the Philippines.

China's overt land grab has led to several confrontations and triggered the development of a DF-21D missile that could unseat the balance of power in the region. Dubbed the "carrier killer" by U.S. naval experts, it can strike targets as far as 1,242 miles away at Mach 10. That's like shooting a missile from New York City and hitting a ship-size target in Miami fewer than twelve minutes later. Current naval defenses have a tough time defending against Mach 5 missiles, let alone something twice that fast. The Chinese have already deployed DF-21D missiles in strategic sites all along the coastline near the South China Sea. These sites can easily hit targets near the Spratlys, as well as Guam, Malaysia, Taiwan, South Korea, Vietnam, and the Philippines.

While the U.S. is developing railgun and other technologies to ward off this threat, it is years away, and in the meantime, the ocean near the Spratlys is about to boil with potential conflicts.

China's Covert Ambitions

The Chinese People's Liberation Army Navy (PLAN) has been updated in the country's recent defense white paper, to include twenty-nine military procurement programs and 250 vessels. Much of the focus is on aircraft carriers and submarines.

China built its first aircraft carrier, the Type 001A, in Dalian and launched the ship in April 2017. The Type 002 and Type 003 represent next-generation designs, and construction of both started in Jiangnan in

February 2017 and December 2017, respectively. These new carriers will allow China to compete with the U.S. in the South China Sea by further tipping the balance in its favor.

Under the waves, China plans to launch four Type 094 *Jin*-class nuclear ballistic-missile submarines (SSBNs) that will each carry twelve JL-2 missiles that can hit the Hawaiian Islands from the South China Sea. Along with China's new "boomers," a dozen fast attack SSNs are planned, including five Type 095s that are expected to enter service in 2020. China now operates almost seventy submarines, a number that rivals both U.S. and Russian numbers. Many of these are diesel-powered, but several have or will soon have newer air-independent propulsion (AIP) systems that are quiet and allow these boats to stay silent and submerged for more than a week.

Like Putin, China's premier, Li Keqiang, is planting flags. China has brazenly informed the world it intends to own all or most of the ten trillion dollars' worth of energy reserves in the South China Sea. For now, the Chinese have used only arm wrestling and elbowing to warn the U.S. and other nations to steer clear of their sand islands. What will happen as tensions escalate? Will China use its new aircraft carriers, advanced submarines, and Assassin's Mace missile systems to start punching noses? If so, how will the U.S. and its allies respond?

Are we headed toward skirmishes in this region, and if so, will they send us headlong toward another world war?

North Korean Threats

Are North Korean submarines, armed with nuclear torpedoes, preparing to attack U.S. western seaports? Years ago, U.S. government and military officials were focused exclusively on land-based ballistic missiles, and offered assurances to the world that North Korea was not yet capable of accurately hitting Western targets. In more recent years, these same sources have been strangely silent about the ability of the Korean People's Navy (KPN) to arm submarines with nuclear torpedoes or ballistic missiles.

I published an article in 2018 about the threat of North Korea arming *Sinpo*-class submarines with nuclear missiles, and it seems my warning has come true. On January 6, 2020, U.S. satellites snapped SAR imagery at the Mayang-Do naval base of a *Sinpo*-class submarine equipped with ballistic missiles. Do these missiles contain nuclear warheads? If so, and should the U.S. become embroiled in a distracted conflict with Iran, will Kim Jong-un be motivated to launch these weapons of mass destruction against the U.S.?

In 2013, Russia's Ministry of Defense issued an Urgent Action bulletin to all Strategic Missile Forces to prepare for a potential nuclear strike, but not from land-based launchers. Intelligence reports confirm that on February 12, KPN conducted an underground nuclear test, its third within seven years. Shortly thereafter, Russian defense analysts raised concerns about several highly suspicious transfers of unknown materials from the Punggye-ri nuclear test facility, located in Mantapsan, about a mile west of the Hwasong concentration camp, where North Korea disposes of its political prisoners. The unknown material was believed to be highly enriched uranium, or plutonium-239, derived from a 5 MWe nuclear reactor. The material was transferred to the heavily protected submarine base located on the east coast island of Mayang Do. This base is where the KPN parks its ten *Yono*-class miniature submarines.

While many Americans believe the U.S. military can easily vanquish the KPN, this may now fall into the category of wishful thinking. North Korea's military is one of the largest in the world, with the ability to deploy almost one million active, reserve, and paramilitary personnel. The KPN has 5,400 tanks, and the Democratic People's Republic of Korea (DPRK) can scramble up more than eight hundred combat aircraft. With more than 780 vessels, the North Korean Navy is now the world's third largest. It has almost eighty submarines, including twenty-two Chinese-made *Romeo*-class (1,800 tons), forty *Sang-O*-class (300 tons), four former Soviet *Whiskey*-class, and ten *Yono*-class midget subs (130 tons).

A *Yono*-class submarine has been blamed for the torpedo attack on March 26, 2010, that sank the Republic of Korea Ship (ROKS) *Cheonan*, a South Korean *Pohang*-class corvette. Forty-six sailors lost their lives in the attack. Evidence recovered at the site points to a CHT-02D torpedo. Experts believe the North Koreans may have more recently outfitted several of these torpedoes with nuclear warheads and loaded them into five or more *Yono* subs. While these minisubs have a range of only five hundred nautical miles and are not typically used for long-range missions, it is possible that the North Koreans have created several underwater refueling areas scattered across the Pacific Ocean. They may also be using fuel-laden vessels disguised as fishing trawlers. Lastly, the *Yono* subs may be decoys for the larger *Sang-O*-class subs, which have a range of 1,500 nautical miles.

Yono, *Sang-O*, and *Romeo* subs run on diesel-electric power. They can operate on batteries for around two or three days, and then must surface or snorkel and use a diesel engine to charge the batteries and recirculate the air. When running on battery power, they are nearly silent and very difficult to find by ASW forces. Even the sophisticated sonar used by the U.S. Navy's most advanced *Virginia*-class submarines has a hard time locating these subs. Furthermore, the Navy has deemphasized ASW technologies and training since the Cold War, and many officials lament that recent budget cuts have severely crippled the Navy's ASW capabilities.

Validation of this fact may have occurred on April 5, 2013. The Urgent Action bulletin issued that day warned that up to five *Yono* subs had evaded U.S. and South Korean ASW forces and could not be located. Russian military analysts feared that *Yono* or *Sang-O* subs may have been headed toward South Korea's port of Busan or Japan's port of Yokohama, and perhaps a few were using hidden refueling points to reach the West Coast of the United States. If so, they may have been targeting the shipping ports in Seattle and in the California cities of Oakland and Long Beach.

A day before the Urgent Action bulletin was released, North Korea's state news agency broadcasted a stern warning from Pyongyang: "Now that the U.S. is set to light a fuse for a nuclear war, [our] revolutionary armed forces...will exercise the right to a preemptive nuclear attack to destroy the strongholds of the aggressors."

In my book *Red November,* I document how four Soviet *Foxtrot* submarines successfully evaded U.S. forces during the Cuban Missile Crisis. All four were carrying nuclear torpedoes, and all came within moments of firing on the U.S. fleet, which would have triggered World War III. If only one North Korean submarine reaches a U.S. or allied shipping port and explodes just one nuclear-tipped torpedo, the entire world could be plunged into an economic nightmare.

Iran's Revenge

Iran's top general was executed in a U.S. air strike in Iraq on January 3, 2020. U.S. Secretary of State Mike Pompeo said the strike was lawful and called for as General Qasem Soleimani was likely plotting an imminent attack against the U.S. As expected, Iran's supreme leader, Ayatollah Ali Khamenei, threatened "severe retaliation." Geopolitical experts warned against anything from terrorist strikes to naval battles in the Persian Gulf. Most have scoffed at Iran's ability to win such battles, but few are aware of Iran's secret weapon.

Iran's military has been planning for a fight in the Persian Gulf for decades, as it's aware of the strategic importance of the Strait of Hormuz. Many transport ships use these waters frequently to deliver natural resources and goods to a hungry world. Iran now has twenty-one homegrown *Ghad-ir*-class minisubmarines based on the North Korean *Yono*-class design. These 120-ton vessels can hit about eleven knots submerged, and they carry two 533-millimeter torpedoes. Shallow littoral waters favor diesel-powered subs, as they are hard to detect due to refractions and interference from crashing surf and jagged rocks. Complementing the *Ghadir* subs, Iran also has three larger and more formidable Russian *Kilo*-class diesel-electric subs. These are typically deployed in the Indian Ocean.

In recent years, Iran also built its own *Fateh*-class submarines, which use more modern and quiet air-independent propulsion systems; these allow them to stay deep for over a week without needing to recharge batteries. These subs are around 150 feet in length and displace about six hundred tons submerged. They can dive to around six hundred feet deep, have four torpedo tubes in the bow, and carry six to eight torpedoes. Their top speed is about twenty-three knots submerged.

The Fars News Agency claims that the *Fateh*-class subs can remain away from port for five weeks and venture up to 3,100 miles from home—allowing them to patrol the Arabian Sea. To bolster the fleet even more, Tehran is planning to build two *Besat*- or *Qaem*-class submarines in a similar weight class to the *Fateh*'s. Of greater concern, however, is Iran's new weapon, designed after reverse-engineering a Russian Shkval rocket torpedo.

Iran's new Hoot ("Whale") supercavitating torpedo, in similar fashion to the Shkval, can hit speeds up to two hundred knots underwater—again, almost four times the speed of a MK-48 ADCAP. The Hoot also uses rocket exhaust heat to vaporize water in front of the torpedo and create a gas bubble around the nose to reduce drag resistance. Iranian television broadcasted the first Hoot tests in 2006, and the weapon completed sea trials in May 2017. Experts believe it is now in service and mounted aboard Iran's latest submarines. Should tensions escalate in the Persian Gulf, how many U.S. submarines will be destroyed by Iranian Hoot (Shkval) rocket torpedoes?

As noted earlier, almost 90 percent of everything we consume gets to our shores by way of ships. Transport vessels must traverse a half dozen choke points, including the Strait of Hormuz, to reach their destinations. In June 2019, the U.S. Navy's Fifth Fleet, stationed in Bahrain, received two distress calls from vessels in the Gulf of Oman. Both ships were on fire and sinking from attacks perpetrated by Iran. Not long after U.S. National Security Adviser John Bolton threatened retaliation, four oil tankers were damaged by mines placed by Iranian divers. These attacks escalated tensions between the U.S. and Iran that eventually led to the assassination of General Soleimani and propelled both countries toward the brink of war.

Iranian navy divers are adept at placing mines, and the U.S. Navy's geriatric minesweeping force in the Persian Gulf consists of only four 1980s-vintage *Avenger*-class ships that are now obsolete and unreliable. Imagine a scenario wherein several transport ships are destroyed by Iranian mines, disrupting the flow of oil and other goods. The minesweeper USS *Devastator* is tasked with clearing the mines and is escorted by the USS *Abraham Lincoln* carrier group. The Iranians anticipate this move and set a trap.

While we'd all like to believe the deal cut with Iran limited their nuclear weapon production capability, but military experts know better. If a *Fateh*-class submarine fired one nuclear-tipped Hoot rocket torpedo, given its 200-knot speed, U.S. Navy ASW forces might have a low chance of stopping the weapon before it evaporated a dozen U.S. warships. Should this happen, it would obviously trigger a war with Iran and cause a massive disruption of seaborne trade through the Strait of Hormuz. And that scenario could have a serious impact on the U.S. economy and our livelihoods.

In early 2000, U.S. intelligence sources feared what might happen if Russian Shkval torpedoes—which destroyed the *Kursk*—were sold to China, Iran, North Korea, or other countries with aggressive regimes. That's why various assets, like Edmond Pope, were desperately trying to get their hands on the plans for this weapon. That's also why the NSA and NSG were highly motivated to have two U.S. submarines risk everything to gain close-up information on this formidable weapon. And that's why the sinking of the *Kursk* may go down as a pivotal historical event that catapulted the world toward self-annihilation.

CHAPTER 17

CONCLUSION

*"In the Asia-Pacific region, tensions over the South China Sea have
increased, with relations between the United States and China
insufficient to re-establish a stable security situation."*

—DOOMSDAY CLOCK SCIENTISTS

The Petrodollar War

The U.S. and NATO countries are at war with Russia and China, and have
been for decades. The Cold War started in 1946 but an economic war began
when President Nixon shifted the U.S. off the gold standard on August 15,
1971. Nixon's actions turned George Washington's face into the symbol of
the world's reserve currency.

The good news? Dollars were no longer tied to gold. The bad? They were
no longer tied to anything, so the U.S. and most other governments could
create money out of thin air. They just printed it. Money really did grow on
trees, or at least came from them. Inflation ran rampant, and the purchas-
ing power of the dollar plunged. In fact, it has declined almost 80 percent
since the early seventies.

To address this problem, Nixon invented the petrodollar. Instead of gold,
black oil backed green dollars. Nixon flew Secretary of State Henry Kissinger
to Saudi Arabia, where Kissinger cut a deal with the ruling House of Saud.
The U.S. swore to protect the Saudi oil fields with military might, and even

sell Saudi Arabia some weapons along the way. Old ones, of course. Protection from Israel and Iran was assured. In exchange, Kissinger asked for two things: one, all oil sales would be made exclusively using U.S. dollars. Two, oil profits made by the Saudis would be invested in U.S. Treasuries.

At the time, Saudi Arabia was a proverbial dichotomy. Most of the country was dirt poor, the infrastructure was dismal, its neighbors wanted to do it harm, and capitalizing on all that "black gold" required substantial investment. To the Saudis, the U.S. offer seemed like a nice deal. They signed up in 1974, and a year later the rest of the Organization of Petroleum Exporting Countries (OPEC) tagged along.

Decades of oil prosperity followed and kept the U.S. at the top of the economic ladder. When the Soviet Union bit the dust in 1991, the resurrection of Russia came at a snail's pace. Then Putin entered stage right. He immediately saw the potential for his country to dominate world energy markets. Due to his vision and leadership, oil and gas now account for 68 percent of Russia's exports. The Russians own almost 20 percent of the world's gas sales and around 12 percent of the oil market. As noted earlier, Putin wants more and will apparently stop at nothing to get it.

Recall that Saudi Arabia, at the behest of Nixon, agreed to stash large chunks of its oil profits in foreign reserves—primarily in the U.S., and they are backed by the U.S. dollar. We're talking about three-quarters of a trillion U.S. dollars. No doubt someone in Washington leveraged this fact to convince King Abdulaziz, when he was alive, to temporarily create an oil glut to punish Putin for Ukraine. The Saudis voiced no objections, as the glut also made it harder for Iran to move forward on its nuclear weapons program.

In October 2014, Venezuelan President Nicolás Maduro said, "What is the reason for the United States and some U.S. allies wanting to drive down the price of oil? To harm Russia."

The oil strategy employed by the U.S. and OPEC had a dramatic effect on Russia. When the price of oil tanked, one of Russia's primary sources of income fell off a cliff. Coupled with the economic sanctions, things got bad in Russia and investors dumped rubles and sent the Russian economy into a tailspin.

Moscow yanked the stick upward to pull out of the nosedive, but the ruble still plunged more than 25 percent, down to a new low of eighty rubles per U.S. dollar by December 2014. In response, Russia's central bank raised interest rates to 17 percent, the largest single-day increase since the 1998 recession. Inflation surged in Russia to a troubling 10 percent while the ruble plummeted to almost half its previous value during the latter six months of 2014. Russia relies on oil revenue to fund more than half its state spending and, like most OPEC countries, needs oil prices to hover at around one hundred dollars per barrel to maintain a stable budget.

Furious, Putin wagged a finger at the U.S. while informing the world that Russia had plenty of reserves and could weather any storm, and warned of serious retribution if the screws were turned any tighter.

The Economic Tornado

The screws have been turned tighter, and Putin needs three properties on the Monopoly board to assure future income: the Lomonosov Ridge, the Peanut Hole, and the NSR. The first two all but guarantee trillions of tons of oil and gas, and the latter ensures he controls the real estate needed to ship his spoils while charging others for the same privilege. Once these properties are firmly in place, which is imminent, he can use them to unwind the petrodollar standard. This move may one day prove to be far more devastating to human life in the U.S. and EU than any terrorist act we can imagine.

In late 2010, Putin and Chinese premier Wen Jiabao agreed to settle trades in rubles and renminbi (yuan) for many of their transactions. This agreement, the first of its kind, was a direct assault on the petrodollar and on the U.S. as the world's economic leader. If Russia and China win the pet-rodollar war, the U.S. economy will tank, perhaps even overnight.

What will happen to the U.S. if Russia and China shift the world away from the petrodollar? The best-case scenario is a slow fade into oblivion, but Putin will probably push for a more rapid unwinding, in which case the breakup will happen within a few short years. In the worst-case scenario, interest rates will skyrocket. The rate on the thirty-year Treasury bond could once again hit 15 percent, which is where it was in the 1970s. Existing bond prices could be chopped by more than half.

The Federal Reserve will have little choice but to cut down more trees and print more worthless dollars to buy the bonds sold by foreigners, but the eventual effect will be a further devaluation of the dollar. If we thought the U.S. bank meltdown in 2008 was bad, we'll long for those days again when interest rates cause a huge gap between prior loan rates and current loan rates so wide that it pushes many banks toward insolvency.

The Fed will print even more money. Interest rates will climb higher, maybe up to 20 percent. Main Street America and small businesses will pay through the nose for loans to stay afloat, if they're lucky enough to get approval. Then the dominoes in financial markets will topple. Banks, hedge funds, stock brokerages, insurance companies, and others will see their derivative investments unravel. Simply put, all these institutions have investment values based on other investments that derive their value from various assets. As those assets, such as real estate, rapidly lose their value, everything "on top" will lose its value. Remember when gas prices went through the roof? If you owned a gas-guzzling car, you couldn't sell it to your brother for more than a few bucks. That's what will happen to the assets owned by these firms.

When that occurs, the fallout will cause massive panic attacks and perhaps even suicides. Stockbrokers may once again jump from buildings like they did in 1932. At that point, whoever is unlucky enough to be the president will be forced to require the U.S. to default on its foreign debt. That means countries like China will stop getting interest payments. When the Chinese start blockading sea-lanes with their new and formidable warships to force the U.S. to pay, things will get ugly fast.

The president's advisors will "suggest" that it's time for a measure of last resort: the U.S. government must raid the savings accounts of almost every American. I say "almost" because we know that congresspersons, senators, union bosses, and campaign donors will remain untouched. Those registered with the political party opposed to the president will probably be first in line. If you think this is impossible because it's illegal, you have a short memory span. Recall that the IRS went after conservatives with unbridled passion prior to the 2012 election. Your IRA, 401(k), or whatever you have will be cleaned out to pay for your government's inability to win an economic war, and it won't be the government's fault. It will be your fault. After all, you elected the president and legislators. If you failed to consider whether the persons you elected could compete against the likes of Putin, you have only yourself to blame.

You might be hopeful that your favorite political candidate will tip the scales in your favor for immigration reform, the environment, gay rights, education, medical insurance, retirement benefits, gun control, social security, or whatever you're passionate about. These issues may be important and worthy of attention, but pale in comparison to the most important concern: the global economic war. If the next president and his or her team are clueless about global business and foreign affairs or are too weak to stand strong against Putin and other world leaders, they will be eaten for lunch and the U.S. and European economies will pay the price.

When the above proverbial stuff hits the fan after Putin destroys the petrodollar, middle-class America will be in shock. A trip to Costco today is enjoyable for most of us, but if Putin has his way, it could become a nightmare. Commodities like milk, eggs, flour, hamburger meat, fruit, vegetables, snacks, and even coffee will become luxury items. Starbucks, Taco Bell, and McDonald's will see massive layoffs as people stay home and reuse coffee grounds and eat the cheapest noodles they can find. Pink slips and foreclosure notices will be commonplace.

The hardest hit will be the ones who have incomes tied to unions and the government. Government employees, teachers, auto workers, electricians, and scores of others will be laid off and forced into soup kitchens as organizations and whole cities file for bankruptcy. Blue-collar workers will be on the street first, but even bellwether technology companies will start axing engineers as their customers freeze spending. Then the riots and looting will start.

People living in gated communities will soon realize that gates are worthless against starving mobs with guns. Martial law will be enforced, with the National Guard patrolling neighborhoods in trucks and even tanks. As the U.S. continues to default on its loans to foreign nations, those countries will retaliate with sanctions, blockades, and eventually even shots fired. The two nations most likely to start shooting to force payments are China and Russia. They have already become economically connected at the hip and will be motivated to assist each other in the collection of debts. After all, if China can't pay Russia four hundred billion dollars for the gas it recently bought because the U.S. isn't paying China, how motivated will Putin be to fire warning shots across the bow of American tankers?

Perhaps the above scenario seems improbable or even impossible to most of us. How could our government and others allow such a thing to happen? How could it possibly get that bad? It can't, right?

That's what they said in 1932.

As discussed in the previous several chapters, "they" are already allowing it to happen by making bad chess moves. Again, it is not up to "them" to avoid a future filled with poverty; it is up to us. If we continue to elect leaders who do not know how to lead, and who do not have the strength, business acumen, chess-playing skills, and courage to stand up to foreign bullies, we will sow what we reap. And what we reap will be an economic war followed by a fighting war—most likely over Arctic resources—that may leave the U.S. and its European allies devastated and defeated unless immediate actions are taken to avoid such an outcome.

Two Minutes to Midnight

According to the experts at the Bulletin of the Atomic Scientists in Washington, D.C., it's now only two minutes to midnight. The Bulletin has maintained the infamous Doomsday Clock since 1947, which metaphorically evaluates how close the world has ticked toward self-annihilation. Whether or how much the clock's minute hand moves each year is decided by the organization's Science and Security Board, which includes a dozen Nobel laureates. In 2018, the organization published a report detailing why it believed the world had only two more minutes to live. The report said:

> The greatest risks last year arose in the nuclear realm. North Korea's nuclear weapons program made remarkable progress in 2017, increasing risks to North Korea itself, other countries in the region, and the United States. Hyperbolic rhetoric and provocative actions by both sides have increased the possibility of nuclear war by accident or miscalculation.
>
> But the dangers brewing on the Korean Peninsula were not the only nuclear risks evident in 2017: The United States and Russia remained at odds, continuing military exercises along the borders of NATO, undermining the Intermediate-Range Nuclear Forces Treaty (INF), upgrading their nuclear arsenals, and eschewing arms control negotiations.

The group published a similar report in 2019, stating that the clock had not moved from two minutes due to continued threats from nuclear weapons and world instability.

Small pebbles dropped into the ocean of world history have created ripples that turned into tsunamis. During the World War II battle of Midway in the Pacific Ocean, the Japanese fleet could not locate the U.S. aircraft carriers. The launch of two Japanese scout planes were delayed by catapult system malfunctions. The one plane that did become airborne found the U.S. ships, but could not warn the Japanese fleet due to a broken radio. These minor delays created a chain reaction that eventually led to the loss of four Japanese carriers and helped turn the tide of the war in the Pacific.

Decades later, Vladimir Putin might not have been elected in March 2000 if not for the *Kursk's* mission success six months earlier. If not for the tragic loss of the *Kursk* in August 2000, wresting control of oil and gas wealth from the oligarchs might have been far more difficult for Putin, if not impossible. Without oil and gas profits, Putin could not have rebuilt

Russia's military and reignited a dangerous new cold war. His ability to wage an economic or shooting war would have been mitigated substantially.

If the most terrifying incident in submarine naval history had never occurred, the world might have more than two minutes left to live.

NOTES AND SOURCES

Books, articles, references, and interviews with numerous individuals listed below were used as validating and supporting information for this book. Special thanks to Ramsey Flynn, author of *Cry From The Deep*—an excellent book about the *Kursk* incident—for his input, information, and references. Those interested in personal stories about the *Kursk's* crew and their families will find this book remarkable.

Special thanks also to Mark Medish, former advisor to President Bill Clinton as the National Security Council senior director for Russian Affairs, for his recollection of events. Also, to Igor Kurdin, former Russian submarine captain first rank and currently the president of the International Submarine Association branch in Saint Petersburg for his technical assistance. Finally, to my fellow submariners who served aboard the USS *Memphis* and *Toledo*. While none divulged any classified or sensitive information, their honest input helped illuminate the dark corners of the past. A few who have served in the silent service will take exception to the revelation of any information pertaining to submarine operations, but the utmost care was taken to ensure accuracy without sacrificing secrecy. After two decades of agony, the families of those on eternal patrol deserve at least some measure of closure.

Kursk Incident/Salvage/Interviews/Accounts

Aleksin, Retired Rear Admiral Valery Ivanovich, former chief navigator of Navy who published pro-collision article in *Nezavisimaya Gazeta,* Sept 12, 2000.

Archipchenko, Igor, communications operator who was fired for disclosing sub-surface *Kursk* communications. Appeared in NTV documentary.

Argelander, Konstantin, Russian diver involved in *Kursk* rescue attempt.

Arsenjev, Anatoly, Russian diver involved in *Kursk* rescue attempt.

Baranets, Victor, military observer for *Komsomolskaya Pravda*

Baranov, Igor Leonidovitch, *Kursk's* chief designer at Rubin.

Borisov, Capt. Tengiz Nikolaevich, former head of Russian government committee on underwater rescue in mid-90s, worked on *Komsomolets* issues.

Boyarkin, Vice Admiral Yuri, Chief of the Combat Training Directorate of the Russian Northern Fleet and executed dismissal orders from Putin.

Bressel, Alexei, a surviving *Kursk* crew member who was on leave, transferred to the crew of the *Voronezh*.

Buglak, Alexey, Assistant Commander of the Russian flotilla.

Burtsev, Vice Adm Oleg, submarine flotilla commander. Headed first Krosnoznamennaya Flotilla. Later fired by Putin.

Cherkashin, Nikolay Andreyevich, writer at *Rossiskaya Gazeta*.

Chernavin, Vladimir, Former Russian military Commander-in-Chief, became a submarine club leader.

Dobroskotchenko, Vice Admiral Vladimir, assistant to the Northern Fleet Commander who told widow Khalima Aryapova that her husband Rashid authored the second note.

Dygalo, Capt 1st Igor, Russian naval spokesperson.

Ezhov, Sergey N, former Commander of the *Kursk's* second crew.

Felgenhauer, Pavel, Moscow-based defense analyst who wrote authoritatively about the technical and socio-political aspects of the *Kursk* disaster.

Filatov, Rear Admiral Valery, Russian submarine Flotilla Chief of Staff, later fired by Putin.

Geletin, Capt. Vladimir, coordinator of rescue effort. His 25-year-old son, Lt. Boris Geletin, was on board the *Kursk*. Held a press conference Wed, September 20, published on September 23, in which he blamed the disaster on the Russian economy and crumbling military.

Gizatulin, Renat S, Russian *Regalia* diver from 40th Research Institute in St. Petersburg, involved in *Kursk* salvage operation, who filmed the discovery and reading of Koleshnikov's note.

Gusev, Yuri V, Russian *Regalia* diver involved in *Kursk* salvage operation.

Ilchenko, A.G., Russian *Regalia* diver involved in *Kursk* salvage operation.

Ivanov, Sergei, Putin's Security Council Secretary, received Berger's intel at Waldorf Hotel on Sept. 12, 2000.

Karakhanov, Capt. 1st Ruben, Northern Fleet technical base commander, later fired by Putin.

Kasatanov, Capt Vladimir, Senior officer on *Peter the Great* who ordered the crew at 0300 to look for rescue buoys. They were promised free vacations if they found a buoy.

Khandobin, Rear Adm Vladimir, Chief of the Northern Fleet Directorate, carried out dismissal orders for Putin.

Khondotov, Vladimir Alexandrovich, former head of Russian torpedo control.

Khramov, Anatoly, Russian diver involved in rescue mission.

Kolkutin, Victor, medical examiner involved in *Kursk* forensics.

Koloskov, Vladimir, aboard *Regalia* during body recovery.

Kozevatov, Lt. Col. Alexander, Commander of Russian Northern Fleet ASW airborne unit who flew one of the two IL-38 craft from the Sev-1 Airfield, carrying torpedoes and sonar buoys, tracked by Norwegian forces.

Kuroyedov, Admiral Vladimir, Commander-in-Chief of the Russian Navy.

Kuteinikov, Anatoly Valeryevich, Designer General and Director of Malachite, which designs Russian torpedo systems.

Kuznetsov, Rear Adm Mikhail, Submarine Division Commander, later fired by Putin.

Makarchuk, Nikolai, deputy to Admiral Verich.

Mikhailov, V.V., Russian *Regalia* diver, involved in salvage operation.

Mikheyev, Vice Admiral Nikolai, head of the Main Commandment, naval training; executed dismissal orders from Putin.

Motsak, Mikhail, Russian Northern Fleet chief of staff.

Navrotsky, Vladimir, spokesman for Russian Navy's northern fleet.

Nikonov, Sergei V., Chief Surgeon for Russian naval divers.

Novikov, D.V., Russian *Regalia* diver.

Ovcharenko, Capt 1st Sergey: Russian naval officer aboard *Peter the Great* who told newspaper *Zhizn* on Aug 31 that the ship had fired Vodopad rockets at 1130 and saw an explosion and worried they'd sunk an American sub.

Popov, Adm. Vyacheslav, Russian Navy's Northern Fleet Commander.

Semizarov, D.M., Russian diver involved in salvage operation.

Sergeyev, Igòr, Russian Defense Minister who called and notified Putin in Sochi at 7 a.m. on Sunday regarding loss of *Kursk*.

Shmygin, Sergei, Russian diver involved in salvage operation.

Sidorov, Ivan: Commander of Russian submarine *Veronezh*.

Skorgen, Rear Adm, head of Norway's rescue effort.

Smirnov, Capt. 1st Victor Andreyovich, head of diving training and salvage department in St. Petersburg.

Spassky, Igor, head of Rubin Design Bureau that built the *Kursk*.

Sukhachyov, Yuri Aleksandrovitch, head of Emergency, Diving, and Deep-Sea Works Institute No. 40 in Lomonosov, Russia.

Teslenko, Capt, 1st Alexander, head of Northern Fleet's rescue service.
Timashkov, Colonel Sergey, former military liaison officer at Russian mission to NATO who liaised on *Kursk*.
Tomko, Vice Adm Yegor, former Commander of Russian Northern Fleet nuclear submarine division.
Ustinov, Vladimir, prosecutor general, former head of the *Kursk* criminal case.
Velichko, Capt. Vasily, Russian diver involved in rescue attempt.
Verich, Rear Adm. Gennady, Chief of Russian Navy Search-and-Rescue Directorate.

Technical / Content Consultants

Ball, Garry, *Seaway Eagle* Dive Supervisor
Dinessen, Paal, *Seaway Eagle* Diver
Greenawald, Kenneth, STS1 (SS), technical consultant
Kreuzberger, Charles, LT, Operations Officer, U.S. Navy Undersea Rescue Command (URC)
Lehman, John, USN (ret), technical consultant
Martin, Ramsey, Stolt Submarine and Salvage Expert
Scott, Tony, *Seaway Eagle* Diver

USS *Memphis* Crew Consultants

Chin, Michael, CDR (SS)
Ferretta, Joseph, NC1(SS)
Smith, Del E, MM1(SS)
Kunz, Thomas R, YNC (SS)
Chaparro, Oscar, (SS)

USS *Toledo* Crew Consultants

Atkinson, Al, CMDCM (SS)
Freyer, Scott, TMC (SS)
Grace, Todd M, TM2 (SS)
Montafia, Stephen, EMC (SS)
Moore, Patrick W, FTC (SS)
Nahs, Alan, CSC (SS)

Book References

Anderson, Alun. 2009. *After The Ice*. Smithsonian; 1 edition.

Anderson, William R. 2008. *The Ice Diaries*. Thomas Nelson Inc.

Bamford, James. 2001. *Body of Secrets*. DoubleDay.

Byers, Michael. 2010. *Who Owns The Arctic*. Douglas & McIntyre; First edition.

Burleson, Clyde. 2002. *Kursk Down*. Grand Central Publishing.

Emmerson, Charles. 2011. *The Future History of the Arctic*. Vintage Books USA.

Fairhall, David. 2011. *Cold Front*. Counterpoint.

Feifer, Gregory. 2014. *Russians*. Twelve.

Fishman, Ted C. 2005. *China Inc*. Scribner; 1st edition.

Flynn, Ramsey. 2004. *Cry From The Deep*. HarperCollins.

Goldman, Marshall E. 2008. *Petrostate*. Oxford University Press; 1 edition.

Howard, Roger. 2010. *The Arctic Gold Rush*. Continuum; 1 edition.

Katusa, Marin. 2014. *The Colder War*. Wiley; 1 edition.

Ladd, Adrian. 2009. *Go Get A Woolly Hat*. AuthorHouse.

Leary, William M. 1999. *Under Ice*. Texas A&M University Press; 1st edition.

McClaren, Alfred R. 2008. *Unknown Waters*. University Alabama Press; First edition.

Moore, Robert. 2007. *A Time To Die*. Crown.

Pope, Edmond D and Shachtman, Tom. 2001. *Torpedoed*. Little, Brown and Company.

Reed, W. Craig. 2011. *Red November*. William Morrow Paperbacks; Reprint edition.

Rickards, James. 2011. *Currency Wars*. Gildan Media, LLC.

Riker, H. Jay. 2009. *The Silent Service, Los Angeles Class*. HarperCollins.

Shirk, Susan L. 2007. *China Fragile Superpower*. Oxford University Press.

Truscott, Peter. 2003. *Kursk*. Simon & Schuster.

Websites Accessed

https://www.theguardian.com/commentisfree/cifamerica/2011/jun/08/dick-cheney-halliburton-supreme-court

https://www.thedrive.com/the-war-zone/30728/russia-sends-ten-subs-in-to-north-atlantic-in-drill-unprecedented-in-size-since-cold-war

https://en.wikipedia.org/wiki/Piper_Alpha

https://www.shephardmedia.com/news/imps-news/analysis-china-seeks
-dominate-seas/

https://nationalinterest.org/blog/buzz/dead-submarines-5-worst-sub
-disasters-all-time-72486

https://www.parttarget.com/Naval-Sea-Systems-Command_nsn-parts_
5599392-1_585-6404865.html

https://www.parttarget.com/3040-01-497-5152_3040014975152_566-
7067171.html/-B3402650-8FBB-4BF0-A6D3-9716AE6B628D

https://permalink.lanl.gov/object/tr?what=info:lanl-repo/lareport/
LA-UR-00-4261

https://www.nytimes.com/2000/12/15/world/american-jailed-as-spy-in-
moscow-is-freed-on-putin-s-orders-us-welcomes-gesture.html

https://nationalinterest.org/blog/buzz/russia-wants-four-submarines-
armed-nuclear-warhead-drones-can-cause-tsunamis-73606

https://nationalinterest.org/blog/buzz/here-chinas-plan-nuclear
-war-against-america-73646

https://www.cbsnews.com/news/us-diver-helps-in-kursk-rescue/

https://blackopspartners.com/chinas-secret-plan-topple-us-worlds-super-
power/

https://nationalinterest.org/blog/buzz/russia-wants-four-submarines-
armed-nuclear-warhead-drones-can-cause-tsunamis-73606

https://www.maritime-executive.com/editorials/us-china-tensions
-unmanned-military-craft-raise-risk-of-war

https://www.shephardmedia.com/news/imps-news/analysis-china
-seeks-dominate-seas/

https://www.washingtonpost.com/graphics/2018/world/arctic-cli-
mate-change-military-russia-china/?utm_term=.d9c82839f0e6

https://nationalinterest.org/blog/buzz/how-russia-getting-ready-war
-arctic-37667

https://www.maritime-executive.com/editorials/has-russia-already
-won-the-scramble-for-the-arctic

https://www.rt.com/news/un-okhotsk-enclave-russia-804/

https://www.usni.org/magazines/proceedings/2019/july/russias-activities
-arctic-cannot-go-unchecked-either?utm_source=U.S.+Naval+
Institute&utm_campaign=43e3613155-Proceedings_This_Week_
2019_7_25&utm_medium=email&utm_term=0_adee2c2162-
43e3613155-232343681&mc_cid=43e3613155&mc_eid=d52d3d1c15

https://www.washingtonexaminer.com/policy/defense-national-security/
northcom-commander-warns-the-arctic-is-an-avenue-of-approach-
for-russia

https://www.shephardmedia.com/news/imps-news/analysis-china
-seeks-dominate-seas/

https://nationalinterest.org/blog/buzz/see-submarine-photo-its
-how-america-would-crush-china-war-72831

https://tass.com/defense/1072724

https://www.cnbc.com/2019/08/07/china-nato-is-monitoring-beijings-in-
creased-presence-in-the-arctic-circle.html

https://nationalinterest.org/blog/buzz/how-russia-and-america-plan-
track-and-sink-each-others-stealth-submarines-43562

https://features.propublica.org/navy-accidents/uss-fitzgerald-destroyer
-crash-crystal/

https://www.express.co.uk/news/world/1048690/world-war-3-us-china
-nuclear-submarine

https://abcnews.go.com/Politics/us-withdrawing-cold-war-nuclear-arms-
control-treaty/story?id=60777071

https://thebulletin.org/2018-doomsday-clock-statement/

https://nationalinterest.org/blog/buzz/russia-wants-four-submarines-
armed-nuclear-warhead-drones-can-cause-tsunamis-73606

https://nationalinterest.org/blog/buzz/rip-us-navy-how-much-damage
-can-irans-submarines-do-war-74001

https://www.newsmax.com/newsfront/nuclear-submarine-navy
-military/2019/08/18/id/928952/

https://www.dailymail.co.uk/news/article-7368667/Military-expert-says
-Australia-rely-protect-Beijing.html

https://nationalinterest.org/blog/buzz/1981-british-submarine-smashed-
russian-sub-armed-nuclear-weapons-66882

https://www.newsmax.com/newsfront/nuclear-submarine-navy
-military/2019/08/18/id/928952/

https://www.dailymail.co.uk/news/article-7368667/Military-ex-
pert-says-Australia-rely-protect-Beijing.html

https://en.wikipedia.org/wiki/Kursk_submarine_disaster

https://www.strategypage.com/htmw/htsub/20190820.aspx#foo

https://taskandpurpose.com/esper-navy-submarine-fleet-russia-china

https://thearabweekly.com/russias-naval-cooperation-iran-compli-
cates-western-calculus

https://www.forbes.com/sites/hisutton/2019/08/17/russia-testing-nuclear
-powered-mega-torpedo-near-where-deadly-explosion-occurred/
#697e42cc2d7f

https://nationalinterest.org/blog/buzz/us-navy-should-watch-out-chinas
-submarine-force-rise-56107

ACKNOWLEDGMENTS

I would like to acknowledge the excellent contributions provided by those who were directly involved with this tragic event in naval history, including Mark Medish, former and current Russian naval officers and government officials, U.S. submariners at the scene, and the dive teams and supervisors involved in the *Kursk* rescue attempt and salvage operation.

ABOUT THE AUTHOR

W. Craig Reed is the *New York Times* bestselling author of the award-winning *Red November*, *The 7 Secrets of Neuron-Leadership*, and *Tarzan, My Father*, co-written with the late Johnny Weissmuller, Jr. Reed served as a U.S. Navy submariner and diver during the Cold War and earned commendations for completing secret missions, some in concert with SEAL Team One. Reed's military experience and inside contacts help infuse his writing with intrigue and realism and inspired his latest novel, *STATUS-6*. Reed holds an MBA in Marketing and is the cofounder of Us4Warriors, an award-winning Veterans Non-Profit. Reed serves on the Board of Aretanium, an employee productivity firm that leverages the neuroscience research in the *The 7 Secrets of Neuron Leadership*.